Washington's Sport of Kings

Views of a Fisheries Insider

Frank Haw

Why You Should Read This Book:

I recommend this book to everyone who has an interest in fish and fishing, no matter which fish or what place, and it should be required reading for every college student studying fisheries, as well as their instructors, as well as fishery managers who might benefit from a new perspective on their responsibilities.

—**Richard R. Whitney, PHD; Retired Professor, School of Fisheries, University of Washington.** Professor Whitney taught Fisheries Management (1961-1994); and from 1974-1979 served as Fisheries Technical Advisor to Honorable George H. Boldt, Senior Judge, United State District Court for Western Washington in the case United States v. the State of Washington.

If you love salmon fishing like I do and care about our salmon, then you should get this book. Frank Haw, better known as the "Guru" by those of us lucky enough to call him friend, has written a marvelous book on the history of saltwater salmon angling in Washington State. Be aware and be delighted that this is not your typical "fishing book". This is a comprehensive book that includes personal insights into the coast wide management of salmon, the effects of the Boldt Decision and the Endangered Species Act, and the critical need to protect salmon habitat. How all these factors interact is set against a rich and entertaining history of salmon fishing in our state. Salmon anglers, historians, students and policy makers will enjoy and learn much from this excellent book.

—**Norm Dicks, Congressman (D-WA), 6th Congressional District, 1976-2013**

All inquiries should be addressed to:
Frank Amato Publications, Inc.
P.O. Box 82112
Portland, Oregon 97282
(503) 653-8108
www.AmatoBooks.com

Cover Image: Director of Fisheries Donald Moos with
a tethered male Wannock River Chinook salmon.

ISBN-13: 978-1-57188-536-4
UPC: 0-81127-00389-1
Printed in The United States

10 9 8 7 6 5 4 3 2 1

Table of Contents

Foreword

Salmon are an iconic symbol of the American Northwest. For centuries Native Americans built their settlements at the mouths of rivers and collected abundant clams and oysters. They waited patiently for the returning salmon seeking their traditional breeding grounds. Tribes harvested enough fish to sustain their yearly food supply and respected the cycle that annually brought them sustenance.

This balance was smashed as settlers moved in, rivers were polluted, dams were built that blocked returning salmon, and commercial fishermen chased declining salmon runs. Frank Haw, as a young boy, experienced the results of this remarkable transition. He was hooked, proverbially, at an early age on fishing and eventually experienced the unique thrill of working, playing and landing a muscular King salmon. That created a lifelong devotion to angling and to a career as a fisheries biologist and leader of Washington State fisheries management.

I first met Frank when I became Governor of Washington State and he was a young fisheries biologist in the Department of Fisheries. I was invited on a fishing trip and Frank initiated my fisheries education. He taught me to the proper way to cut a herring so it would roll to attract the big fish and the proper calm and patient reaction to the gentle nibble of the King salmon toying with the bait. Most of all he taught me the joy of fishing when no fish were striking. It was being on the water, breathing the richness of salt air, watching seabirds and seals fight for dinner, and occasionally witnessing the stately procession of a pod of orcas searching for the same salmon we were chasing. Forty years later he introduced our eight-year-old grandson Jackson to cutthroat fishing on Hood Canal. We trolled close to shore as the tide rolled in, passing bald eagle sentinels perched on huge granite boulders. When a good sized trout struck Jackson's bait the grin on his face was magical.

Frank became the top scientist and deputy director of the Washington State Department of Fisheries in the mid-1970s during a time of extraordinary turmoil. Federal court judge George Boldt interpreted an ancient treaty between Indian tribes and the U.S. Government to award half the harvestable salmon to Native American fishermen. That decision created conflict and even open warfare on the waters of Puget Sound. Purse seiners, charter-boat operators, gill-netters, Native Americans, environmentalists, sports fishermen all fought to catch or preserve the last salmon and only reluctantly did cooperative management of the salmon fishery prevail.

Written here is a remarkable history of salmon sport fishing in the Pacific Northwest and the details of the human, scientific, economic, and political forces that have battled over salmon for the past century. More importantly, Frank Haw uses his lifetime of fishing experience and biology knowledge to make a persuasive case for the economic value and personal challenge of the sport salmon fishery. He also questions the transparency and effectiveness of current fish management.

This book should be read by every fisheries manager, every commercial fisherman, every tribal leader, every sports fisherman, and every legislator charged with preserving our great salmon heritage. These remarkable fish, after a lifetime in the open ocean, return unerringly to the streams where they were hatched. During their return they are preyed on by voracious seals and orcas, tantalized by exotic lures, challenged by the nets of Native American and commercial fishermen, but some survive, breed the next generation and give their exhausted bodies to the bald eagles waiting patiently to feed. This cycle has been repeated for eons and deserves to repeat for ages to come. Frank's wise words will contribute to this remarkable life cycle.

—Daniel J. Evans, "Mr. Washington", Governor 1965 – 1977
U.S. Senator, 1983 – 1989

"The Cast"

Figure 1. Chinook salmon
Photo courtesy of the Washington Department of Fish and Game.

Chinook salmon, *Oncorhynchus tshawytscha,* are the largest of the Pacific salmon and have various aliases. Large specimens approaching maturity are king salmon and immature fish are blackmouth to Puget Sounders. Canadians refer to Chinook as springs, while reserving tyee for fish exceeding thirty pounds. Sexually precocious males, usually two-year-olds, are jacks. Fall-run stocks native to the lower Columbia River, lacking fat characteristics of up-river fish, are called tules. Quinnat, an archaic American term, are New Zealand Chinook that were introduced from the Sacramento River over a century ago.

The species is native to the larger rivers from California's Ventura River to western Alaska, the Aleutians and corresponding latitudes of the Asian Pacific coast. Juvenile fish rear in freshwater for periods ranging from a few months to a year or more and most mature from two to six years of age. Large numbers are caught by commercial hook-and-line fishermen (trollers) and anglers along the Northwest coast. Chinook salmon originating in Washington typically move north to forage along the coast of British Columbia and as far as S.E. Alaska.

Most local Chinook (falls) return to our rivers during September and spawn in October. Other races (springs and summers) favor the headwaters of large cold streams and return earlier in the year to spawn during the falling temperatures of late summer and early fall. Prime Chinook salmon, rich in tasty fat, command the highest per unit of weight price of any of the Pacific salmon species.

Figure 2. Coho salmon.
Photo courtesy of the Washington Department of Fish and Game.

Coho salmon, *Oncorhynchus kisutch*, are, in numbers, the most important saltwater sport salmon from Oregon through S.E. Alaska. They are also taken in large numbers by commercial trollers. The red flesh of the species ranks third in per unit of weight value among the five species of Pacific salmon. Other common names for the species are silver salmon and hooknose – the latter term reserved for the largest mature fish which include males with distorted snouts. Canadians refer to smaller fish residing in Georgia Strait as blueback.

Coho are relatively uncommon south of the Oregon border and range northward to the Alaskan coast through the Aleutians. They are also native to the opposing Asiatic coast. The species typically utilizes small coastal lowland streams for spawning and rearing where they spend about half of a three- to four-year life span. Local stocks are almost entirely comprised of fish that mature at age three, although coho jacks mature at age two having spent only a few months at sea. Coho exhibit a variety of migration patterns but do not range as far from home as Chinook.

Homing migrations of local coho salmon begin in September, peaking at mid-month into Puget Sound, and into freshwater during the freshets of late September and October. Spawning activity peaks in late November.

Pink salmon, *Oncorhynchus gorbuscha*, are the smallest and most numerous of the Pacific salmon. Streams in the Puget Sound region essentially constitute the southern limits of North American pink salmon spawning. Pinks are also called humpies or humpbacks because of the more prominent hump on the backs of mature males. They are distributed north to the Arctic and eastward along the Asian coast as

Figure 3. Pink salmon.
Photo courtesy of the Washington Department of Fish and Game.

far south as northern Japan. Pink salmon are two years old at maturity and local stocks, apart from a few minor exceptions, spawn only in odd-numbered years (2005, 2007, etc.). Even-year runs can be dominant elsewhere. Thus, each Puget Sound pink run is directly descended from the previous cycle so that genetic interchange between even-and-odd year spawners is limited. This is unique among other breeding populations of Pacific salmon that are comprised of fish of various ages (e.g., two, three, four and five year olds). Young pinks migrate to saltwater soon after emerging from the gravel.

From late July through the first week of September of cycle years, pink salmon moving from offshore through Juan de Fuca Strait toward the Fraser and Puget Sound rivers comprise a significant fraction of Washington's sport catch. The vast majority of harvested pink salmon are taken in purse seine and prices paid for them are the lowest per unit of weight of the five local species. Upstream migration peaks during September and the two-year life span ends in October. Curiously, Pink salmon established by accident in Lake Superior are capable of living beyond two years.

Figure 4. Chum salmon
Photo courtesy of the Washington Department of Fish and Game.

Chum salmon, *Oncorhynchus keta*, are also called dog or fall salmon. The former name refers either to the canine-like breeding teeth of the males or the implication that the fat-deficient chums should be fed to man's best friend. Chums were once relatively rare in sport catches but that has changed in recent years. The species ranges from Northern California northward well into the Arctic and east to the Mackenzie River, and in corresponding latitudes along the Asiatic coast.

After completing a three- to-five year life cycle, maturing fish typically begin arriving in local waters during October, ascending spawning streams during mid-fall freshets, and quickly spawn and die in the lower reaches of rivers and creeks – some of which are dry for much of the year. Shortly after emerging from the gravel, the young fish enter saltwater where schools of feeding juveniles are a common spring-time sight along Puget Sound beaches.

Figure 5. Sockeye salmon
Photo is courtesy of the Washington Department of Fish and Game.

Sockeye salmon, *Oncorhynchus nerka*, are called red salmon in Alaska and blueback in the Columbia River. Landlocked lake-dwelling fish, a favorite of anglers, are kokanee. Anadromous sockeye are a relatively recent addition to Washington's recreational catch. The deep-red fatty flesh of prime sockeye, primarily harvested in purse seines and gill nets, commands high prices. The species ranges from the Columbia River to Alaska's Bristol Bay and eastward to Russia's Kamchatka Peninsula and the Okhotsk Sea.

Sockeye are almost always associated with deep, cold lakes with outlets providing access to the sea. One such lake, Redfish Lake in Idaho, once hosting a large run, is 900 miles from the Pacific and 6500 feet above it. These fish spawn in lake tributaries and less frequently in outlets or in suitable lake beach gravel. After emerging from the gravel, the fry usually rear in the connected lake for a year or more before migrating to sea.

Sockeye typically range from three (jacks) to five years of age at maturity.

Sockeye returning to Washington lake systems begin arriving during the spring (Quinault, Ozette) but others runs peak during the summer months (Wenatchee, Pleasant [Quileute system] and Lake Washington.) Osoyoos Lake sockeye swim up the Columbia and Okanogan rivers to reach their spawning grounds in British Columbia. By relying on stored body fats, mature sockeye typically spend weeks holding in the cool depths of their nursery lakes before spawning in October.

Introduction

Angling for the original salmon (*Salmo salar*), native to the North Atlantic region, primarily involves late-spring and summer fishing for adults returning to spawning streams. Fishing for Atlantic salmon has been traditionally reserved for those who can afford the often exorbitant costs of paying for the privilege. Such was not the case on Puget Sound where pioneers and Native Americans long before learned that there were salmon available to all that could be taken in saltwater throughout the year.

As a fishing-obsessed youth in Seattle during the 1940s when, in terms of catch, Puget Sound probably hosted the world's most important salmon sport fishery, I often wondered why saltwater salmon fishing was largely ignored by *Field & Stream* and other such East Coast magazines. I read everything available to me about fishing and was captivated by the writings of Roderick Haig-Brown. My only disappointment in the accounts of this gifted writer/angler, who left England to settle at Campbell River on Vancouver Island, was a lesser interest in saltwater salmon fishing. If he had become a saltwater angler I could only imagine his descriptions of salmon slashing through schools of baitfish, the frantic seabirds, and the speed and power of a Chinook salmon diving into the depths or racing for the horizon.

Haig-Brown's *A River Never Sleeps*[1] is my favorite book and, apart from a chapter on pike, it is exclusively devoted to trout and salmon and I had it with me during my three-year USAF tour in Europe. I was so taken with the author's boyhood memories of a giant pike lurking under a railroad bridge on an unnamed English salmon river that, 50 years later, following a remarkable bit of detective work by an English friend, I peered into that same pool from a dilapidated structure over Wiltshire's River Avon.

That book is so descriptive that one is constantly reminded of similar experiences and observations that have languished below the conscious level. The author's rivers and their surroundings come alive and one can almost feel the pressure of the current and takes of the fish. But it seems to me that he missed an opportunity to describe an astonishingly productive "river" at the door step of his adopted home – a river of saltwater that only briefly naps at the change of tide, forming countless channels and eddies that are special places for prey and predators. The people who originally lived here, and those who followed, understood tides and currents like all those dependent upon paddle and sail. Learning from the Indians, newcomers soon took to salmon angling in this flowing and fertile environment. Their experience and techniques eventually spread far beyond the Seattle waterfront where saltwater salmon angling, as we know it today, all began.

Until recently, salmon caught in saltwater have historically accounted for more than 90% of Washington's recreational catch[2,3]. This was the case even though salmon angling in the Columbia River system has been popular for many years. Salmon anglers in the Puget Sound region were so oriented to saltwater that many viewed fishing for salmon in rivers as unethical and something that should be banned. The silver luster of a salmon at sea, in contrast to the darker hues of maturing fish was, and remains to some, a characteristic as highly valued as size. Saltwater salmon sport fishing was once far more important to the quality of life in Washington than it is today.

I was about five years late in qualifying for Tom Brokaw's *Greatest Generation*, but I have vivid memories of the decade preceding Pearl Harbor when Seattle's Smith Tower dwarfed its surroundings; Hooverville's shacks occupied nine acres west of "Skid Road" (modern Pioneer Square); and the streamlined ferry *Kalakala* was a shining harbinger of a rosier future. A time when motoring east from Rainier Valley toward Snoqualmie Pass, involved circumventing Lake Washington through Renton, past smoldering piles of coal from abandoned mines, and traversing the two lanes of Sunset Highway through Issaquah, Fall City, Snoqualmie and on to North Bend at the gateway to eastern Washington. A time when youngsters organized their own games and knew little if anything of professional baseball east of the Pacific Coast; believing that Leo Lassen, radio voice of the Seattle Rainiers, whose nasal delivery all kids tried to imitate, was the greatest announcer of all time. And when President Harry Truman learned, when he visited Seattle in June of 1945, that one of the greatest treats a local could bestow on a visitor was a salmon fishing trip on Puget Sound.

During the late 1960s, when it was my job to know such things, Washington's saltwater salmon sport catch exceeded the combined sport salmon catches of California, Oregon, and British Columbia and Alaska. In 1977, the first year of three major-league sport teams in Seattle, the number of saltwater salmon angler trips in Washington nearly equaled the combined attendance of the Sonics, Mariners and Seahawks teams.

There are still those around, older than I, who grew up and remained in the Puget Sound area. But the numbers are dwindling and I am unaware of anyone remaining who shares the experience that I have, relating to Washington's salmon sport fishery. Although this will appear to be a relatively insignificant subject to most contemporary residents, particularly those who are too young or are relatively recent arrivals, salmon angling was a priceless treasure to many and it contributed significantly to the quality of life in Washington State. This document represents an attempt to preserve the memory of what we once had and could have again.

1   The Development of an Angler

In *A River Never Sleeps*, apart from its stimulating thought and perception, the author is unable to determine why he and others choose to fish. I am not alone is suggesting that we enjoy fishing because for only a blink of an eye in our existence, natural selection favored successful fishermen and hunters. Since those who enjoy fishing and hunting tend to be better at it, could it be that nature has protected those who derive pleasure from it?

My addiction to fishing began at a family picnic to a campground and trout farm on Raging River above Preston in King County. I was eight years old and my father paid for me to catch a fish on a rented cane pole with a length of line attached to the tip. I can still recall the feel of the bite telegraphed through cane. Apart from this event, my perpetual desire to fish was independent of family influence. My father, who built our home in Rainier Valley, was a good and hardworking English immigrant, a WW I veteran of the Royal Flying Corps, who supported us during WW II by making and repairing boilers for ships. Although he was totally disinterested in fishing and forever puzzled by my addiction, it never seemed to displease him and was even a source of amusement.

Because of a fondness for fishing in rural surroundings, I spent weeks of my boyhood summers of the 1940's in Fall City with my maternal aunt's family, where the local streams and still waters had much to do with my education. Various species were available in the Snoqualmie River at the mouth of Raging River only a stone's throw from the house. For bait, my younger cousin and I used fat yellow caddis larvae from the rocks of the warmer tributary, dug angleworms, or used "single" preserved salmon eggs that were the standard trout bait of the day. To avoid fumbling with the lid and small jar containing the eggs, I can still taste the spares held in my mouth. During June we caught spawning peamouth ("chubs") that then swarmed up the river and, to our delight, discovered that by squeezing the orange-striped males, sperm could be squirted half the width of Raging River. Mountain whitefish and juvenile steelhead, protected only by a six-inch minimum length and a twenty-fish bag limit, comprised the bulk of our catch here throughout the summer months. By far the largest fish we encountered were the large-scale suckers that were particularly fond of caddis larvae. These fish, weighing well over a pound, would break the cheap olive drab leader material available during wartime when we attempted to hoist them from the water. This experience introduced us to the concept of playing and beaching a decent-sized fish.

Small colorful cutthroat inhabited the tiny un-named spring creeks in the valley – trickles so small that grass on opposing sides could intertwine. These fish could be easily caught on three feet of line and leader tied to a switch. An angle worm, collected under a properly aged "cow pie", was the bait of choice. The trout favored miniature plunge pools, undercut banks and other lies providing cover and depth. A worm dropped into the right spot would instantly disappear, often in a puff of silt, as the fish returned to its refuge. Sixty-five years later, I sometimes dream of tiny creeks and cutthroat trout and, upon wakening, hope that they are still there.

Live larval lamprey (ammocoetes) shoveled from the muddy sediments of a nearby creek, were our favorite bait for pan-sized largemouth bass at Rutherford Slough – an oxbow of the Snoqualmie River. During summer evenings, we fished from a cow bridge spanning the dark water with cane poles lacking guides or reels. The squirming ammocoetes were so deadly that they seemed to seek the open mouths of the bass, sometimes slithering through the gill openings so that the unfortunate fish could be hoisted onto the bridge without being actually hooked.

Seattle's Seward Park was about a three-mile walk east of our Rainier Valley home. Peamouth and northern pikeminnows (squawfish), along with greedy ducks, were attracted to floating pieces of stale bread and were my most common catch, along with an occasional fat yellow perch. Laws protecting our shorelines arrived too late to save the shallow cove at the foot of Genesee Street next to Lakewood Boathouse. From late spring through summer the cove was covered with blossoming pads and lined with cattails, and by May husky largemouth bass nested there along with fat pumpkinseed sunfish. At sunset, as if awakened by bellowing bullfrogs, brown bullheads ("catfish") came alive and often kept us there until midnight. White cork bobbers, partially illuminated by a kerosene lantern, were important parts of our nocturnal gear. Night crawlers, a

European invasive species, were not as widely distributed as they are today and our source was the tilled rose bed at the Columbia City library. More than once our flashlights attracted the attention of Seattle's finest working the night beat.

Figure 6. A miniature cutthroat trout from a small western Washington creek.

It always seemed easy to hitch-hike a ride while carrying a fishing rod, and during winter it took us to the "gravel dock" on the far side of the Lake Washington bridges on the East Channel. My pal Vaughn Parker was my usual companion. We occasionally caught a nine- or ten-inch cutthroat that succumbed to a single preserved salmon egg cast from the end of the dock and allowed to soak on the bottom. We would lay our rods down, try to keep warm, and watch the tips of our steel telescopic or cheap bamboo fly rods for movement. On one such trip, during the late fall, we walked to the mouth of Coal Creek fascinated with the foot-long red fish (kokanee) visible against the black residue remaining from an earlier east-side industry.

Hitch-hiking also provided transportation to the Maple Valley area during spring where the lakes held yellow perch and small bass; and trickles of permanent spring water flowing into Cedar River contained tiny, but mature cutthroat. These native fish were, and hopefully remain, widespread in Western Washington and are deserving of more scientific attention. They undoubtedly occur in many permanent trickles of water that currently lack official recognition as "fish bearing" and thus lack the protection they deserve.

At Columbia Grade School my friend Clint Burt was much admired by his peers for his toughness and athleticism. At no more than ten years old, I remember him laughing during recess as he pulled a small dried-up trout from a pocket – another probably held cigarettes and matches. He had taken the trout the previous school day from Taylor Creek, a Lake Washington tributary south of Rainier Beach. Clint got me seriously interested in saltwater when we took a city bus to West Seattle's Fauntleroy ferry dock. "Sea perch" were often visible in the clear water, and at many other Puget Sound piers and docks, as they grazed among the anemones and mussels encrusted on the supporting pilings. From the dock railing, and my limited experience, the fish appeared huge, though the largest probably weighed less than two pounds. However, our attempt to catch fish on this occasion was hampered by a lack of suitable equipment and bait, as well as active enforcement of a no-fishing rule.

We eventually found docks where we could lower hand lines into the schools of perch with relatively little harassment: Healy's Boathouse and an adjacent dock where old ferries were moored during WW II on the west side of Elliott Bay, and, best of all, the Vashon Island side of the Fauntleroy ferry route where the perch were abundant and the no-fishing rule was seldom enforced. The finicky perch tugged hard on our hand-held lines and they relished marine worms, shrimp, shore crabs, and the flesh of crushed mussels and barnacles. We discovered that by scraping these organisms from the pilings we could attract feeding perch to the resulting carnage. Striped seaperch are among the most beautiful of all local fishes and the fact that the members of this family give live birth to fully developed young added to our fascination with them.

Once or twice during the WW II years, we delivered our catch to the Seattle Public Market where vendors paid us ten cents a pound for perch in the round. My catch once raised $3.00. In addition to our usual catch of striped seaperch and pile perch we were occasionally rewarded with rockfish ("rock cod"), cabezon ("bull cod") or thrilled by an occasional skate that appeared to slowly fly into view. In those days anything other than salmon, flatfishes, or dogfish sharks were considered to be a "cod" of some kind. Real cod were, and remain in some circles, "true cod".

Although many small salmon were caught from some of the piers along the Seattle waterfront in those days, most salmon fishing basically required a boat and relatively sophisticated equipment. My pal's father, John Parker, owned a 1.5 horse power Johnson outboard and other equipment and he took me fishing. In March of 1947 we went out from Brown's Bay Boathouse just north of Edmonds. The trolling equipment consisted of short-stubby "rods", star drag reels, solid Monel metal lines, six-ounce sinkers, huge spinners (Shovel and Rudder) attached to an additional yard-long string of smaller spinners (Pop-Gear), and a short leader baited with angle worms. We remained in the vicinity of the boathouse and each of us caught the limit of six 12- to 16-inch resident coho. Following a slight tug, the dreadful assortment of gear filtered any feeling of life at the end of the line and success was only indicated by a bend in the retrieved row of spinning blades The water was glassy-calm on that particular day and we were often surrounded by finning fish, feeding on zooplankton, that could have been easily taken on a cast fly or weightless lure. At the end of the trip, there was a beautiful fish, huge in comparison to ours, hanging from the boathouse scale and reference to blackmouth, spinning, and a place across the water called Point No Point.

During the summer of 1947, at age 15, I somehow arranged a stay with an older couple (the woman was a distant relative) in Pincher Creek – a small town in the foothills of southwest Alberta. I had no interest in meeting the couple but my instincts told me that fishing had to be good there. An overnight trip on a Greyhound Bus carried us over the Rocky Mountains and at dawn beheld a beautiful open country of grass-covered hills and clear streams. The town, with its board walks and dusty streets, resembled a set for a western movie, including pig-tailed Indians in Stetsons and horse-drawn wagons containing black-clad members of a nearby Hutterite community. The old man who met me off the bus was a native of Ireland and a grave digger who traveled to and from the job by horse and buggy. His wife took care of the Catholic clergy in the local parish and rented out rooms in their two-story frame house located nearby.

The only chore that I performed during my three-week stay was to provide Friday fish for the clergy. Rainbow trout and mountain whitefish – "grayling" to locals – were the standard fare, but I caught cutthroat that looked nothing like our coastal fish and a good-sized bull trout. The trout were far bigger than ones I caught at home and managed to activate the clicker on the cheap fly reel attached to my three-guide steel telescopic rod.

Walking through town from a fishing location near the graveyard one afternoon, I was stopped by a local merchant who was curious about what I had in my bag. He was obviously impressed with the two fifteen-inch rainbow and some smaller fish and later took me on two memorable day trips to the Carbondale River where it flowed into the Castle and to Waterton River just below Waterton National Park that is a northern extension of Glacier Park. He carried dead minnows in a jar of brine for bait that were caught after being herded through the shallows of Pincher Creek into a V- shaped stone trap terminating in a net pocket.

I learned that good-sized trout eat fish and I showed him that they also eat preserved salmon eggs. Fifty years later I returned to Pincher Creek, caught a rainbow trout on a Parachute Adams next to the town historic center and there learned that my fishing companion had died years earlier after having served as town mayor. I have had many exotic fishing adventures since then, but the fondest memories of all are those of that summer in Pincher Creek.

My developing angling skills during the following decade had little to do with salmon, but I managed to boat a 32-pound Chinook salmon at Sekiu in August, 1952. My fish was the smallest of three that we caught on dodger and herring trolled just outside of the kelp bed in front of "the Caves". Again, I was with my good friend who had first taken me salmon fishing at Brown's Bay Boathouse. A few weeks later I was watching flying fish from the bow of a troop ship bound from New York, via Puerto Rico, to Germany. Five years as an enlisted man in the Air Force, most of it in Europe, and three-plus years as a married father at the University of Washington's College of Fisheries on a "G.I. Bill" interfered with my ability to pursue the sport.

From the moment that I learned in the ninth grade at "Career Day" at Franklin High School[b] that there were people who were paid to work with fish, my course was never in doubt. The opportunity to learn more about salmon angling came in 1958. While a student at the University, I was hired by the Washington Department of Fisheries to collect salmon sportfishing information on weekends and during the summer from anglers landing at boathouses and ramps throughout the Puget Sound area. Part of my responsibility was to determine the ratios of rental and private boats fishing for salmon. Since the number of rental boats was theoretically known, through the mandatory submission of reports, the number of private boats could be calculated from the ratios established by counting the boats engaged in fishing. Rentals were easily identified by their relatively uniform appearance and the names of the boathouses or resorts painted on the hulls. The counts were made from small aircraft and boats rented for the purpose. This information was used to estimate the total sport catch.

The Department provided me a 15hp outboard, took care of the rental fee, and on such occasions I would embark on such missions very early in the morning to fish for salmon, follow with the boat count, and return to the boathouse before the first anglers had returned. This, in combination with an intense interest, a sympathetic supervisor, and the opportunity to talk to hundreds of anglers, provided a "crash course" in saltwater salmon angling. On many such boat-counting excursions I was back with a limit catch before the first angler had returned to the boathouse.

Most of my 26 years with the Washington Department of Fisheries involved working with the sport fishery but during the latter portion of my career, as the agencies top-ranking fisheries professional, I served as both Deputy and Acting Director of Fisheries. This spanned, what I believe, was the most contentious and difficult period in the history of the Department. Following retirement from state service in 1984, I worked for Northwest Marine Technology as a biologist for 30 years but remained involved in salmon management.

Having now achieved octogenarian status, I still love to mooch for salmon, but have seriously taken to fly-fishing and, like those early thrills of seaperch tugging a hand line, have become addicted to feeling the line pulled from my hands when a good fish takes; and take pride in having caught more different members of the salmon family than anyone I know. I greatly miss fishing year-round in Puget Sound, particularly during the winter months when there are fewer boats and more wild things to see. I mourn the loss of a healthy south Puget Sound resident salmon population that is only partially mitigated by the tenacity of wild sea-run cutthroat that are available year-round in the Sound.

These are exciting fish that appear as a silver flash from nowhere as they take the fly. One would consider cutthroat, along with other local cold-water species, as particularly sensitive to urbanization and pollution. However, while other native fishes such as coho salmon and sculpins have become less abundant in Puget Sound's urban small streams, cutthroat have somehow managed to hold their own, aided by a no-kill restriction. Wild cutthroat are also doing well in Lake Washington, and apparently Sammamish as well, where they have established a pelagic lifestyle foraging on "land-locked" longfin smelt and growing to sizes exceeding those of their anadromous counterparts. Elsewhere, in the lower Columbia River system, my knowledgeable acquaintances tell me that wild sea-run cutthroat have nearly disappeared.

2   Early Angling in Puget Sound

Clarence Bagley arrived in Seattle from the east in 1860 and his *History of King County[4]* includes a chapter on "Fish and Fisheries". He describes the Puget Sound Country as a sportsman's paradise, and relates how his friend loved to arise early and troll a spoon from his canoe off Seattle's Alki and Five Mile rock; and how local Indians made fishing lines from the tough lower stems of kelp, and that food rather than sport motivated the native anglers. He identifies hook-and-line fishing by the local Indians as a primary method for initially supplying salmon to the fishing industry on Puget Sound. Twenty-five years later, the Sound's first salmon cannery opened at Mukilteo in 1877 with equipment moved from the Columbia River. In 1880, the cannery moved to West Seattle. According to Bagley, in 1853 the pioneer Dr. David S. Maynard had asked Chief Sealth/Seattle to direct him to the best fishing ground and the Chief brought Maynard to the mouth of the Duwamish River on Elliott Bay. The river at that time was much larger since it included flows

Figure 7. Sea run cutthroat trout (Oncorhynchus clarki) from Case Inlet, Puget Sound.

from the Black (Lake Washington outlet), White, and Cedar rivers which have since been diverted into other systems. But the old chief knew what he was talking about and if a "birthplace" of the Northwest's saltwater salmon sport fishery is ever designated it would have to be at the mouth of the Duwamish in Elliott Bay.

A number of years ago, on the bank of Ireland's River Eriff, I learned that Chief Seattle's fame had spread at least as far as the European continent. I had innocently strayed from my assigned salmon "beat" and struck up a conversation with a visiting German angler who was resting after fruitlessly casting to the "stale" fish that were awaiting a freshet and impatiently surfacing throughout the pool. Learning that I was from Seattle, he began reciting the eloquent and prophetic passages from the Chief's famous speech. I had not the heart to mention that these words first surfaced more than 30 years after allegedly given at the Treaty negotiations of 1854, and were apparently written by Dr. Henry A. Smith – a man Bagley describes as "a poet of no ordinary talent".

The United States Exploring Expedition, under the command of Navy Lieutenant Charles Wilkes, visited Puget Sound in 1841[5]. The expedition remained in the vicinity of Hudson Bay Company's Fort Nisqually from May through early July using the location as a base for exploring the region. The narrative of the expedition has this to say regarding hook-and-line fishing in the adjacent marine waters by the Nisqually people: *"During the salmon fishery, vast shoals of young herring are seen, which the Indians take with a kind of rake attached to a paddle. The herring are used for bait for the salmon. Their hooks are made in an ingenious manner of the yew tree and are strong and capable of catching large fish. They are chiefly employed trailing for fish."*

Early surveys conducted by the U.S. Fish Commission on Puget Sound and adjacent waters also document the importance of hook-and-line fishing by local Indians[6]. In 1888, when Seattle's population was about 30,000, J. W. Collins observed: *". . . the Indians employ trolling hooks and spears in the sound and small streams tributary thereto, and parties fishing for pleasure also use spoon hooks and trolling lines. In autumn, when salmon are most numerous in the sound, Seattle Bay is literally covered with pleasure boats for days in succession."* A year later Richard Rathbun, in another U. S. Fish Commission Report[7], described hook-and-line fishing for "quinnat" (Chinook) salmon in the Puget Sound region: *"The fishermen are chiefly Indians, and the season is principally the winter beginning in November. The method followed is trolling with both bait and spoon at various depths below the surface, dependent upon the position of the fish. Herring is the bait usually employed."*

Figure 8. Author's concept of how a Makah fish hook may have been baited with herring.

James G. Swan abandoned his wife and children in Massachusetts and joined the California Gold Rush in 1850. Two years later he moved to the Washington Territory and initially settled on Willapa Bay. His experiences there, then known as Shoalwater Bay, resulted in the 1857 publication of *The Northwest Coast* – which includes an invaluable ethnographical description of the region. Of Swan's many activities and talents, none is more valuable than the meticulous documentation of his observations and conversations with native people. Beginning in 1859 he periodically visited and resided among the Makah Indians at Neah Bay. His book, *The Indians of Cape Flattery*[8], describes the soaking, stretching, and joining process required to make kelp fishing lines and compares their strength with "the best of hemp cod lines". Swan considered the Makah method of catching salmon on hook and line as "most excellent sport", and it seems that at least some of the Indian anglers must have shared these views. But halibut, rather than salmon, were the most important fish in the Makah diet. As further evidence of the strength and utility of kelp lines, such line hauled these powerful fish from the off-shore banks north and west of Cape Flattery. Halibut commonly weigh more than 100 pounds; they

lack the buoyancy of other species, and make powerful rushes for the
bottom when hauled toward the surface.

Figure 9. Lummi men trolling for salmon.
University of Washington Libraries, Special Collections NA689.

The Nootka people, of the west Coast of Vancouver Island, are closely
related to the Makah at Neah Bay. John R. Jewitt, an armourer aboard
the trading vessel *Boston*, was one of only two surviving crew members
of the Indian attack at Nootka Sound in 1803. His metal-working
skills, recognized by "King" Maquinna, were Jewitt's salvation and he
was added to the king's cadre of slaves, remaining captive for three years
before rescue. During this time he maintained a fascinating record of
local customs, practices, and events (including his marriage). Hook-and-
line fishing (trolling) for salmon is described as follows: *"One person seats
himself in a small canoe, and baiting his hook with a sprat (small herring),
which they are careful to procure as fresh as possible, fastens his line to the
handle of the paddle; this, as he plies it in the water, keeps the fish in constant*

motion, so as to give it the appearance of life, which the salmon seeing, leaps at it, and is instantly hooked, and by a sudden and dexterous motion of the paddle, drawn on board. I have known some of the natives take no less than eight or ten salmon of a morning, in this manner, and have seen from twenty to thirty canoes at a time in Friendly Cove thus employed."

There is no mention in any of these accounts, including those involving Bagley's friend, of a rod or pole being used. However, Puget Sound Indians were quick to adopt manufactured lines and hooks when they became available, although Swan reported that the Makah continued to favor their own specialized halibut hooks. Among the most common artifacts found in archaeological investigations in the vicinity of Cape Flattery, are various kinds of fish hooks fashioned from wood and bone.[10]

These early observers have clearly documented the importance of subsistence hook-and-line fishing for salmon in the Puget Sound region that predated the arrival of the first "white" settlers; and that feeding salmon occurred year-round. Indian fishing with gillnets, the most common method currently employed by Treaty Indians, is not

Figure 10. This photograph of another form of hook-and-line fishing by the Makah, was taken from a 1938 U.S. Bureau of Fisheries Bulletin with the following caption: "Modified floating hook-and-line gear used for coho salmon by the natives at Neah Bay before white fishermen operated in that district. The bone hook was baited with a whole herring." The text of the accompanying article further describes the gear as consisting of ". . . a bladder float to which is attached a line of twisted sinew suspending a stone weight. A second line is fastened to the weight, and the free end is attached to a shank of whalebone bearing a double hook of bone lashed with bark. As many as thirty of these units were attached together, each hook was baited with a whole herring, and the string was drifted from a canoe. Both types of gear were fished close to the surface, and the principal catch was coho salmon, preferred by the natives because of its suitability for drying."

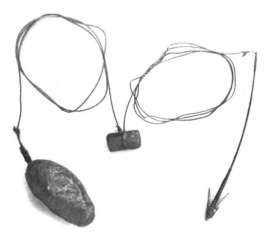

mentioned in any of these accounts.[11] A 1940 Department of the Interior document[12] describing in detail the array of fishing methods originally utilized by Indians throughout the Columbia River basin, concluded that ". . . no definitive information is available on that type of fishing." The narrative states that the first gill net used on the Columbia River was brought from Maine in 1853.

With few exceptions, such as with the Makahs at Neah Bay, this reliance on hook-and-line fishing appears to be given up by modern Indians. The year-round abundance of feeding salmon in the protected waters of Puget Sound clearly facilitated development of Indian salmon angling. There are countless early accounts of local use of weirs, traps, seines, dip nets, spears, gaffs and other devices by Indians, but these were primarily used to harvest mature salmon returning to local streams that were only seasonally available.

"Fish in Puget Sound" was the title of a brief article that appeared in December 1886 in *The American Angler*. J. P. Hammond, the author, had a business in dogfish oil, salting and smoking salmon, and herring. He was located across from Seattle at Port Madison and describes catching *"winter salmon"* from November to March in locations where he also

Figure 11. Yelm Jim's weir on the Puyallup River (C.A. 1885). These remarkable structures for capturing salmon were among the many devices widely used by Indians throughout the Pacific Northwest. Courtesy of the Washington State Museum.

caught herring. The salmon were pickled and shipped to San Francisco. Although the salmon species are not indicated, the winter fish were almost certainly "blackmouth" – immature Chinook salmon.

Angling for salmon quickly became a popular activity in the growing communities around Puget Sound. A Washington Department of Fisheries publication[14] describes typical salmon gear of the early 1900s as consisting of a cotton hand line with a short steel leader and a single-hook, brass spoon that was often homemade. In 1916 the Seattle Rod and Gun Club stipulated the kind of gear its members were required to use to qualify for silver and gold award buttons.

Salmon angling at the mouth of the Columbia River, and in the vicinity of Ilwaco and Chinook, was reported to have occurred before 1912 when a few local anglers discovered that in August and September, during safe incoming tides, salmon could be taken by trolling[15]. This activity targeted maturing up-river-bound salmon rather than the mixture of immature feeding and maturing fish that were sought on Puget Sound.

Elsewhere to the south, a US Bureau of Fisheries survey, published in 1908, describes a relatively advanced saltwater salmon sport fishery, involving an early version of the "downrigger", that had developed in California's Monterey Bay[16]: *"On the Pacific Coast the salmon congregate in Monterey Bay before entering the rivers. At Monterey, Santa Cruz and Capitola they are fished for from boats – the professional fishermen with big boats, using hand lines and heavy sinkers, in water 40 or 50 feet deep, with sardine bait, but the sportsmen using rod weighing 9 ounces, with a 9-thread line and a 7/0 hook baited with smelt, anchovy, or sardine. A sinker is needed, and an ingenious device is used to release the sinker and enable the man to play the fish. The line near the hook is connected by a thread to a pipe sinker of lead. When the fish strikes the thread breaks, releasing the line and the angler plays the salmon, which comes to the surface and leaps, making a fine play. Large catches are made."*

SPOONS

Trolling involves towing the lure or bait through the water column. Following the example of the local Indians, trolling with herring and spoons was the standard technique used by early Puget Sound anglers.

Although Indian trollers were apparently quick to adopt the use of metal trolling spoons, they had independently used "spoons" made of the glossy portions of mollusk shells. Following this lead, "Pearl wobblers", commercially made from abalone shell, were popular salmon lures for many years on Puget Sound. Due to the natural variations in the configuration of the shells the lures varied slightly in shape and "hot" wobblers were highly valued.

Ever since, trolling has always been the most common method of fishing for salmon in the Puget Sound region. For many years trolling with "jigger spoons", such as the FST, McMahon and Canadian Wonder, was very popular. Salmon spoons were intended to imitate flashing baitfish and were designed to wobble rather than spin. They were made of thin metal, rendering them impractical to cast, and were finished in silver, brass or "half and half". Depending upon depth of the quarry, current and trolling speed, sinkers of various weights were required for the spoon to reach the desired depth. Most of the salmon trolling spoons, plugs and attractors, such as "dodgers" used here and elsewhere for saltwater salmon fishing, were apparently developed and manufactured in the Puget Sound area. Trolling with spoons pre-dated the use of wooden plugs which gained popularity during the early 1930s.

Mission Bar, located off Mission Beach in the Tulalip Bay area, on the Tulalip Indian Reservation where many non-Indians had leased tribal land, was once a mecca for Puget Sound salmon anglers. The most popular fishing area was apparently the northern edge of the Snohomish River delta where adult salmon bound for that river, and the Stillaquamish and Skagit river systems to the north, tended to congregate. In addition, feeding immature salmon were abundant in the area, along with sea-run cutthroat and native sea-run char (Dolly Varden and/or bull trout). Adult Chinook salmon that congregated off the area from late July through early September were the prime attraction.

An unpublished report prepared in July, 1932 for the State Supervisor of Fisheries and the Director of the Department of Fisheries and Game, blends cynicism with philosophy in describing trolling for salmon in the "Mission Beach District", located north of Everett in the vicinity of the Snohomish River. Included, are observations surrounding the first salmon derby on Puget Sound. At this time sport-fishing activists, primarily interested in preventing steelhead trout from being commercially caught were campaigning for Initiative 62, which did away with the existing Department of Fisheries and Game and created two new state agencies – the Washington Department of Fisheries and the Washington Department of Game. I-62, championed by sportsmen and its supporting industry, clearly threatened the security of the employees of the existing fisheries management agency and influenced the content and tone of the document:

"There are in this district about one hundred and fifty boats for hire and privately owned rowboats and pleasure craft available for salt water sport fishing. Jim Remp at Hermosa Pt. and the Everett Boat House are the important boat renting resorts. Mission Beach consists of mainly summer homes and private boats at the present time. During the summer months about 25 boats varying in description operate at intervals from this point. Potlatch Beach consists mainly of summer cabins and a picnic ground and is not important as a fishing resort. The beach operates four or five boats while a few privately owned boats are operated from this point. Everett has a large number of small yachts and privately owned small row and outboard motor boats. Priest Point is a summer resort and a few private boats are operated from this point. The Mukilteo Boathouse also supplies a few for hire boats to the Mission Beach fishing area.

"A few larger power boats come from the Seattle District over holidays and weekend thus bringing the total sport fishing potentiality to well over a hundred boats at one time or another during one fishing day at Mission Beach District.

"It is not unusual during the fishing season for the large boats to rig poles to operate four lines in pursuit of salmon and cutthroat trout. Jim Remp offers as a service two of these poles on all boats rented regardless of size. It is the opinion of the sportsmen however that more than two lines on a small boat is not satisfactory hence these poles are only a convenience to the sportsmen and does not necessarily cause an increase in the number of lines operating from each boat. A large boat however can operate quite readily four lines and the catch is necessarily increased but not in proportion as a rule. The beach mentioned previously is the only resort giving this service and these poles are not used to any extent by other boats except the larger power boats operating from the yacht clubs. The usual procedure when trolling and not using the

outrigger poles is to either have two small whip sticks fastened to the sides of the boat or to hold the line in the hands. The latter is the less common of the three methods of fishing procedure. As a rule a group of fishing boats average about two lines during the week and two or less operators. At this time if the limit was observed the average catch per boat could not be as great as on holidays and weekends when the boats average about three people per boat. Only one man may fish at a time with convenience but the total catch is increased by the increased number in the boat as all may take turns fishing.

"In regards to tackle the total investment represented by one hundred boats fishing probably runs into the hundred dollars as it is the rule to have an assortment of spoons. According to reports it is the idea of Ben Paris to bring out during the process of his famous fishing contest a new spoon in order to create an increase in business. Among the fishermen a pet spoon or killer arouses more argument than any other article of his fishing equipment. The amateur also looks to the sportsmen with a "rep" for advice in this connection and as none of them agree as to the type or size he will probably, if he can afford the expense, buy a collection. The sporting goods houses can capitalize on this feature by having a new spoon in the contest that can catch fish this spoon is thus born amongst the fishermen as the fishing contest is attended by all the "important" and thus receives its necessary advertisement. The so-called freak was instituted last year at the fishing contest according to reports and now ranks amongst the required spoons of the average fisherman. Sitting in a round circle amongst a group of sportsmen on the beach an amateur rapidly feels sort of out of place with his small catch and listens with awe to the tales of how many fish and their respective cleaned weight that so and so caught with a so and so spoon. He came out to have a good time and was originally pleased with his catch which probably consisted of two or three blackmouth averaging from one to four pounds or a few cutthroats. He had had his recreation and enjoyed the outing very much. Upon listening however he learns that the other men have reps and never mention so small a catch as his and just sort of hides them away in their basket so no one can see them unless perhaps they have thirty or so of them and then numbers cause an entrance into the community competition.

"As the conversation proceeds the so called amateur gradually feels like the semi pro baseball player watching a big league game. He finds much to his surprise that fishing is not for recreational purposes except as a secondary *consideration and that the size and weight of the catch is the primary purpose throughout. He modestly keeps quiet and at the end of the display of large catches and extensive words he corners one of the "reps" with an entire new outlook. Gone is his appreciation of Washington great outdoors and in its place is born the modern idea of capitalistic competition. No longer does he play the game for pleasure with a simple idea of efficiency but his number of strike-outs, errors, hits and runs fill his whole mind. He retires to Seattle with the advice to go to Ben Paris or other well-known recreational supply houses and get a standard setup of equipment outlined by the chief who includes the so-called killers or special spoons. Of course, this costs several dollars but in order to be acknowledged with a smile around the boat house instead of just a nod with a half sneer or no word of greeting at all he must use this equipment in all his spare time to learn their technique and finally bring in a half row boat full of fish. With the advent of this the reps all gather around and congratulate him and if he does it frequently through the summer he too gets a rep and becomes a brother in the bond.*

"All this has been born in the advertising methods of the sporting goods houses not only in Seattle but in the other larger towns of the District. Fishing contests and newspaper classification of individual catches and the front store display cases and the birth of hero worship by newspaper publicity which is similar to the case of a famous swimmer or flyer have polluted our salt water fishing grounds and changed them to areas of commercial competition instead of a great recreational center and a tourist drawing card through a proper channel such as the chamber of commerce.

"Last year Ernie Hahn and Louie Peterson, men having the famous "rep", caught seventy Chinooks averaging from twenty to forty pounds during the short period of the adult chinook run late in the summer. This run usually does not arrive until about the first of August and continues throughout the month. Just as the Chinook run dwindles the silver run comes in and the catch poundage increases still further. A man that tends boats for Jim Remp reported catches of eighteen silvers totaling over three hundred pounds in one day and only stopped at the appearance of a patrol boat. He advocated getting a commercial trolling license to take advantage of the wonderful fishing opportunities at this time. No actual breaking of the limit has been observed to date this year, although one man took in thirty pounds of fish to the relief in Marysville or Everett. Fishing conditions have prevented to a great extent

the possibility of exceeding the poundage allowed. There are two or three individuals however that fish the greater part of each day and no doubt catch an excessive amount of fish. On July seventeenth one man caught fifteen fish but they were not seen to observe the total poundage. Very few fishermen operating a small spoon usually used for blackmouth or young chinook only fail to catch from one to five, six to ten inch Chinooks. Whether these fish are kept or not causes a serious mortality due to the size of hook used. Any injury to the gills causes death and the hook being of such size invariably severs some portion of this delicate and mortal spot.

"The sportsmen including Jim Remp and a man named Cliff are petitioning the Director of Fisheries to have the Mission Beach District closed to commercial fishing. No doubt this is founded on the desire of the reps to catch a greater number of large Chinooks during the run and to be able to break the poundage limit further probably the only reason that the commercial trollers are not included is that one cannot tell the difference between them and Jimmie Remp's rigged cruisers and the pleasure yachts during fishing operations. The sportsmen feel that this being political year they can get anything they want and are thus striking while the iron is hot".

"On the day of the Ben Paris fishing contest finals a portion of the bay is staked off and guarded by the Coast Guard. No commercial fishermen or other craft are supposed to enter this area at that time. Jim Remp gets a large portion of the rake off from the boat rentals and the finals are held with his place a headquarters. About one hundred and twenty five boats are to be entered in the contest besides a large number of spectators. Everyone in this district is fairly enthusiastic about the whole affair as it does mean a talking point in renting a boat. "To Qualify!" That is the slogan of the boat owners to the fishermen. However qualifying is simple as only a three pound fish is necessary and every fisherman can do this without difficulty. It is during the qualifying that the sporting goods men take their profits through the sale of spoons. Jim Remp estimates that during the past few years over a thousand dollars worth of spoons have been lost either on the bottom of the sound or in large fish. Judging from the spoons that several fishermen questioned have lost in this period this estimate is probably not exaggerated to any great extent."

ATTRACTORS

An "attractor" is a device that entices fish by flashing and/or providing alluring movement to the trailing bait, spoon or other lure. My understanding was that the flashing was thought to resemble salmon slashing through baitfish and attract quarry to the scene, but the more recent popularity of colored attractors belies this assumption. Much of the information that follows was taken from the book *Tacoma Tackle*[17]. The Shovel and Rudder, a huge spinner with a rudder to eliminate line twist, was an early attractor (c.a. 1930s) and the Herring Dodger, first marketed in 1932, was another. Both were manufactured in Tacoma. Ralph "Pop" Geer was the creator and manufacturer of the Shovel and Rudder which, for good reason, has disappeared from use. However, Geer also made "gang trolls" (a series of spinners spaced along 40 inches or so of wire) which remain popular for catching trout and kokanee in lakes. Although Geer and his company no longer exist, "Pop Gear" remains the common name applied to gang-trolls regardless of the manufacturer. Prior to the late 1950's, trolling for juvenile coho salmon with Pop Gear baited with angle worms accounted for thousands of these fish each year.

The Herring Dodger was first marketed in 1932 by Les Davis who was also located in Tacoma. The dodger was designed to wobble rather than spin, although later versions ("flashers") were intended to rotate. Unlike the Shovel and Rudder, the dodger in many different forms and colors has remained popular on the Pacific Coast and for catching transplanted Pacific salmon in the Great Lakes.

A once-popular trolling sinker, that appears to have been developed locally, incorporated a clip that was attached to the line at an appropriate distance above the terminal gear. A strike would unclip the sinker and allow it to slide down the line so as to allow a hooked fish to be brought to net or gaff. The throbbing drag of attractors, the weight of sinkers required for trolling, the constant smell and noise of the engine, or the effort of rowing, were all reasons why many anglers chose other methods of fishing.

PLUGS

At least as much as anyone would ever want to know about salmon plugs is included in Jim Lone and Mark Spogen's book *Salmon Plugs of the Northwest*[18]. According to the authors, plugs began to catch on in about 1910 when salmon showed more than a casual interest in freshwater bass plugs offered by an innovative angler. However bass plugs lacked the durability required to catch these larger and more active fish and they also inadequately represented salmon prey. Salmon plugs began to be manufactured in Seattle in 1927 and the number of local manufacturers eventually increased to "75 or so". Variations in products primarily involved how the hooks (usually two trebles) were attached, along with color and finish. Salmon plugs were originally made of Alaska cedar and later plastic. Unlike plugs made for other fish, they are relatively consistent in size and shape, averaging from five to six inches in length. A typical salmon plug was unlike those used for other fish. Excepting their beveled front ends, driving them downward when trolled, they were tear-shaped and round in cross section.

Salmon plugs were trolled without attractors. A slip sinker was clipped on the line 20 or so feet from the plug to facilitate action. A strike pulled the line from the clip allowing the sinker to slip down to a swivel attaching the line and leader. Plug-fishing experts typically "tune" their lures; by adjusting the plug's eye, to ensure that the side-to-side darting action is vevenly balanced rather than biased in one direction. Care is also taken to provide a loop, rather than a tight knot, in attaching the leader to the eye of the plug. Salmon plugs were apparently intended to imitate herring and for years were the standard lures for catching maturing Chinook throughout Puget Sound. Slight variations are inherent in the manufacture of wooden lures and most plug fishermen possessed a tooth scarred treasure or two that was considered "hot".

Eddie Bauer's original establishment in Seattle was a sporting goods store. In 1940 he advertised that they had "secured proven killer plugs" in order to "permit perfect reproduction". Photographs of two tooth scarred killers are included in the ad, which goes on to say, "Bauer Precision Tested Plugs are available in sizes 5, 6 and 7, Rosegard type, and in 4 1/2, 5 and 6, Martin type. They cost no more . . . get yours now and enjoy your fishing." Plugs were, and to a lesser extent are still, a favorite of the commercial salmon trollers and have been shown to reduce catches of sublegal-sized fish and more selective to larger Chinook salmon. Plugs remain a popular year-round lure in the Tacoma Narrows area since they can be effectively fished in deep water with strong currents while avoiding dogfish sharks and other nuisances. Lost salmon plugs once ranked with glass floats as collectables on the outer coast.

For many years plugs were the only lure at the nearly forgotten, but once famous, trophy Chinook salmon fishery at Hope Island on Skagit Bay. Skagit River summer-run Chinook, averaging around 30 pounds, were the attraction here and for years plugs were the lure of choice, although during Hope Island's waning years large "Canadian Wonder" spoons prevailed. The popularity of Hope Island, and the narrow confines of the area where the fish rested, resulted in anglers following a specific trolling pattern, at the east (flood tide) and west ed (ebb) ends of the island, that was described on a map provided by the two local boathouses. Mooching, or trolling with bait, never caught on at Hope Island.

Enos Bradner, the outdoor writer for the *Seattle Times* from 1943 to 1969, began in the early 1950's to keep an "unofficial" record of fifty-pound-plus Chinook salmon taken by anglers in Washington[19]. Because of the location of his readers and local interest being saltwater oriented, his list of "lunkers" probably under-represents Columbia and coastal river catches of qualifiers. Bradner's list includes nine fish ranging from sixty to seventy pounds taken at Hope Island. The complete list of fish over 50 pounds includes 43 from Neah Bay and Sekiu, 41 from Hope Island, 28 from Westport and 9 from Ilwaco. The largest king was a 70.5-pound fish taken on September 6, 1964 by Chet Causta out of Sekiu, edging Mrs. Ray Shy's 70-pound fish taken at Hope Island in 1954. The September catch and size of Causta's fish indicates that it may well have been a white-fleshed Harrison River (a Fraser tributary) fish, but I have no way of determining this. In 1968 Arne Goett, an addicted expert at fishing at Hope Island as well as an outspoken advocate for eliminating the local gillnet fishery, had previously boated a 60-pounder. Arne invited me to fish with him and suggested that the best time for big ones would be between mid-June and mid July. Unfortunately, I was unable to put together the trip but later, around the summer of 1970, I was treated to a trip with Maury Miller who caught a 66-pounder on a Rosegard plug in 1951. We never touched a fish.

Following World War II, interest in plug-fishing declined with the growing popularity of mooching, the use of herring for bait, and trolling with flashers. However, during the summer of 1962 interest in plugs revived with news accounts of a young U.S. Coast Guardsman who was consistently catching huge kings on plugs somewhere off the delta of the Snohomish River. Apparently refusing lucrative guiding offers, although cashing in on a salmon derby or two, he chose to fish alone and quietly embarked from Everett Boathouse and returned with his catch. My job with the Department of Fisheries at that time included periodic visits to boathouses as a part of the system for estimating sport salmon catches and I met with Stan Petersen, owner of Everett Boathouse, when all this was occurring. Stan, a well-known old-time salmon angler was previously the operator of Hope Island Resort when he played a key role in exposing fraud in the 1940 *Seattle Times* Salmon Derby. He fell hook, line and sinker for the validity of the young man's feats and could talk of little else. A few days later, at 10:30 PM on August 9, a burglar who had

Figure 12. Trolling gear: 1940's era rod and reel, ("jigger") spoons, plugs, rotating flasher and herring dodger.

been habitually stealing only one or two of the largest kings, was arrested at Whiz Fish Company in La Connor – it was the Coast Guardsman. Interest in plug-fishing took another dive. As had occurred in the 1940 salmon derby scandal, the fish in question appear to have originated in the Swinomish fish trap located at the mouth of the Skagit River.

COMMERCIAL TROLLING

The bartering of hook-and-line-caught salmon from Puget Sound among local Indians doubtlessly began thousands of years ago. The initial transaction with Europeans may have involved Lieutenant Peter Puget himself when, in May of 1792, he acquired "fine fresh salmon" while his crew was camped on Anderson Island near present-day Steilacoom[20]. The Indians providing the salmon appear to have been from the same tribe described by Charles Wilkes[21] as being proficient with hook and line. Sales of hook-and-line-caught salmon to settlers commenced on a much larger scale upon their arrival to the shores of Puget Sound.

Independent of these occurrences, commercial fishermen, apparently noting the success of anglers in Northern California's Monterey Bay, began wind-powered trolling in the late 19 Century[22]. They soon learned that the method was effective elsewhere along the coast. Stimulated by the development of reliable gasoline engines and the mild-cure process of preserving and shipping large high-quality Chinook salmon to markets in the East, commercial trolling rapidly spread northward. Since it occurred largely in the ocean beyond the jurisdiction of the states, commercial trolling was essentially uncontrolled. Utilizing multiple lines and lures, the troll fishery soon became the principle suppliers of fresh Chinook and coho to local markets along the Pacific Coast.

For many years, commercial troll licenses in Washington were very inexpensive and were purchased annually by hundreds of otherwise recreational anglers to defray expenses, exceed bag limits, or to simply make money. This fishing was often conducted using standard sport-fishing equipment and boats. Participants in this activity were known as kelpers because they intended to remain inshore in contrast to larger troll vessels that ranged as far north as Southeast Alaska. This practice continued into the mid-70s.

SPINNING TO MOOCHING

Relatively early in the 20 century, anglers casting from the piers of Seattle's Elliott Bay discovered a new way of catching salmon. Salmon fishing from Elliott Bay piers, such as at Bell Street, remained popular throughout the 1940s. The typical fishing outfit consisted of a long, light, home-made natural cane rod, with a single ferrule, agate guides, and a simple reel. A 1935 *Fishing Guide to the Northwest*[23] describes the process of making a proper bamboo cane rod, lamenting the fact that the current price of $0.50 was ten times the previous price of cane. Long casts were required and were accomplished using "raw" silk lines previously soaked and coiled on the deck or in a bucket to avoid tangling. The primary function of the reel was to store line, and to retrieve or give line when a fish was tight to the reel. Banana-shaped sinkers, weighing an ounce or two, were swiveled at both ends. Bead swivels at the terminal end of the sinkers were critical since baits, hooked onto a six- to eight-foot gut leader, were rigged to spin through the water and anything less would result in a hopelessly twisted leader.

Anglers usually allowed the sinker to touch bottom and then retrieved by "stripping". Stripping was similar to the retrieve used by fly-fishers but the strips were a foot or two, rather than inches, in length. With sufficient tidal current, the bait would spin without being stripped and this often produced the desired result. This new technique was called "spinning", referring to the action of the bait rather than casting with a fixed-spool reel – a technique that was to come much later. Anglers of Japanese ancestry were among the more skilled practitioners of the art, including cutting and rigging the bait. A gentleman of near legendary status was K. Kawaguchi – known simply as "K.K". He may have been among the first to master the art of cutting "spinners" from the sides of large herring – a skill that helped win prizes in the annual *Seattle Times* Salmon Derbies. Salmon fishing from Seattle docks, such as at the foot of Bell Street, remained popular for many years as noted in the 1949 Annual Report of the Washington Department of Fisheries: *"During the winter, as many as 100 fishermen a day fished from Seattle docks. Their take of salmon, often as great as that of the boat fishermen ..."*

Roscoe *(call me Harry)* Dunagan was no spring chicken when I first met him at a Seattle Poggie Club-bait cutting class during the mid-60s where he took great pride in demonstrating his skill in producing perfect spinners and plug-cut herring with his genuine *Bill the Greek* knife. I later learned that he was an angling mentor to Pete Bergman – my colleague and" "partner in crime" at the Department of Fisheries. During the 1940's, Harry had introduced Pete to the west end of the Strait of Juan de Fuca where they camped and successfully trolled salmon plugs at Pillar Point. At the time of our meeting I had asked Harry what he knew about the origins of spinning and mooching. He knew a great deal and in 1965 he provided me with a rare and written account of what was occurring a century ago on Seattle's waterfront:

"Just wondering how many remember way back around 1911 when we didn't have the modern tackle we have today! Of course we didn't particularly need it as we were blessed with an abundance of the 'Silver Horde'.

"The average tackle then consisted of natural bamboo or Calcutta rods. As to guides, most of us used just plain glass white porcelain guides taped on with surgical tape. We used a product known as raw silk, a by-product of silk processed with glue which came in tests of about two to 50 pounds, and of course for spinning we usually used a test of 8 pounds.

"Very few people fished from row boats and those that did used hand lines and spoons. Several brands were on the market: F.S.T. made by F. S. Tucker in Ballard, McMahon, Seattle Spoon and others. Reels were practically useless, only to coil your line on as the line had to be wet or damp to make it pliable enough to cast. In these years, around 1911 to 1915, most of the sports salmon fishing was done off the docks or hand line trolling and even then a lot of the docks prohibited fishing as there was constant danger of fishermen being hurt when ships were docking. I remember the only docks we were really welcome on were the Coal Dock which still stands south of Coleman Dock at the foot of Jackson Street. North of Coleman Dock was the Grand Trunk Dock which is now Black Ball Freight Lines. North of there was dock no. 99 off which we fished and from there to the next welcome dock was pier no. 10 where the wholesale fish markets were. On further north there was the Seattle Lumber Company pier 12 and some fishing from the dock at Smith Cove.

"At that time salmon eggs were a drag on the market and were dropped

through the planking into the bay from the fish houses which attracted the
salmon trout, making fishing extra good at these docks.

"*This is where I first met Harry Dines and Frank Lundstrum but didn't*
acquire names but met them on the docks at different times fishing. In later
years, at Dines' resort on Whidby Island we reminisced about the old times
and the dock fishing in earlier days. The resort was located at Dines Point
(Note: near the herring trap in Holmes Harbor. The trap was a primary

Figure 13. Harry Dunagan's Seattle waterfront (ca. 1911).
University of Washington Libraries, Special Collections SEA2170.

source of adult large, firm spawned-out herring that were popular for
cutting spinners.) I asked Harry who was the first man to use spinners cut
from herring and he said to his earliest remembrance they were first used
around 1908 and 1909 and gave me the name of the man which I can't
recall at this time. He and Harry Dines fished together and he thought they
were the first to use cut spinners and cast for salmon off the docks. Slits were
first used cut from small sea perch but were too fragile and would not stay
on the hook and herring were found to be better.

"*The majority of the people who fished at that time on docks used light*
fly-type rods and fished with fresh eggs. Tegusa leaders were not too plentiful

and we could only procure them from Japanese stores. They were a silk cocoon product of China, controlled and marketed by the Japanese. They were graded from quite light to maybe six or eight pound test. They usually had a flaw and needed testing, soaked and retied before being used. The egg fishermen used lighter leaders and often had difficulty in holding the larger fish, but we who were spinning used heavier leaders and caught larger fish as a rule.

"The Japanese who fished off of the docks at that time fished in a very peculiar manner. They used a very long cane rod, sometimes 15 feet long, and cast their line upstream on the tide with little or no lead and one small chunk of fresh eggs, and as the line ran down with the tide they usually hooked into a trout by the time the line started up with the tide (Note: small Chinook and coho salmon were called "trout"). Our biggest difficulty in those days was in getting our fish up on the dock but someone usually had a net upturned on a 20 foot curtain rod. Then it was quite a trick to get a floundering fish into it and we lost many.

"I fished the docks quite often and sometimes we encountered southwest winds which blew so hard in fall and winter we had difficulty in casting our lines into the wind. Our lines would dry out so fast it was trouble to keep them from bird-nesting. When these conditions prevailed we would take the ferry from Coleman Dock to West Seattle, at a cost of only five cents, and walk south to the old Globe Mills and fish from that dock where we were protected from the southwest winds. This dock was located just north of where I think the first boat house was erected, the West Seattle Boat House. I fished with a fellow by the name of Shorty Hicks, a very good fisherman, and I often wonder if he is still about.

"If there were any boat houses around 1911-1915 I can't recall them. I was away in WW I during 1916 and returned early in 1918 and my first experience fishing from a boat house was at Ray's in Ballard, don't recall if it was called Ray's then. (Note: Ray Lichtenberger's boathouse in Ballard dates back to 1939. Before this Ray's Boathouse was located on Harbor Island in Elliot Bay). When I returned the boat houses had caught on and were selling fishing to the general public. Two boathouses were now on the East Waterway, one at the foot of King Street known as Straley's and one at the foot of Connecticut Street. Straley's Boathouse was quite popular and Mrs. Straley was a very clever fisherwoman. She let me in on a secret that really worked. As I mentioned before, leaders were really a problem and once used

*were not safe to depend on for a second trip because the light would make
them brittle and useless. She discovered that getting them fresh from Japanese
stores and keeping them soaked in mineral oil saturated pads would toughen
and preserve them and not affect their clearness or scent, and by all means
kept away from light.*

*"At the other boathouse on Connecticut Street is where I first met "Wild
Bill Daugherty" or rather heard him as he was surely a wild cuss. If he was
anchored out in the stream in front of the boathouse you would be sure to
know it as he blasted a blue streak of foul prose every time he hooked a fish
and if it was a "bow-wow" (spiny dogfish) you could hear him up to the
Smith Building. I remember on one of our fishing trips to Hat Island out
of Everett, arriving there around 1 p.m., we kicked (traveled by outboard
motor) toward the island and anchored about a half a mile south and east of
the island. Bill sat in the stern of the boat and I in front. He had two sets of
tackle, plain old can poles, don't remember if they were jointed or not, white
guides and tips secured with surgical tape. He was using a fairly light line
with two ounces of lead, one rod from each side of the boat and hardly would
he have one line down he would have a fish hooked, we would sock that one
and reach over and hook the other and just alternate back and forth with
a fish on at all times. I sat there wondering what his method was as I only
caught a fish occasionally. I just stopped and watched him cut spinners and
noted his method of hook-up. I had been cutting spinners since 1911, but
from that day on I never deviated from Bill's spinner and hook-up. Bill used
practically the same dead spinner method as Bill Lindberg, fed his line out till
it hit bottom, pulled it 10 feet off and let it set and work in the tide. Bill was
not particular about the looks of his rod as long as it had fairly good bend in
the tip, but from the sinker to the razor sharp hook it was a work of art. Bill
did not use the heavier leaders, he would use about the medium weight.*

*"I was helping the late Eddie Vine at his salmon class at the YMCA one
night and he said to me, "You sure copy my spinners Harry, "and I looked at
him and said "No Eddie we both copy Wild Bill's spinners." And he finally
admitted Wild Bill taught him the art of cutting a perfect spinner."*

Although Dunagan's account recognizes Frank Lundstrum as an
early dock fishing acquaintance, he does not credit him with inventing
spinning. However, an article in the 1940 *Fishing Guide to the Northwest*
does just that and gives the date as 1898.

Spinning from a boat involved anchoring in flowing water as deep as 125 feet. This requires a good, long anchor line, and a length of holding chain that was usually attached to a Danforth anchor. In addition to stripping the line to provide the desired results, salmon were also taken by simply allowing the tidal current to work the bait. Anchoring gear was often available for rent at boathouses. This method of fishing, involving light tackle, became very popular among the Sound's salmon angling elite. An excellent description of spinning is included in *Northwest Angling*[24]. It later became obvious that the basic technique, without the long cast required for dock fishing, was also effective from a drifting or slowly rowed boat, and that cut spinners were not the only effective bait since plug-cut herring and properly rigged whole herring and sandlance also caught fish. This off-shoot of spinning became known as "Mooching" and its popularity was enhanced with the availability of monofilament nylon lines and leaders. Although spinning, or at least cutting spinners, has long ago become a lost art on Puget Sound, a modern form is currently popular around Sitka, in southeast Alaska, where boats anchor, in precise locations, in depths upwards of 200 feet and, although working mainly "plugged" herring on the reel, rather than stripping, they are essentially "spinning".

Mooched bait is either simply allowed to descend into the depths from the weight of the sinker or is cast a short distance, and allowed to sink, so as to prevent the bait from tangling with the sinker and line. As reliable outboard motors became available, some anglers discovered that the options of free drift or powered motion, both forward and reverse, could be very effective for determining the most productive depth and presentation. For example, slowly backing into the current or wind sinks the bait while forward movement produces the opposite effect. This technique became "motor mooching". The advantage of mooching is that it provides two dimensional movements to the bait rather than a horizontal path resulting from trolling. One of the most common takes of a mooched bait occurs on its descent which, to the novice angler, as though the sinker has grounded. Mooching tackle, usually requiring heavier sinkers, can also be effective by simply trolling with it.

The technique of mooching eventually spread from Puget Sound to wherever anglers sought salmon along the Pacific Coast of North America.

It was also an important factor in the development of the charter fishery off the Washington Coast since it allows more anglers to fish at one time from a drifting boat than is practical when trolling.

My first mooching experience occurred during August of 1949, shortly after attending a bait-cutting class at the Seattle YMCA. The instructor, a member of the Seattle Poggie Club, may have been Gus Zarkades but I don't remember. A few days later, two us who attended the class, rented a row boat, tackle, and a landing net at Ray's Boathouse in Ballard. It was well past the hour when one, no less rank neophytes, was apt to catch a fish. Somewhere off Golden Gardens, with me rowing, my companion caught a twenty-plus-pound "king" which qualified him for the finals of the *Seattle Times* Derby.

My preference for this method of fishing is that one is more in touch with the fish. Long, light rods are in order and sinker weight can usually be reduced to a maximum of three ounces if line diameter is reduced. Although line manufacturers appear to consistently under-rate breaking strength, catching salmon of thirty or so pounds in open water on line rated at eight pounds breaking strength is not that difficult. The sense of contact with the fish can be further enhanced by using the pressure of a thumb on the spool for drag requiring that one must judge when to give and take line. This to me is far more entertaining than relying on the drag built into most reels so that playing a fish is essentially a matter of cranking regardless of what the fish is doing. However, the alternative requires using a "direct drive" reel or one providing that option and such reels are becoming difficult to find.

My introduction extolls the writings of Roderick Haig-Brown – the consummate fly-fishing aesthete – and laments his disinterest in saltwater salmon fishing. However, in his *Fisherman's Fall*[5] he condescends to compare the relative merits of flasher trolling with mooching and grudgingly recognizes the skill associated with the latter. He describes flashers, attractors, and dodgers as "*the ultimate horror*" in being "*ugly, clumsy, and awkward to fish with*" in that "*they get in the way in the last stages, when a fish is being brought to net and, most serious of all, they grossly inhibit the activity of the fish when it is hooked.*"

Figure 14. A page from State of Washington Department of Fisheries Development of Washington State Salmon Sport Fishery Through 1964 (Research Bulletin No 7, 5/67) showing common terminal gear of the 1960s.

① COHO FLY
½ ACTUAL SIZE

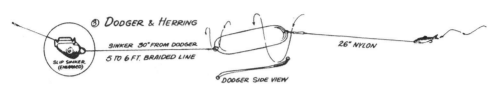

③ DODGER & HERRING
SINKER 30" FROM DODGER
5 TO 6 FT. BRAIDED LINE
SLIP SINKER (ENHANCE)
26" NYLON
DODGER SIDE VIEW

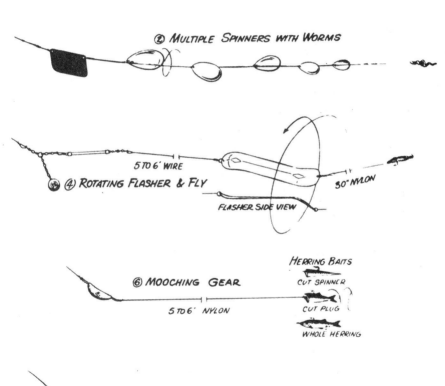

② MULTIPLE SPINNERS WITH WORMS

5 TO 6' WIRE
④ ROTATING FLASHER & FLY
30" NYLON
FLASHER SIDE VIEW

⑥ MOOCHING GEAR
5 TO 6' NYLON
HERRING BAITS
CUT SPINNER
CUT PLUG
WHOLE HERRING

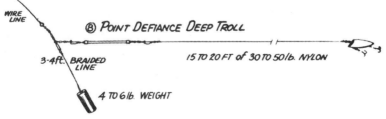

WIRE LINE
⑧ POINT DEFIANCE DEEP TROLL
3-4ft. BRAIDED LINE
15 TO 20 FT of 30 TO 50 lb. NYLON
4 TO 6 lb. WEIGHT

Figure 14 continued. A page from State of Washington
Department of Fisheries Development of Washington State
Salmon Sport Fishery Through 1964 (Research Bulletin No
7, 5/67) showing common terminal gear of the 1960s.

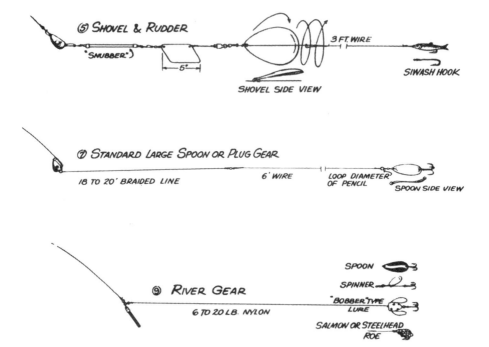

⑤ SHOVEL & RUDDER

"SNUBBER")

|—5"—|

SHOVEL SIDE VIEW

3 FT. WIRE

SIWASH HOOK

⑦ STANDARD LARGE SPOON OR PLUG GEAR

18 TO 20' BRAIDED LINE   6' WIRE   LOOP DIAMETER OF PENCIL   SPOON SIDE VIEW

⑨ RIVER GEAR

6 TO 20 LB. NYLON

SPOON
SPINNER
"BOBBER" TYPE LURE
SALMON OR STEELHEAD ROE

3   Herring and other Baitfishes

Generally speaking, spinning and mooching were techniques utilized by the Sound's more proficient anglers. Many were meticulous, perhaps unnecessarily so, in cutting and rigging the bait so that its spinning action was just right – even to the extent that using a specific hand-made knife was important. "Bill the Greek" (Niforas) was renowned as a maker of bait-cutting knives and to a lesser degree as a salmon angler. When I knew Bill, apart from an occasional female visitor, he lived alone in a loft above Lloyd's Boathouse on the west side of Elliott Bay, where he ground knife blades from discarded hack-saw power blades. Possessing a Bill the Greek bait knife, with its Alaska cedar handle and case, was a status symbol of the first order. Bill, a short powerful native of Greece, was one of many remarkable characters that frequented Lloyd's. I had a great deal of respect for Lloyd Sanborn who was very supportive of the Department of Fisheries and had once worked for Ray Lichtenberger (later owner of Ray's Boathouse in Ballard) when he operated a boathouse on Harbor Island. Judge William Long, although having lost an arm, was also a salmon angler, a Lloyd's customer, and a friend of Bill's. Although my knowledge of the incident is second hand, Bill was once arrested by a nasty "fish cop" for shooting a confused beaver swimming near the boathouse that was mistaken for a seal. At the time there was a cash bounty for seal noses and Bill thought he was doing the proper thing. However, instead of being seven dollars richer, he was faced with a hefty fine. Bill had the good fortune of appearing before Judge Long and was promptly acquitted.

For years, many of Seattle's most skilled salmon anglers were Lloyd's Boathouse customers when it was the site of the Tengu Salmon Derby held on weekends during November in Elliott Bay. Mooching was the only fishing method allowed and although the original organizers were of Japanese ancestry the contest was open to all.

The frequent occurrence of herring heads and parts in salmon stomachs, discarded in the process of cutting bait, did little to diminish the perceived need for ritualistic precision. "Gus" Zarkades, and other Seattle Poggie Club members, dedicated much of their spare time to conducting bait-cutting classes. Zarkades, another native of Greece, was a true gentle-

Figure 15. Bill the Greek blade case (replacement), bait knife, plug-cut herring and spinner.

man and a disciple of his art. *Life Magazine* once featured Gus in his quest for king salmon at Neah Bay.

The Sound's more skilled anglers were primarily interested in the larger salmon: Chinook salmon ("blackmouth"), maturing coho during the summer months and adult Chinook ("kings") from August to mid-September. Although herring is the most common bait, Pacific sandlance (erroneously called "candlefish" by local anglers) were also popular in northern Puget Sound where, like herring, they were held alive in bait tanks for sale at some boathouses.

In the beginning local anglers collected their own herring for bait. The herring rake, copied from a device used by Northwest Indians, was made of a long, narrow piece of blade-shaped wood. A row of sharp nail-like points projected from the edge of the rake's business end. The rake was sliced through a school of fish, in a motion similar to paddling a canoe and follow-through, carrying the impaled fish into the boat. This obviously created a terrible mess, but the blood, scales and injured herring often attracted hungry salmon to the scene. Indians originally used sharpened points of ocean spray (iron wood) or splinters of bone for rake tines. Since few herring rakes exist outside of museums, the need for a recent state regulation outlawing their use seems hardly necessary. Herring can also be jigged, with an array of tiny plankton-resembling hooks arranged vertically on a line kept taught by a sinker at its lower end, or dipped from a "ball", although the latter option could have been rather difficult without a speedy boat. Herring balls are usually formed when fish-eating marine birds, notably rhinoceros auklets, cause the fish to school into increasingly tight masses that eventually surface. The ball can be so dense that it breaks the surface and creates a sound not unlike bacon frying in a hot pan. Gulls, diving into the mass, give the ball away from a great distance and with a deft approach and swipe of the net hundreds, if not thousands, of the preoccupied fish can be captured in a single dip. Many times during my forays into south Puget Sound during the 70s and 80s, I took no bait and depended entirely on dipping or jigging a supply.

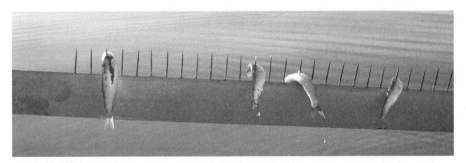

Figure 16. Peter Bergman with the herring rake he patterned after those used by Northwest Indians, and made for "kelping" at Neah Bay.

By 1953, the use of herring for salmon angling on Puget Sound and elsewhere created such a demand that almost all of the annual commercial herring catch on the sound was used to satisfy that market[26]. Bait herring was sold alive, fresh and in frozen packages of a dozen. Prior to the shift in the market, tons of adult herring were caught, many in traps located around the Sound, for commercial Pacific cod, halibut, and shark fishing. During the years of World War II, prior to synthesizing vitamin A, there was a high demand for shark (primarily spiny dogfish) livers. These commercial hook-and-line fisheries used adult herring for bait and the traps to catch them were located in major herring spawning areas. In 1930 there were 19 licensed herring traps in Puget Sound and by 1947 the only such trap existed at Holmes Harbor on the east side of Whidbey Island. A requirement of operating this herring trap was to allow the fish to spawn, before they were harvested, on brush that collected the masses of adhesive eggs. The brush, usually Christmas tree Douglas fir, was submerged along the lead into the trap and in its terminal end ("pot").

Apart from those capable of filleting "spinners" from adult herring, they are not the bait of choice for the vast majority of salmon anglers. The demand is for herring ranging in length from about four inches ("minnows") to seven inches ("plugs"). Such fish are in their first and second year of life. Bait herring were caught by beach seining, off-shore in seines by "round-hauling" (purse seining was illegal), by trapping, and by "ball fishing". Herring commercially caught for salmon bait were placed in live tanks aboard vessels and transported to holding pens. "Ball fishing", requiring the participation of rhinoceros auklets or murres and gulls, may be unique to Puget Sound. The diving birds ball the bait and drive it to the surface, the gulls, visible at considerable distance, swarm over the ball and telegraph its presence to a "chase boat" teamed with a larger vessel fitted with a live tank. These small fast boats speed to the ball, coast in and surround the oblivious fish with a large dip net. Racing to a particular ball could be competitive and a source of conflict among ball fishers. The live fish are then loaded into the live tank and transported to a net pen for "starving"– a process that reduces fat and results in a firmer product that tends to stay on a hook. Much of this bait was packaged and frozen for later use. Some was hauled daily and sold fresh at major sport-fishing ports.

In addition to herring, other species also entered the Holmes Harbor trap. Biologists from the Department of Fisheries took advantage of this in May, 1955 by tagging and releasing more than a thousand 20- 24-inch juvenile sablefish (black cod)[27]. Subsequent returns demonstrated that these fish soon left the Sound and moved northward along the outer coast. Six and seven years later three of the tagged fish were caught by Japanese vessels in the Bering Sea after having grown at a rate of about 1.4 inches per year [28]. Hungry salmon were also attracted the perimeter of the trap and some of the biologists would take advantage of the opportunity by baiting a hook with a live herring and tossing it over the side while working at the trap.

Herring are not the only major forage fish that local Chinook and coho salmon depend upon. Both species consume large quantities of sandlance when they are available and they were a popular bait fish in the waters surrounding Whidbey Island for many years. Commercial sandlance fishermen, such as at Jim and John's Columbia Beach Resort, caught them in beach seines and anglers sometimes raked them from sandy beaches at low tide. Sandlance also "ball" but do not bite the hooks of a jig. Both herring and sandlance are the primary forage fish in Puget Sound and throughout the Strait of Juan de Fuca and along the northern portion of the outer coast. Anchovies are prime forage for salmon from Grays Harbor south and are the primary species used for catching albacore when they appear during late summer and early fall in the warmer waters located well off-shore. Anchovies are occasionally abundant in Puget Sound and Chinook and coho salmon are quick to take advantage of them. Some of the most spectacular fishing I ever enjoyed in Puget Sound occurred during the summers of the early 1970s when anchovies were massed against the north-western shoreline of Camano Island and provided a ready source of both bait and husky salmon. In recent years anchovies have been relatively common in the Olympia area. Although surf and other smelt are abundant in Puget Sound, they appear relatively uncommon in the stomachs of Chinook and coho salmon and are seldom used for bait.

4   Evolving Fishing Methods

Fly-fishing – For many years it has been known that artificial flies could be used with great success for catching coho salmon. This method appears to have originated at the mouth of the Cowichan River in British Columbia – where it is known as "buck-tailing"– although polar bear hair was a much preferred material. For many years, a 32-pound coho salmon, caught at that location, stood as the world record. A 1938 technical publication of the U.S. Bureau of Fisheries goes so far as to state: "At the present time the Campbell River is best known for fly-fishing for kings, and many coho are taken by this method at the mouth of the Cowichan River"[29]. Although I question if fly-fishing for Chinook salmon was ever popular at Campbell River or elsewhere at the time, the mouth of the Cowichan was indeed well known for coho buck-tailing. The method involves trolling a weightless, four- to six-inch fly, a short distance astern of a boat moving at a speed of about five knots. The waking fly is most effective on coho feeding on baitfish that have been chased to the surface. The method is so effective that small-boat commercial fishermen operating out of Neah Bay have been known to use it in preference to other methods. The off-shore tide rips in the vicinity of Cape Flattery, from mid-July through early September, provide the State's best fly-fishing for large coho. Conventional fly casting is gaining in popularity here and it has the potential of becoming a world-class attraction.

Fly casting for coho has also become popular on inner-Puget Sound where coho in their third year of life are sought from early winter – as foot-long fish – throughout the summer when resident fish approach their maximum average weight of three or four pounds. Early in the year the schools of juvenile fish are often abundant along the shorelines of south Puget Sound where they can be seen feeding on the surface or, for no apparent reason, leaping into the air. Although mature coho staging off Puget Sound are often very abundant, they are far more difficult to catch on bait or lures. Nevertheless, an increasing number of fly-casters are targeting them during the early fall. Chinook salmon typically feed well below the surface and are only occasionally taken by conventional fly-fishing either as immature or mature fish. The large numbers of pink salmon that have returned to Puget Sound in recent cycle years have created an unprecedented opportunity for fly-anglers, and casting from beaches en route to major spawning streams is gaining in popularity. Much of the mystique of taking a fish on a fly has been erased by what appears to be an accelerated level of competition among the fish to be first to reach lure, bait, or fly.

Interest in fly-fishing for salmon was spurred with the 1985 publication of *Fly Fishing for Pacific Salmon*[30] authored by three local anglers who spent considerable time in research and developing fly patterns imitating the bait fishes, crustaceans and other organisms comprising the diets of salmon. Bruce Ferguson, the senior author of the book, was a good friend and chose to live at the entrance to Wollochet Bay where, in past years, flocks of Boneparte gulls ("Coho birds") were often busy picking krill from the edges of rips. Bruce was forever on the look-out for the subtle rings of feeding resident coho that often appeared within casting range of his beach. I was honored when Bruce asked me to write the Foreword of their book.

Jigging – Anyone who has spent much time mooching has noticed that salmon frequently chase a sinker as it is brought to the surface. Before jigs became popular, my mentor Al Lasater made very effective rockfish jigs by simply threading his line through four or five inches of "pencil" lead and tying a treble hook to the end (sandlance imitation?). Commercial salmon jigs appear to have originated elsewhere and they have become very popular for salmon and rockfish throughout the Puget Sound region and the outer coast. Jigs made of lead, or other heavy metal, come in a number of shapes. Those designed for salmon angling appeared to originate in British Columbia where *Buzz Bombs* cast from boats, piers and shorelines, or simply lowered into the water column, created a sensation. *Buzz Bombs* are diamond shape in cross section, elongate, and tapered toward the ends. Jigs that are cast are typically allowed to sink and retrieved in a series of twitches; whereas, those lowered to and maintained at the desired depth, are continually twitched and lifted with the rod and allowed to drop back. Salmon are often attracted to the fluttering action of the falling lures. Jigs currently come in a variety of shapes – most of which are currently shaped to resemble bait fishes (usually sandlance). Jigs have the advantage of being less attractive to dogfish that can be a serious nuisance when fishing with natural bait.

Downriggers – During the 1960s, Chinook salmon eggs from Green River Hatchery near Auburn, along with coho salmon eggs from Washington hatcheries, were provided to the Michigan Department of Natural Resources for stocking Lake Michigan. It was hoped that the introduced predators would both feast upon and reduce the enormous and troublesome population of alewifes – a small member of the herring family – that periodically died off in such numbers as to cause public – health concerns; and shore up an ailing sport fishery. The alewifes themselves were not native to the Great Lakes and had reached the basin, from the Atlantic Ocean, via man-made canals or by other unnatural means.

Following the remarkable early success of the introductions, we were contacted and later visited by Stan Lievense, an angling specialist with the Michigan Department of Natural Resources. Stan was working to increase angler efficiency so as to take better advantage of the thriving salmon population. Stan visited us in Olympia and we had a fine time mooching for resident Chinook salmon at Johnson Point. Stan also visited Les Davis and, by Stan's account, had a very successful day with Davis – no doubt trolling with the Tacoma tackle manufacturer's products. Mooching never caught on in the Great Lakes but a new method did. A letter to me from Stan, dated July 1, 1971, contained the following paragraphs:

"Our charter boat captains are now professionals. They use electric thermometers expertly, they use chart type depth sounders, they use downriggers and outriggers, they use radios for communicating with each other, and they now have good sea-worthy boats.

"Downriggers are a development by our Great Lakes fishermen to get trolling lines down without the need of adding heavy sinkers. The downrigger is merely a means of lowering a 4 to 7 lb. lead ball on a measured cable from which a release mechanism is attached. The fisherman lets out 20 feet or so of the terminal end of his fishing line, takes a tuck of the line into the release mechanism of the downrigger and then simultaneously the two are lowered to the right temperature level".

Downriggers quickly became the standard method used in the big lakes to troll artificial lures through productive depths where temperatures range from 50 to 60 degrees. Upon being hooked, the fish pulls the line from the release mechanism and free from the cumbersome sinker. Downriggers have since become very popular for salmon angling in Washington, and unlike the Great Lakes where artificial lures prevail, are frequently used with herring. Most boats rigged for saltwater salmon angling now appear to have a downrigger or two affixed near corners of the stern. They have become quite sophisticated with telescoping booms to separate the cable from the hull, digital depth display, electronic retrieval, and a feature that automatically maintains a fixed distance to the bottom. Downriggers, along with fast-sinking small-diameter synthetic braided lines, have resulted in the disappearance of solid-wire fishing lines that once filled many local salmon reels.

Some of us who prefer to mooch have often had problems in popular fishing locations when downrigger cables have severed fishing lines. This is particularly likely to occur at unfortunate times when a large hooked fish makes a long surface run near an inattentive downrigger troller.

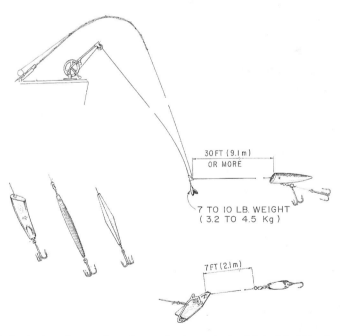

Figure 17. A simple downrigger, salmon jigs, and a down-planing "sinker" that trips to reduce drag when a fish is hooked.
Washington Department of Fisheries diagram.

Bait fishing for chum salmon – Mature chum salmon return in large numbers to Puget Sound from October well into December and anglers are paying far more attention to them than in years past. The problem has been hooking them in a manner consistent with the principles of "fair angling". A significant breakthrough occurred in 1999 when Greg Cloud, an Olympia angler, discovered that milling chums would readily take anchovies suspended vertically under a float. The gear is simply cast among the milling fish and allowed to dead drift. Cloud emphasizes the importance of anchovy, rather than herring, bait. This fairly recent development has the potential of contributing significantly to opportunities for local salmon angling as would be a similar "breakthrough" if it were to occur with maturing coho.

Recent developments in terminal trolling gear – A variety of dodgers and flashers, roughly patterned after shapes of the originals, are now available to salmon anglers. Many are now made of plastic and, rather than virtually all being finished in polished nickel or brass, a variety of bright and fluorescent colors are now used to attract salmon to their trailing lures. Fish Flash Flashers, a significant new design that "rotate around a linear axis", have become very popular since they both catch fish and reduce the drag associated with other attractors. Planing sinkers that trip when a fish is hooked are also helpful in this regard. Contemporary spoons, no longer just silver and brass, come in a variety of brilliant hues and taking the trend to the extreme some,

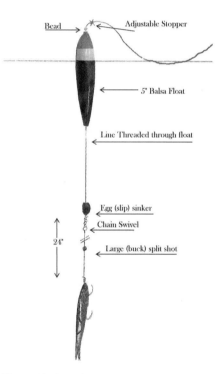

Figure 18. Greg Cloud's chum salmon bait rig.

dissatisfied with the natural color of herring, are dying it blue!

Boats, motors and electronics – During my life on the water, fishing boats have evolved from those made of wood, to plywood, to fiberglass and aluminum. Planing hulls, powerful and dependable motors (especially outboards), have vastly increased the range of a large segment of the fleet. It seems that only yesterday, venturing 40 or so miles off-shore in a small boat in search of albacore would be unheard of, but it has become commonplace; and private fishing boats have replaced the charter-boat fleet in accounting for the majority of the ocean sport salmon catch.

In the recent past, serious salmon anglers relied on navigational charts to locate promising submerged contours for fishing and would attempt to locate them by triangulating features on the land. Testing for depth with a sinking line also played a role in locating the proper area. Sea-bird watching/identification were important fish finders. Although diving, screaming gulls or fleeing baitfish spraying from the water are obvious signs of the presence of salmon, more subtle clues were such as things knowing that one should essentially ignore the rafts of western grebes, or a few pigeon guillemots, and concentrate on the likes of the rhinoceros auklets and murres. While quietly drifting in dense fog, only the sound of screaming gulls has led me to fish.

Although I am annoyed by ceaseless CB radio and cell phone chatter while fishing, it has played a significant role in connecting anglers and fish. Inexpensive sonar has essentially unraveled the mysteries of the depths. Salmon anglers have become so dependent upon it that it is as important to them as their rods and reels. Affordable GPS provides the means of traveling to and from productive fishing areas and, to the detriment of some rockfish populations, locating reefs and small underwater pinnacles and other features that were former havens for these fishes.

5   Fishing Areas, the Catch and its Origin

DETERMINING ORIGIN BY TAGGING

During the latter portion of the 19th century, it was commonly believed that salmon at sea remained within the vicinity of their rivers of origin since it was difficult to imagine the true extent of their homing ability. The much greater distances of salmon migrations was later demonstrated when salmon caught at sea and tagged, usually with colorful dime-sized disks pinned under their dorsal fins, were recovered in rivers vast distances from where they were tagged.

Since then, tagging has become far more sophisticated and much more is known about the origins of Chinook and coho salmon caught at sea. Over the past 40 years more than a billion Pacific Northwest salmon, the vast majority Chinook and coho salmon originating in hatcheries, have been coded wire tagged. About 10 million of these have been subsequently recovered and analyzed. The minute stainless-steel tags, about the size of two-day-old whiskers (1.1 mm) and bearing unique inscriptions, are implanted into the snouts of fry and fingerlings prior to their release.

In a coordinated coast-wide effort, technicians from California to British Columbia and Alaska sample catches and collect the tags for analysis. Coded wire tagging has provided a wealth of information on where Chinook and coho salmon go and how many are being caught. It also enables managers to evaluate options relating to hatchery operations and provides critical information relating to international and Indian fishing treaties compliance. In addition to coded wire tagging, important information has also been gained from earlier fin clipping and other means of identification.

Coded wire tagging has also demonstrated that different stocks of Chinook and coho salmon maintain specific migration and foraging patterns. For example, Chinook salmon native to the outer Washington Coast are far north migrating stocks that contribute heavily to catches in northern British Columbia and Southeast Alaska. In contrast, Lower Columbia River fall-run Chinook primarily forage off the coasts of Washington and Vancouver Island. Cowlitz River coho salmon primarily

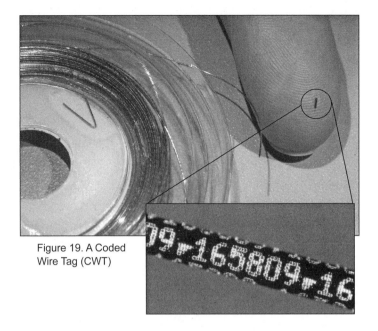

Figure 19. A Coded Wire Tag (CWT)

forage off the Washington Coast; whereas, coho from a Cowlitz tributary, the Toutle River, turn left along the Oregon Coast.

PUGET SOUND

Puget Sound provides the environment for three different salmon life phases: a nursery for rearing juveniles, a home for resident fish, and a staging area for salmon returning from the ocean to spawn in local streams. Coho, Chinook and to a lesser degree, pink salmon are of primary importance to anglers. Many such fish, less than 12 inches long, are destined to leave this nursery for feeding areas north of the Canadian border. In days past, Chinook and coho salmon of this size were commonly referred to as "salmon trout". Since real trout of this size are a desirable freshwater catch and conditions on the inner Sound are somewhat similar to those in local lakes, one can understand why people would target juvenile salmon if allowed to do so. These fish were very abundant, they occurred near the surface, and were easy to catch on equipment very much like that used for trout fishing. From the earliest recorded times fishing for small salmon was popular on Puget Sound and rules to curtail these catches were generally resisted by the public at large.

Figure 20. Significant salmon sportfishing locations on inner Puget
Sound. From Washington Department of Fisheries Research
Bulletin No. 7 (1967).

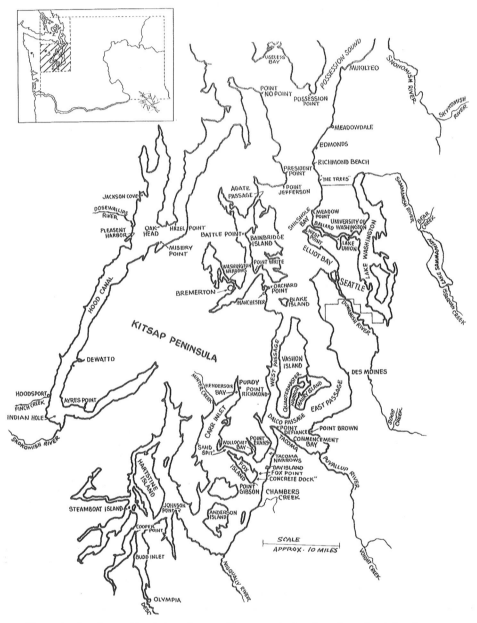

Figure 1. Locales pertinent to salmon angling on central and southern Puget Sound.

Resident coho salmon – Resident salmon, in terms of numbers caught, were historically the most important to Puget Sound anglers[31, 32]. Tagging experiments have shown that these fish, Chinook, coho and, in the past, pink salmon, primarily originate in local streams and spend most of, if not their entire marine lives within the Sound. Resident salmon tend to be smaller than their ocean-reared contemporaries. They are important because they are feeding, and thus "bite", and occur in protected water near population centers where anglers can fish for them throughout the year.

For many years resident coho were the Puget Sound anglers' "bread and butter". Washington Department of Fisheries sport-catch estimates began in 1938 and from then until 1957 these fish dominated catches. During a typical year, fish in their ultimate (third) year of life are expected to average 14 inches in January and about 20 inches in August, averaging three or four pounds at maturity, while Neah Bay fish would then be expected to be about 4 inches longer in August and about twice the weight of resident fish at maturity.

Figure 21. The catch in the photo, taken during the early 1930s at a boathouse in the Meadowdale area, appears to consist largely of resident coho salmon. The size of the fish indicates it to be early summer. Since the average number of anglers in a boat of this size was about 2.5, the photo represents the catch in two or more boats. University of Washington Libraries, Special Collections SOC1573.

Resident coho tended to be widely distributed throughout Puget Sound during the winter months of their final year. Later in the spring and summer they tended to congregate in areas rich in zooplankton. Analyses of stomach contents showed that amphipods, krill, crab larvae and similar creatures constituted the bulk of their diet until mid-summer when they relied more on sandlance and herring[33]. Admiralty Inlet, the south end of Whidbey Island, and the Tacoma Narrows were notable for resident coho angling

The former abundance of these fish was noted in 1918 and 1919 when, E. Victor Smith, a University of Washington scientist, investigated the waste associated with harvesting immature salmon in the various commercial salmon fisheries[34]. Smith concluded that the *". . . most inexcusable slaughter takes place in Puget Sound during the 8 or 10 weeks that follow the opening of the (commercial) season, April 15. These silver salmon are in their third year, but at the time the fishing season opens they do not weigh more than one or two pounds and many of them weigh less than one pound. The region where the most of these young fish are taken is Possession Sound and the banks just south of Whidby Island."* According to Smith each commercial troller took an average of 20 to 30 fish daily, while gill netters averaged not less than 200 with a maximum of over 2,000 per night. Inexcusable as this fishery was, Smith's assessment was based upon the incorrect assumption that these fish would average from six to ten pounds if allowed to mature – rather than the lesser weight now known to be typical of resident fish. A commercial troll fishery for these fish continued into the 1940s.

Prior to 1958, from January through March when 12- to16-inch resident coho were still relatively abundant, fishing with angle worms trolled behind a string of yard-long spinners ("Pop Gear") was very popular. The addition of a heavy sinker and a giant shovel and rudder to the head of the string was often added to such an outfit. This arrangement was selective to small coho and relatively few Chinook salmon succumbed to the gear. Uproar occurred in 1958 when the salmon size limit was increased from 12 to 16 inches thus curtailing a brisk winter/early spring business in renting boats from Edmonds to Mukilteo and across the sound at Manchester and Eglon. Unfortunately, the size limit change did little to stem the downward trend in the resident coho abundance. Currently, with greatly reduced resident coho populations, fish of this size are highly valued by fly-fishermen, most of whom prefer to release their catch.

Resident Chinook – These fish have always provided anglers with an opportunity of hooking a good-sized fish at any time of year. Tagging studies have shown that some of the Chinook that originate in local streams and hatcheries remain within the Sound for all or most of their marine lives; whereas, most migrate toward the ocean at a small size and, if fortunate enough to avoid the various hazards, grow to maturity primarily off the west coast of Vancouver Island. Resident Chinook salmon are the favorite target of most skilled Puget Sound anglers whenever adult Chinook ("kings") and large adult coho are unavailable, and unlike coho salmon, are fish-eaters from the get-go. An examination of the stomach contents of Puget Sound sport-caught Chinook salmon in 1947-48, many of which were just over 12 inches long, revealed that herring and sandlance comprised the overwhelming bulk of their diet[35]. Chinook are drawn to concentrations of herring, sandlance and the occasional presence of anchovies.

Popular fishing locations, as well as the most productive tidal stages, tend to be well known to the extent that sportfishing boats will usually be clustered at specific locations while vast areas of the Sound will remain vacant. The typical pale flesh color of these fish, in contrast to crustacean-induced red of coho and most ocean-reared Chinook salmon, appears indicative of a diet consisting primarily of fish.

Resident pink salmon – In past years, resident pink salmon were sporadically abundant in Puget Sound. These fish primarily foraged among the tide rips of the Tacoma Narrows and ranged to and fro from Toliva Shoal to the southern tip of Vashon Island with the ebb and flood of the tide. Specialized gear, "humpy rigs", consisting of a spinner with a trailing herring strip or other bait, were designed and sold for catching these fish. "Humpies" were sought from late winter through early summer of cycle years. Schools of these attractive fish were often visible surface feeding on plankton and, if they existed today, would be targeted by the increasing number of fly-fishermen. A Washington Department of Fisheries study involved tagging resident pinks in the Narrows during the early summer of 1955[36]. Subsequent tag recoveries indicated that most of that year's population of resident pinks originated in the Stillaquamish River.

In a typical year during early summer, resident "humpies" would be about 17 inches long when pinks at Neah Bay and Sekiu were 23 inches and four times heavier. Into the 80s, the annual Washington State sport-catch reports indicate that small numbers of resident pink salmon were being caught between May and June in the Tacoma area. Sadly, my last encounter with them was during the 70s.

In an experiment to test the feasibility of artificially enhancing the population of resident pink salmon, fertilized eggs were collected from the Stillaguamish River in 1971 and 46,000 were reared for an extended period and to an exceptional size of about five inches, although juvenile pinks normally migrate to sea soon after emerging from the gravel at a length of less than 1.5 inches. This process of "extended rearing" was intended to emulate the success experienced with coho salmon to facilitate Puget Sound residents[37]. These fish were released after 45 days of rearing into Chambers Creek near Steilacoom. Unfortunately, they were not coded wire tagged. Adult returns of these fish to Chambers Creek appeared to number about 1,000 fish. However, the size of these fish was typical of ocean migrants rather than Puget Sound residents.

The significance of Puget Sound resident salmon has faded in both fact and memory. Despite overwhelming evidence to the contrary, contemporary critics of utilizing hatcheries to enhance these populations even erroneously suggest that they are unnatural additions to Puget Sound that would consume small wild salmon[38]. The fact is that, as previously documented, there were historically large numbers of naturally occurring year-round populations of Chinook, coho and sometimes pink salmon in Puget Sound that were utilized by natives and newcomers for food, commerce and recreation. Stomach analyses of resident Chinook salmon also show no evidence of predation on smaller salmon species, although the same cannot be said for Puget Sound's wild anadromous cutthroat trout and char.

The decline in the populations of resident salmon in Puget Sound should provide a valuable lesson to those interested in optimizing the sustainable benefits resulting from recreational fishing. Along with the decline in resident fish, adult Chinook and coho salmon returns to Puget Sound hatcheries dramatically increased during the 1960s. The vast majority of the fish returning to the Sound, from feeding grounds located in

Canadian waters, were in an advanced state of maturity and not actively feeding when they arrived in the waters of the inner-sound. The peak abundance of coho in the most publicly accessible waters also follows the prime recreational season. The clear and simple lesson is that feeding, i.e. *biting*, fish are required over an extended period at the right time of year to maximize their recreational value.

Sea-run cutthroat and char – In its southern extremities, and perhaps elsewhere in Puget Sound, sea-run cutthroat remain available along the beaches throughout the year. These fish appear to have been an even more important game fish in earlier times. All of the early local fishing guide books that I have, including *Taft's 1925 Sportsman's Guide and Handbook*, devote a chapter to fishing for them. Their forays into local small streams for spawning appear to extend from the late-fall freshets into early spring but individual adults may only spawn on alternate years. The smallest fish a saltwater angler is likely to encounter appears to be about seven inches and anything over eighteen is a notable catch. Perhaps their most distinguishing characteristic is preference for the shallows, often no more than a foot in depth, where they forage on a wide variety of organisms, including juvenile salmon. Cutthroat trout avoid clear sandy or mud-covered beaches in preference to the gravel and shell substrate hosting their preferred forage. Due to the array of sizes and shapes of prey, they appear relatively indiscriminate in their choice of fly patterns to the extent that an *olive* Wooly *bugger* does just fine. As is the case with fishing for trout in a river, analyzing near-shore tidal currents and looking for surface activity is important. Unfortunately, during the warm-water months, the bodies of south sound sea-runs often become distressingly infested with huge unsightly parasitic copepods (*Argulus pugentis*).

Another fascinating sea-going member of the salmon family roams the shorelines of Puget Sound and Washington's outer coast. Bull trout and Dolly Varden (named for a Charles Dickens character noted for her brightly colored clothing) are members of genus *Salvelinus* and technically "char". Both are native to western Washington and visually separating the two appears impractical. Although more is to be learned regarding the relationship of these fish, in our state Dolly Varden appear confined to the upper reaches of some cold mountain streams west of the Cascades (e.g., Dungeness, Quinault), whereas bull trout are more widely distributed in mountain origin streams on both sides of the state, with those in west making the forays into saltwater. In other parts of the Northwest, bull trout are considered fish of inland waters and Dolly Varden a coastal species, but the reverse appears to be the case in western Washington. These char once commonly occurred along with cutthroat in shallow-water catches from the mouth of the Snohomish and northward. To the south a small but apparently growing population still ascends the Puyallup River where they are counted when hauled above Mud Mountain Dam. Our native char, like all others native to the world's northern waters, are fall spawners utilizing glacial and other mountain-water streams. In Puget Sound, the Skagit system provides the population's stronghold. Most of the local adult and what appear to be sea-run char that I have caught have ranged from one to three pounds, although I weighed a six-pounder from the Sauk during late summer and released one from that same river, caught on a fly during April, that appeared to exceed ten pounds. However, the very largest specimens appear to remain in freshwater systems associated with deep, cold lakes with suitable spawning tributaries.

Figure 22. Bull trout.

Killer Whales/Orcas

Another Puget Sound resident population, killer whales or orcas, has recently joined Chinook salmon on the ESA list and the latter species has been identified as the former's preferred food. Serious consideration is currently being given to further curtail fishing to provide more Chinook to feed orcas. Although the people of the region may now consider this to be a reasonable alternative, I doubt that it would be the case prior to the mid-1970s when most of those aware of orcas were fishermen who considered the salmon more valuable than "blackfish". This was the common name given to the animals when few locals realized they were actually killer whales. A 1948 scientific report describes the whales and dolphins known to occur in Washington waters, including observations, by the authors and other contemporary observers on killer whales[39]. The document contains several references to orcas being shot or otherwise purposely killed, as well as the "*disastrous effects on salmon fishing*" that they can have inflicted. This was reported to primarily impact Chinook salmon staging off river mouths with much reduced impacts on "blackmouth" and other salmon species. The authors foresaw the possibility that the flesh of these whales "*. . . will prove a welcome commodity and its products, such as oil, meal hormones, vitamins, and ivory, will be utilized.*" They further indicated: "*Trophy hunters, armed with gun or camera, have a worthy quarry in this handsome and spectacular animal.*" However, these views were prudently tempered: "*From a recreational point of view many tourists, sportsmen, and naturalists would willingly concede to the killer whale its daily quota of fish, in return for the privilege of seeing a band of killers plunging along through the Sound.*"

Adult Chinook salmon are still reasonably abundant throughout the region during the late summer and early fall as they migrate toward their streams of origin in Puget Sound and Georgia Strait. This is not the case with resident salmon – fish that provided off-season fare for orcas in years past. As late as the 1970s, orcas were common winter visitors to southern Puget Sound when resident fish, particularly blackmouth, were the only salmon worthy of their interest.

Origin of the inner-sound catch – Some of the most fascinating information resulting from tagging relates to where the various populations are harvested at sea. The vast majority of Puget Sound

Chinook and coho migrate northward into Canadian waters where they are harvested in the local fisheries. Most of this catch occurs off the west coast of Vancouver Island, and in some cases as far north as southeast Alaska. Significant numbers of salmon from streams flowing into the northeastern sound cross the nearby border into Georgia Strait where they contribute to the British Columbia fishery. Since Canadian salmon are also north migrating, Puget Sound anglers are in a less advantageous position to catch Canadian fish.

Chinook salmon from the University of Washington (UW) hatchery were also contributing at a remarkable rate to the Puget Sound anglers. Early maturity, fish maturing at age 3 rather than 4 years, along with high survival, appeared to keep these fish feeding in local waters. Rapid early growth is known to hasten maturity and the conditions at the hatchery were geared to do that.

Figure 23. University of Washington Professor Lauren Donaldson at work with Chinook salmon that contributed heavily to the Puget Sound sport catch. Photo courtesy of the UW.

Data collected during the 1970s provides some interesting comparisons. The UW hatchery, located off the Lake Washington Ship Canal within a mile or two of tide water, is one of two hatcheries located within the Lake Washington basin. Issaquah Hatchery, on the major tributary to Lake Sammamish is the other. The 90-day-reared Issaquah fingerlings weighed about 1/100 of a pound each at release at a time when the UW fish were more than twice as large. Total survival (catch plus escapement) of the UW fish was several times larger than from Issaquah and about 57% of the catch of UW fish was taken by local anglers. More than half of the catch of Issaquah fish occurred in Canada with about 25% entering the local sport catch. In summary, extended rearing, release location, and early maturity appear to be important for keeping hatchery Chinook salmon at home.

With a few exceptions, Chinook salmon reared in Puget Sound hatcheries are of a single fall-run stock originating in Green River Hatchery. The seasonal designation refers to the time when the fish enter their home streams from the sea. Hatcheries on the Nooksack and White rivers rear spring run fish, Skykomish hatchery fish are summer-runs, the native stock reared in the Elwha are considered intermediate between summer- and fall-run fish. Populations of Puget Sound wild fish currently listed as threatened under the Endangered Species Act, 22 in all, occur in the Skagit, Green, Snohomish, Nooksack, Skokomish, Stillaquamish, Puyallup, and Cedar rivers, as well as minor runs to mid-Hood Canal tributaries.

White River spring Chinook, a stock that was almost extirpated, have contributed at a remarkably high rate to the local catch as have releases of assorted stocks of spring Chinook from Hoodsport Hatchery on Hood Canal. The few races of Puget Sound Chinook that migrate to sea as yearlings, rather than the usual three months, tend to linger or reside in the sound where they are more likely to be caught by local anglers.

Hatcheries located in southern and central Puget Sound tend to contribute most heavily to the sport fishery. During the 1970s, tags from Issaquah Hatchery coho salmon were among the most numerous of those along the Washington coast and throughout Puget Sound. Other outstanding contributors to the sport catch are hatcheries located on the Green, Puyallup, Minter Creek, and Skykomish systems. In recent years Quilcene National Fish Hatchery, on northern Hood Canal, has contributed heavily to sport catches off the coast, in the Strait, and throughout the northern sound.

Unfortunately, Issaquah Hatchery has not maintained this level of productivity. Hatcheries, as well as wild salmon, require an abundance of cool, clean water. The water supply at Issaquah became so degraded that its total annual contribution of coho salmon to the catch declined from a high of 100,000, during the decade of the 1970s, to less than 500 in subsequent years. Due to strong support from a community that took great pride in the hatchery that was the focus of a popular annual celebration, conditions at the hatchery have been greatly improved.

Ocean migrating Chinook and coho – The vast majority of salmon returning to Puget Sound from the ocean are fall-run fish that are primarily available from mid-August through early October. They, particularly coho, become progressively more difficult to catch as they approach their staging areas adjacent to their streams of origin. Although these fish can be very abundant, particularly when congregated off mouths of streams, they are then not actively feeding and only a small fraction are usually taken by anglers. Mature Chinook and coho salmon, milling off a river mouth – such as in Elliott or Commencement bays – tend only to strike at dawn, during other brief periods, or not at all. A notable example of the reluctance of these fish to bite occurred in October, 1970 when a large run of ocean-reared coho returned to the Green River Salmon Hatchery. Leaping coho salmon attracted many anglers to Elliott Bay but very few fish were caught. Frustrated anglers discovered that by tying up to the bulwark of the Spokane Street Bridge, in the West Waterway of the Duwamish River, they could snatch leaping coho from the air with their landing nets. Others resorted to leaving an open boat tied under the bridge as a means of harvesting the leapers.

Figure 24. "Fly dipping" leaping coho in the West Waterway of the Duwamish River (10/3/70). About 40 boats were participating in a small area. The person with the light-colored jacket in the center of the photo has a fish in his raised net.

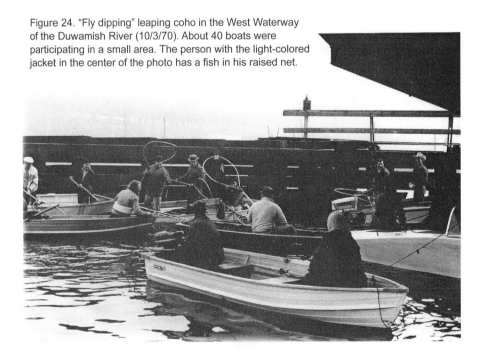

This is just one example, of many, of the fact that it takes more than an abundance of coho or Chinook salmon, for that matter, for good fishing. *Good fishing requires an abundance of fish that bite.*

Many hatchery salmon, particularly coho, are transferred to marine pens and reared for several months prior to release into open water. These fish return to the general area of the release site but tend to mill in unpredictable shallow areas disassociated with potential spawning streams. These fish are particularly noticeable at daybreak, when they are most susceptible to a lure, leaping and swirling on the surface. Most are caught in tribal nets and those that escape capture appear to eventually move into streams near the marine release site.

This is not to say that maturing Chinook and coho salmon returning to Puget Sound are not of great importance to anglers. Both species are actively feeding as they move through the important angling centers from Neah Bay to Sekiu and Pillar Point and eastward to Port Angeles. Fishing for them can be good, as they pass through Admiralty Inlet, but as they approach their home estuaries they have achieved their maximum size, no longer require food to survive through their spawning cycle, and their tendency to take bait or lures is greatly reduced. Nevertheless, the arrival of the kings and "hook-nose silvers", good weather, and the big salmon derbies, attracted the largest crowds of the year to the waters of Puget Sound.

Ocean migrating pink salmon – Large numbers of pink salmon ("humpies") are also available to Puget Sound anglers from early August through early September of odd-numbered years (each run directly descends from fish of the previous cycle). Prior to 2000, angling for pink salmon primarily occurred on the routes to the major pink salmon streams in northern Puget Sound and the Fraser River. Fishing for pink salmon is very popular and achieved a milestone in 1963 when, during an exceptionally large return to Puget Sound (3.2 million), more were caught by Washington anglers than either Chinook or coho salmon. This extraordinary catch (400,000+) boosted the estimated total Washington salmon sport catch to over a million for the first time. Pinks had formerly constituted about 10 percent of the State's odd-year sport catch. A common belief at this time was that a Puget Sound run of this magnitude would never again occur. Forty years later the prognostication was shattered when unprecedented hordes of pinks began returning to the Green, Puyallup, and Nisqually rivers in south Puget Sound. Spawning escapements to these streams totaling only a few thousand in the 1990's exploded at the onset of the biennium, exceeding four million in 2009 – when anglers caught more pinks (558,000) than all of the other salmon species combined. It is noteworthy that 60 percent of this catch occurred in freshwater.

The southern extremity of the North American pink salmon spawning is, essentially, the lower reaches of the Puget Sound basin. In former years, local pink salmon primarily spawned in cooler mountain-origin streams located from the Snohomish basin north – suggesting that the natural range of the species was limited by temperature. As a brand-new full-time employee of the Department of Fisheries in 1959, and to the distress of my wife and toddlers, I was assigned to supervise a crew to count carcasses and collect tags from spawned-out pink salmon in the Puyallup basin. This was part of a joint Washington – Canadian effort to estimate the population size of fish managed jointly by the two countries.

Anxious to perform well in this first major assignment, I was away from home from before dawn till after dark with nary a break for over a month. When *at* home, I smelled like a rotting pink salmon. Nearly all the carcasses that we recovered were in South Prairie Creek, a lowland Puyallup tributary near the town of Orting. Although the main-stem Puyallup is a glacial stream, South Prairie Creek is not and constitutes a glaring exception to my previously stated requirement for the species. The estimated run that year to the Puyallup was only 14,000 pink salmon, with a total Puget Sound run of 541,000. A few pinks showed up in other south sound streams but they were considered strays – fish that got lost. No one would have considered surveying the Green River for pink salmon in 1959, or for many years thereafter, since the highest number recorded in the Green River, over several decades prior to 1984, was thirteen fish[40]. Although the Nisqually appeared to have the characteristics necessary for pink salmon, it was then considered to have none.

During my career with fish, the most extraordinary and puzzling development is the recent explosive increase of pink salmon in southern Puget Sound. Returns of fish to Mud Mountain Dam on the White River, where fish are counted and trucked above a dam, may best illustrate this remarkable phenomenon. So-named for the glacial flour it transports from Mount Rainier, the White joins the lower Puyallup River which flows into Tacoma's Commencement Bay. Mud Mountain, billed as the highest rock and earth filled dam in the world, was completed in 1948 to control floods that plagued the lower valley. Significant wild populations of Chinook and coho salmon, as well as steelhead and anadromous bull trout, spawned above the dam and the U.S. Army Corps of Engineers operated a fish-trapping facility at the face of the dam used to capture the fish for trucking around the dam. The resulting records of the numbers of fish hauled are thus more reliable than on most river systems.

No pink salmon were recorded at Mud Mountain Dam in the cycle years of 1999 and 2001. In 2003 there were 13,000 trapped and hauled. From then on, excluding those spawning in the miles of stream below the dam, counts rapidly increased to more than 600,000 in 2011. Growing overnight from essentially none to a population of hundreds of thousands, pinks swarmed through Seattle's Elliott Bay and the Duwamish to reach the spawning grounds in the Green River. The Puyallup and Nisqually, with modest established runs, have experienced enormous increases numbering in the hundreds of thousands. The trend has continued through the 2013 cycle year. To put this in perspective, the average total pink salmon run to Puget Sound from the Green south to the Nisqually River during the decade of the 1990s was 13,300 fish – by 2009 it increased to several million. At the same time, pink salmon returns to streams in Hood Canal (Dosewallips, Duckabush, and Hamma Hamma rivers) with modest, although established runs and relatively intact habitat, have not responded in a similar manner.

Chum salmon – Until recently, chum salmon were uncommon in Puget Sound sport catches but now they are a significant component of the catch. The only early semi-directed sport fishery that I am aware of occurred during the final weeks of fall in the vicinity of Gig Harbor where anglers anchored and caught both chums and blackmouth while "spinning". Large returns of leaping and cavorting fish in shallow Puget Sound estuaries have since stimulated the interest of opportunity-starved salmon anglers. From late October through mid-November, anglers are commonly shoulder to shoulder, at stream mouths hosting large chum runs. Fishing methods include various spinners, spoons, and strands of yarn – particularly chartreuse, a color also favored by fly-casters. Such fish typically display their spawning colors and are nearly "ripe". Although these chums can be taken by "fair angling", many are also foul hooked. A breakthrough, discussed in a previous chapter, has resulted in a significant sport fishery using bait. Mature chums are typically larger than coho salmon and, when hooked, may be the gamest of our native species.

Sockeye salmon – Millions of sockeye salmon safely migrate past Washington's marine anglers each year. Most are bound for the Fraser River, a handful go to the Skagit River, but in a peak year up to a million head for Lake Washington through the Ballard Locks and the viewing station – a popular tourist attraction . With few exceptions sockeye require a lake for two or more years of juvenile rearing, along with a connected spawning stream or suitable beach.

The construction of the Lake Washington Locks in 1912, allowing vessels to pass between lake and sound, required lowering the lake and diverting the Cedar River into Lake Washington from its natural course into the Duwamish. The lake's outlet, augmented by Cedar River, then flowed into the sound through the Ballard Locks. The unanticipated result of the project was linking the rearing capacity of Lake Washington for sockeye with the excellent spawning habitat of the river. This set the stage for expanding the small native sockeye population that utilized spawning gravel in Bear and Cottage creeks. The vast majority of the lake's sockeye now spawn in the Cedar River. This stock of fish originated in the Baker River, a tributary to the Skagit. During the 1930s and 40s Baker sockeye eggs were collected and taken to Issaquah Creek Hatchery, on a tributary to Lake Sammamish draining into Lake Washington through the Sammamish River. Many of these Baker River fish survived and eventually strayed into Cedar River where the population languished a low level until the mid-1960s when it rapidly increased and eventually thrived. A small population of sockeye also spawn on the gravelly shores on the east side of the lake near Pleasure Point and appear to be descendants of shore-spawners in Baker Lake.

Some years ago Canadian commercial trollers learned how to catch large numbers of sockeye salmon on hook-and-line gear in the ocean. The secret was dead-slow trolling with flashers rigged with small "hootchies" (squid-like lures). Although Washington's saltwater anglers never really developed this technique, a similar method of fishing for sockeye in Lake Washington became astonishingly productive and popular. Dead-slow trolling with dodgers in the cool depths adjacent to the thermocline was the key to success. Lures range from flatfish (a wobbling plug) to bare hooks! The Lake Washington sockeye fishery has the distinction of being Washington's most efficient sport fishery, in terms of harvest rate, on a mature salmon stock. In years when fish are sufficiently abundant, a similar fishery occurs, 1875 feet above sea level and hundreds of miles from the mouth of the Columbia River, in Lake Wenatchee.

From the onset of the build-up in the population of Lake Washington sockeye, the Washington Department of Fisheries established a spawning goal of 350,000 – meaning fishing cannot occur unless returns to the lake exceeded this level. The exception to this rule is that treaty tribes are allowed to take about 5000 of these fish a year, regardless of run size, for "ceremonial and subsistence" purposes. Although sockeye salmon experts from elsewhere have indicated that the escapement goal should be significantly lower, and the run has not favorably responded, the State has steadfastly maintained what appears to be an unrealistic goal. In doing so, over the past 50 years, it appears that salmon anglers in the Seattle area have been deprived of an opportunity of incalculable value for close-to-home salmon angling.

Due to the popularity of the Lake Washington sport fishery, a sockeye salmon hatchery has been developed on Cedar River in an effort to enhance and stabilize returns. The efforts of Frank Urabeck, a recreational fishing proponent, have been instrumental in the fruition of this facility.

SAN JUAN ISLANDS

For statistical purposes, the islands have been considered a part of Puget Sound. It has always been difficult for Washington's fisheries officials to gather information on the salmon sport fishery that occurs among the San Juans. Much of the sportfishing activity occurs from relatively large boats cruising among the islands – rather than from boats that daily return to a launch site where they can be checked and interviewed. As part of my responsibilities with the Department of Fisheries during the early 1960s, I annually visited the resorts on Orcas and San Juan Islands that rented boats for salmon fishing and was left with the distinct impression that vacationers to the islands had a more casual approach to salmon angling than existed elsewhere in the state. During the late 1940s and 50s, Beatrice Cook and her family had a summer home on Orcas island and she authored a series of popular books filled with anecdotal accounts of salmon angling in local waters.

Salmon fishing in the San Juans during the summer months is strongly influenced by fish returning to the Fraser River when its turbid plume is often visible throughout the archipelago. Each year millions of salmon migrate through the islands en route to what may be the world's greatest salmon producer. Unfortunately, as is true of most salmon stocks throughout the region, Fraser River fish forage to the north and, apart from one major exception, do not contribute significantly to catches on the inner sound or the outer coast of Washington. Fortunately, there is a notable exception.

The Harrison, a short but large river flowing from a lake of the same name, joins the lower Fraser near the town of Chehalis, British Columbia. With a spawning escapement goal of upwards of 100,000, a 10-mile stretch of the river below Harrison Lake hosts one the world's largest populations of Chinook salmon. A large run of transplanted Harrison Chinook also exists in the Chilliwack – a hatchery river tributary to the lower Fraser. In addition to being white-fleshed, these fish are unusual in other ways. They are late spawners, with the first returning adult entering the Fraser in September and continuing into November. The fry spend little time in the Harrison and quickly move downstream to rear in channels, sloughs of the Fraser and its estuary before migrating to saltwater as fingerlings.

Harrison fish also contribute generously to Washington coastal, Strait and northern Puget Sound sport catches. To put this in perspective, about 20% of the Chinook taken off the Washington coast originate in the Harrison. Columbia River "upriver brights", a far-north migrating stock of roughly the same size comprises less than 4% of the Washington coastal catch since these fish essentially neither tarry nor take in our coastal waters, with most of the local sport catch occurring within the Columbia River.

Seasoned anglers are well aware of the big, strong "whites" that never seem to give up, that are taken off Washington's northern coast and the approaches to the Fraser. Strong evidence regarding the river of origin is revealed when the thick belly walls and snow white flanks of these fish are revealed. One of many experiences that I have had with these fish occurred while officiating at the 1972 Seattle Seafair Salmon Derby. At that time Seafair Derbies were two-day affairs held during the second week of September. This is past the time when local "kings" are in prime condition since for weeks they have been essentially fasting and transferring fat and tissue into sex products and other body changes. Part of my responsibilities involved gutting derby fish to ensure that none contained unnatural heavy objects.

The big fish carried by the beaming young angler for official weigh-in was something very special. Caught at Point No Point, it weighed over 33 pounds and was silvery bright. Its scales were relatively loose and it dwarfed the dark local twenty-pound contenders. In contrast the thin belly walls of the local maturing Chinook, the cut from the vent to the gills severed thick, fat-laden tissue and revealed snow-white flanks. It was a female and the developing eggs, lacking any trace of red, were bright yellow. In contrast to the empty shrunken alimentary tracts of the local kings, its stomach bulged with neatly packed five-inch hake. This was almost certainly a late Harrison fall Chinook salmon. A few days later I was given a canned souvenir of that event – the label proclaiming it to be a *"Rare Puget Sound Smoked White King Salmon – A $10,000 Taste Treat"*; and in smaller print *"Retail Value: $400.00"* ($10,000 divided by the number of cans from the winning fish). Thirty-five years later I sent the can to the then not-so-young man who caught that fish.

The Fraser is best known for its sockeye that thrive in its unobstructed spawning streams and lakes, but it also hosts major runs of the other four species Pacific salmon, including, an enormous run of odd-year pink salmon that contribute heavily to late summer odd-year catches among the island and throughout Juan de Fuca Strait.

In addition to returning mature stocks, feeding Chinook salmon are attracted to the islands by an abundance of herring. Twenty-pound fish are not uncommon in late-fall and winter catches from the San Juans. North of the Washington San Juans, in Georgia Strait, there exists the

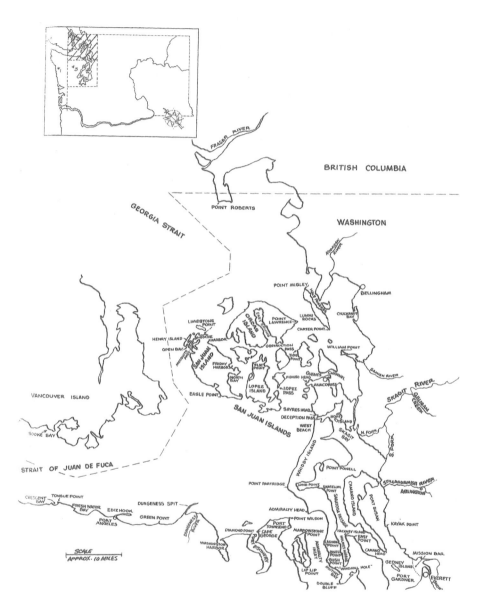

Figure 25. Significant salmon sportfishing locations among the San Juan Islands and the eastern portion of Juan de Fuca Strait. Taken from Washington Department of Fisheries Research Bulletin No. 7 (1967).

Canadian version of a resident coho salmon population. These fish have been a very important part of the recreational fishery and they are occasionally accessible to anglers on the Washington side of the border.

Coded wire tags recovered from San Juan Islands Chinook salmon indicate that Puget Sound hatcheries, especially those located in north Puget Sound, are important contributors to the local sport fishery. Tagged fish from Fraser River hatcheries, and other Canadian facilities, are commonly taken here. Since few if any of the wild Chinook salmon originating in the Fraser River system are ever tagged, these returns do not reflect their importance in local catches. A significant number of fish from Spring Creek Hatchery, located on the lower Columbia River, forage among the islands and also show up in the sport catch. Most of the tagged coho taken by anglers are from hatcheries located in northern Puget Sound and include only a smattering of tags from Canadian hatcheries.

JUAN DE FUCA STRAIT

The character of the salmon sport fishery dramatically changes west of Port Townsend where the open waters of the Strait are exposed to miles of fetch and an ever-present ocean swell. Many anglers with boats considered perfectly adequate for the inner-sound have second thoughts on using them in here and boat-launching sites are few and far between. Port Angeles, with charter boats, boat ramps, and once offering rental boats, is a major center for salmon angling, and small boats can be launched west of Port Angeles at Freshwater Bay. Anglers must travel 40 torturous miles, made even more difficult when towing a boat, to find two launch ramps near Pillar Point – one now privately owned and the other barely serviceable. The next location, a dozen or so sinuous miles away, is Sekiu. It takes 20 miles of even more difficult driving to reach Neah Bay on the Makah Indian Reservation. This is the strait's third important salmon angling center, the jumping off place for fishing the outer coast. The Makah Tribe has recognized the economic benefits of recreational fishing and Neah Bay now boasts a large marina, tackle, launching, charter boats, camping facilities, and other amenities.

Salmon angling at Port Angeles, with its protected harbor and outdoor-oriented population, had early beginnings. The Port Angeles

Salmon Club was well established by the time it held its first fishing derby in 1934. But it wasn't until after World War II that the State Department of Fisheries considered the Strait sport fishery of more than minor importance. In 1934 Alvin Olson, began renting out a small boat or two from his property located at Sekiu. The site, partially protected by natural rocks formations and tucked into the west corner of Clallam Bay, soon began to attract serious anglers who were willing to make the long drive. Olson's has expanded greatly since that time, including a much needed breakwater and is the State's oldest continually operating salmon fishing "resort". Several other facilities followed Olson's example by providing boats, accommodations, camping, private boat launching, and moorage making Sekiu a major center for salmon sport fishing. Rental boats and limited accommodations for anglers probably first became available at Neah Bay following World War II. About twenty-five years earlier commercial trollers (hook-and-line salmon fishermen), attracted by the productivity of Swiftsure Bank, began using Neah Bay as a base of operations.

Chinook salmon caught by anglers fishing the strait are typically larger than those taken from the inner sound. Although feeding Chinook are available throughout the year, they appear to be roving foragers rather than residents. The size limit increases in 1958, from 12 to 16 inches, had little if any impact here since an insignificant portion of the catch was comprised of such small fish. Whenever fishing is allowed, significant catches of "blackmouth" occur during the winter months at Discovery Bay, Port Angeles, and Sekiu. Makah tribal commercial trollers currently target these winter fish in the western Strait. However, salmon sport fishing in the Strait is primarily a June through September affair when maturing Chinook (kings), along with blackmouth, pass through the region. The kings here are still actively feeding on sandlance and herring during the summer months. The Western Strait of Juan de Fuca, from Cape Flattery east to Pillar Point, is the State's prime location for kings although fishing can be also outstanding from Agate and Crescent Beach east to the Port Angeles area. Maturing Chinook salmon passing through the Strait are predominantly mixtures of fish originating in Puget Sound, including strong contributions for its hatcheries, and the Fraser River. Columbia River fall Chinook are also an important contributor to catches from the western Strait. The frequent occurrence of large white-fleshed Chinook is indicative of Harrison River's contribution to the sport catch.

Coho salmon, in their third (final) year of life, are not normally abundant east of Neah Bay until August. From then through September they contribute heavily to sport catches from Sekiu to Pillar Point. These fish are far less inclined to follow the shoreline than Chinook salmon and the fleet is typically scattered for miles off-shore. East of Pillar Point the quality of coho salmon angling becomes less consistent and during some years, when relatively large runs have passed through the region, remarkably few have been taken by angling. Coho salmon are typically abundant throughout the summer months among the tide rips at the west end of the Strait and in the ocean beyond. Anglers frequently report that fish taken near the entrance to the Strait are smaller than those taken from the open ocean.

Pink salmon, during odd-numbered years, begin to appear in local sport catches in July, peak in August and remain abundant through Labor Day. In terms of numbers, as well as providing satisfaction for less discerning anglers, pinks are an important part of the catch. In 1963, when an enormous run of ravenous pink salmon passed through the Strait, resulting in an additional three-pink-salmon bonus, fisheries officers noted many instances of fish having been discarded into waste cans at various camp grounds.

On a day in late July of that year, while making sportfishing boat counts from a small low-flying airplane over northern Puget Sound, I observed a number of anglers in the act of catching fish – something never seen on previous flights. It was obvious that something very special was occurring and it proved to be the vanguard of 10 million pink salmon returning to Puget Sound – twice the size of that year's run to the Fraser.

Although small-boat anglers fishing from Neah Bay often choose to remain within the confines of the Strait, there is an increasing trend to fish in the open ocean. Spectacular tide rips mark the entrance to the Strait and provide summer-long habitat for coho salmon. In past years much of the sportfishing effort for adult Chinook salmon occurred just outside of the kelp-lined shoreline west of Neah Bay and as far south as Cape Alava on the outer coast. Fishing locations were identified by

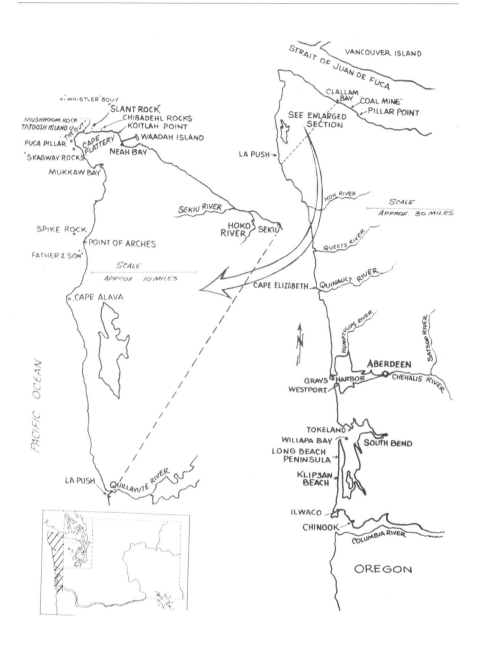

Figure 26. Significant salmon sportfishing locations in the vicinity of Cape
Flattery and along the outer Washington Coast. Taken from Washington
Department of Fisheries Research Bulletin No. 7 (1967).

the names of nearby rocks and other visible features (e.g., Garbage Dump, Midway Rocks, Mushroom Rock, Skagway Rocks, etc.). More recently, with the availability of modern electronics, anglers have utilized productive off-shore locations (e.g., Blue Dot, The Prairie, etc.) that could not be located utilizing visible features. In addition to the salmon sportfishing opportunities at Neah Bay, the bottom structure of the area is a haven for rockfishes and lingcod. The most productive halibut grounds in the lower 48 are located at Swiftshure Bank about 13 miles northwest of the Cape. Unfortunately, the line defining our nation's *Exclusive Economic Zone* (EEZ) angles southwest from Cape Flattery, thus limiting Washington access to this bountiful area. Nevertheless, the natural beauty of the Cape Flattery region alone is more than enough to attract people to Neah Bay.

Puget Sound and Columbia River Chinook salmon contribute heavily to catches at Neah Bay and throughout western Juan de Fuca Strait. Fraser River Chinook are also important. Noteworthy among the contributing hatchery stocks are Spring Creek Hatchery falls and Cowlitz Hatchery fish. Since maturing adult spring Chinook salmon return before the marine sport fishery is operating, these six- to seven-pound Cowlitz springs are a year or two from maturity. Puget Sound and Washington coastal origin coho salmon contribute heavily to the Neah Bay sport catch.

LA PUSH

La Push, the name apparently Chinook jargon stemming from the French *La Bouche* (the mouth), is located south of Cape Flattery on the Quillayute Indian Reservation at the mouth of the Quillayute – the largest river system on the Olympic Peninsula. A significant salmon sport fishery developed here in the early 1960s following the construction of a new jetty, docking facilities, and the growing awareness of its fishing potential. A small charter fleet has operated out of La Push but most anglers have utilized privately owned outboard-powered boats towed to the location. The lack of tourist facilities, its remoteness, and community ambivalence regarding visiting anglers has retarded the development of La Push as a sportfishing center. Nevertheless, during the mid-1970s salmon sport landings twice exceeded 70,000 fish while accounting for more than 40,000 angler days. Since then, largely due to fishing restrictions, catches have dwindled to a few thousand fish a year although in recent years facilities for visitors have improved, accompanied by a surge in fishing.

The narrow entrance to the port lacks the dangerous breakers that are common during ebb tides at harbor entrances to the south. However, locating the entrance to the fog-shrouded harbor while surrounded by wash rocks and pinnacles including The Devils Graveyard, can be a daunting experience without modern electronics. Perhaps the greatest attraction to the area is the magnificence of the coastline that dramatically contrasts to the more popular but featureless beaches to the south.

Coho salmon comprise the bulk of La Push sport catches during the prime fishing season in July and August. Chinook salmon caught at La Push tend to be smaller and younger (immature) than those caught from other coastal ports. The Quillayute River hosts a run of large Chinook but these fish arrive with the fall rains well after the prime season for ocean fishing. During odd-numbered years, significant numbers of pink salmon, bound for Puget Sound and Canadian streams, are taken at La Push.

Coded wire tagged Chinook salmon recovered at La Push are dominated by fish originating in the Columbia River system. Notably among these are fall Chinook from Spring Creek Hatchery and sub-adult Cowlitz River springs. Due to their tendency to migrate northward, Chinook salmon originating in Puget Sound and Canada are only a small part of the catch. Coho salmon originating in Columbia River hatcheries and along the outer Washington coast are important to anglers visiting La Push. Quillayute River Chinook, and other Washington coastal stocks, are predominantly far-north, fall-run fish that contribute primarily to ocean fisheries in Canada and southeast Alaska. As a result, they are available to local marine anglers for a limited time at the tail end of the season.

WESTPORT

Located at the southern entrance to Grays Harbor, Westport grew from a small commercial fishing village in the 1950s to a bustling sportfishing center a decade later. During the mid-1970s, Westport was accounting for more than 250,000 salmon angler days per year and proclaimed itself as the

"Salmon Fishing Capitol of the World" when a third of the state's record sport catch of 1.7 million salmon was taken at Westport.

Although local residents began sport fishing for salmon at Westport during the 1920s, it was after World War II when anglers from other areas, fishing from outboard-powered boats, discovered the exceptional fishing in the ocean beyond the often treacherous Grays Harbor bar. Such fishing, however, was not without its risks and by 1952 there were eight "charter boats" – primarily commercial fishing boats or large pleasure craft – transporting from four to six anglers in relative safety across the bar. Such boats were gradually replaced by larger craft specifically designed to carry 10 or more anglers.

In the beginning, sport fishing was largely confined to near the bar or inside of Grays Harbor. The modern charter fleet, accounting for about 90% of the sport catch during the 1960s, soon began to range south to the Long Beach Peninsula, north to the Quinault River and as far as 20 miles offshore. By 1964 there were more than 200 charter boats operating out of Westport. The rapid growth of the Westport sport fishery is attributed to foraging salmon that are attracted to the area and its proximity to the major migration route of Columbia River and other coho and Chinook salmon stocks, excellent docking and launching facilities, and the effectiveness of mooching – a technique allowing more anglers to fish simultaneously from the deck of a drifting charter boat. Westport was highly dependent upon a source of bait, preferably fresh five- to seven-inch herring transported daily from Puget Sound.

There have been many changes at Westport since its heyday. Restrictions resulting from weak wild stocks listed under the Endangered Species Act (ESA) and federally mandated allocations of salmon to treaty Indian tribes have cut deeply into bag limits and a season that previously extended from mid-April through October. The charterboat fleet, much reduced in size, has attempted to compensate by focusing on rockfishes (primarily black rockfish) and other species as well as whale and seabird watching. By 2001, the numbers of Westport anglers fishing from private boats about equaled those aboard charter vessels and since then private boat fishing has taken the lead.

Although there was originally a 6 1/2-month salmon angling season, about 95% of the sport fishing then occurred from June through early September. Catches peaked in the ten-year period from 1968 through

1977 when annual catches averaged 98,000 Chinook and 252,000 coho salmon. During the decade of the 1990s catches plummeted to an average of less than 7,000 Chinook and 46,000 coho salmon. During the peak catch years at Westport angler trips averaged 219,000 per year, but by the 1990s had declined to 31,000.

A multitude of Chinook salmon stocks contribute to the Westport sport catch, but Columbia River system fish, particularly the lower river fall-run stocks ("tules") that forage off the adjacent coast dominate catches. Coded wire tagged recoveries of lower-river fall Chinook, notably those from Spring Creek and Cowlitz hatcheries indicate that these stocks are important contributors to the catch, as were sub-adult six- to seven-pound Cowlitz springs when hatchery survivals were higher than now. The more numerous north-migrating "up-river bright race" apparently spends little time feeding along Washington's shore line and contributes meagerly to the catch.

Early-season fishing effort generally occurs offshore and shifts inshore as the season advances. Historically, coho salmon tend to dominate the sport catches from July through the rest of the season. Fall-run adult Chinook salmon returning from foraging areas north of the border are taken during September and October in and at the entrance to Grays Harbor. A variety of Washington coastal Chinook stocks contribute to the Westport catch and in some years as many as ten percent of coded wire tags recovered in the sport catch originated in California hatcheries – notably in the Rogue and Sacramento rivers.

Columbia River hatchery coho, particularly the "right turning" late Cowlitz stock, contribute heavily to Westport catches. Although most Chinook and coho salmon stocks originating in Washington demonstrate a strong tendency to forage in marine areas north of their streams of origin, coded wire tagging has shown that the earlier-returning stock reared in lower Columbia River hatcheries turned left at the mouth of the river and contributed primarily to Oregon coastal fisheries. Other important lower Columbia River producers of coho salmon to the catch have been hatcheries on Oregon's Sandy River as well as Washington's Toutle and Lewis rivers. Coho salmon originating in Puget Sound are sometimes present along with those originating along Washington's outer coast. Since there are no significant pink salmon runs south of Puget Sound, relatively few enter the local catch.

TOKELAND AND WILLAPA BAY

The treacherous bar at the entrance to Willapa Bay, in contrast to the relative safety and conveniences at nearby Westport, has prevented Willapa ports from developing into significant centers for ocean salmon fishing. A charter boat or two has operated out of South Bend and the boat-launching ramps in the bay can be busy during late summer and early fall when local Chinook and coho salmon are homing to local streams. In past years a popular small-boat fishery existed at Wash-Away Beach located just inside the bay's northern entrance. Catches here apparently consisted of both local and Columbia River origin fish that were apparently attracted by the abundance of anchovies. The productivity of this location has apparently declined with continuing erosion at Wash-Away. Fishing effort has subsequently shifted to locations well inside of the Bay for Chinook and coho salmon that originate in hatcheries and streams that flow into the bay.

THE PACIFIC OCEAN OFF THE MOUTH
OF THE COLUMBIA RIVER

Salmon angling in the Columbia estuary occurred prior to 1912 when local residents discovered that salmon could be taken by trolling during the safe flood tides near the villages of Ilwaco and Chinook. This activity primarily occurred on weekends in late August and early September when mature salmon were entering the river. Long before this time local Indians trolled for salmon in the lower river, utilizing herring or smelt for bait, with stone sinkers and hooks much like those utilized by the Makah at Neah Bay. The availability of larger, seaworthy power boats during the 1940s, coupled with the abundance and susceptibility of salmon at the mouth of the Columbia River and beyond, attracted a growing number of anglers to nearby ports who had learned that fishing was not solely dependent upon maturing fish entering the river. For those willing to cross the infamous Columbia River Bar, actively feeding salmon were available from June to early September.

Following 1950 the overwhelming influx of anglers, many from Oregon, resulted in the U.S. Army Corps of Engineers constructing new moorage and launching facilities at Ilwaco and Chinook. Initially most of the sport fishing involved outboard-powered boats but a significant change occurred during a ten-year period beginning in 1954 when the number of licensed charter boats on the Washington side of the river increased from 10 to more than 90. Originally, salmon-angling statistics at the mouth of the river included launchings from the Oregon shore as well, but most of the effort originated at or near Ilwaco. The estimated annual angler trips steadily increased from about 40,000 per year in the late 1940s to 115,000 in the early 1960s. Beginning in 1964, angler trips and catches originating on the Washington shore were separately estimated. The popularity of fishing here continued and peaked at 200,000 angler days in 1975 and again in 1976. Later restrictions significantly reduce fishing effort to an annual average of about 60,000 angler days during the 1990s.

From 1946 through 1953 salmon sport-catch estimates for the area included only what occurred from late August through Labor Day – when fishing was concentrated inside of the river mouth. At that time anglers were targeting upriver-bound maturing salmon and catches of Chinook outnumbered coho salmon by more than two to one. Although the catch of Chinook salmon was also increasing, by 1964 the coho catch exceeded Chinook by five to one. This change resulted from shifting from a brief seasonal in-river fishery, involving artificial lures (plugs and spoons), to three months of activity in the ocean where hungry salmon, including immature Chinook, eagerly attacked herring-baited hooks. This change coincided with the increased survivals of hatchery coho salmon, boosted by better diets (e.g., Oregon Moist Pellet). Washington salmon sport catches peaked at the mouth of the Columbia in 1976 when an estimated 433,000 fish – 61,000 Chinook and 372,000 coho salmon – were landed.

Sport-caught Chinook salmon landed at Ilwaco during the early 1960s were sampled in studies to determine their state of maturity. It was found that immature fish, many just over the 20-inch legal length limit and destined to spawn at least a calendar year later, dominated Chinook catches, except during the final three weeks of August.

Columbia River hatchery-origin Chinook and coho salmon are the most important contributors to local catches. Notable among the

Chinook are sub-adult six- to seven-pound Cowlitz River springs and fall-run fish ("tules") from lower river hatcheries, especially those from Spring Creek hatchery located in the Bonneville pool and Cowlitz hatchery. A mixture of stocks from Oregon coastal streams and California contribute at a much lesser rate, although a remarkably strong showing of fish from Oregon's Rogue River and California's Feather River hatcheries have been recorded in some years.

Despite the fact that they constitute the most abundant Chinook run to the Columbia, and contribute significantly to the river commercial and sport catch, remarkably few "up-river brights" are taken by anglers off the mouth of the river or elsewhere along the Washington Coast. Southeast Alaska and northern British Columbia commercial ocean trollers are the primary harvesters of these fish that apparently feed little in local marine waters, but they are prime in-river sport fish.

Perhaps the most highly prized of all the Pacific salmon, in both market and recreational value, are spring-run Chinook salmon. Although not destined to spawn until late summer, these fish enter the Columbia before the onset of the coastal sport season, as early as February en route originally to the river's cool headwaters. Since these spawning destinations are the most heavily impacted by hydro-development, most Columbia "springs" now originate in up-stream hatcheries. The high regard for these fish results from their high fat content and ocean-bright appearance in freshwater. The stored fat provides fuel for their prolonged fast and up-stream journey. However, in contrast to most mature salmon stocks in freshwater, Columbia River springs are readily taken on herring, roe and lures while migrating upstream. They have been found to be feeding heavily on eulachon (i.e., Columbia River smelt) as far upstream as Bonneville Dam. Due to their propensity to "bite", the Columbia River sport fishery has long been capable of fully utilizing any harvestable surplus. This, combined with the fact that a pound of spring Chinook retails for about $30, results in a highly contentious allocation process between the commercial and recreational users.

6   Salmon Derbies

During the depths of the Great Depression in 1931, sporting-goods magnate Ben Paris is credited as having promoted the area's first salmon derby at Jimmy Remp's Hermosa Point Resort on Tulalip Bay. In August of the following year the contest was held there again and the sponsors, clearly at odds with Republican Governor Ronald Hartley and his Department of Fisheries and Game, were campaigning for Initiative 62 which would create two new state fish and game agencies. I-62 was strongly supported by organized steelhead anglers led by Ken McLeod whose primary motivation appeared to be eliminating the commercial harvest of steelhead. In later years, McLeod was also a feature player with Initiative 77 and other campaigns relating to salmon and steelhead. Due to overwhelming support in King County, I-62 was narrowly approved by Washington voters the following November. It divided management of fish and game between two new agencies – the Department of Game and the Department of Fisheries. Game was to manage the species ("game fish") that could not be legally taken commercially and Fisheries controlled the latter ("food fish"). Although it did not directly curtail commercial steelhead fishing, it set the stage for future events that did.

From the dusty files of Fisheries, following are the unedited views of a Department of Fisheries and Game official for the Mission Beach District, who was apparently assigned to keep a suspicious eye on events surrounding the 1932 salmon derby:

"The important feature of the week was the Ben Paris-Seattle Star fishing contest held on Sunday, August 28th. The first preliminary to the contest consisted of a Northwest sportsmen's parade held Friday night, August 26th at 7:30 P.M. in Seattle. This parade did not advertise the contest but was merely a publicity stunt favorable to Initiative 62 A number of floats were entered by the Seattle sporting goods houses including Ben Paris, Piper and Taft, Eddie Bauer, Ernst Hardware and a Japanese sport shop and also by several outside sportsmen's associations including Kent, Sumner, Kitsap County, Skagit County and Silverdale. Puget Sound Power and Light Company and several other miscellaneous companies also entered floats. The former was neutral as to Initiative 62, however, and was merely advertising its own products.

"*The second point of interest in the preliminaries to the contest was the registering of the fishermen qualified for the contest between 10:00 P.M. and 2:00 A.M Saturday evening at Ben Paris's recreational parlor on Westlake Avenue. Without a doubt this set hour for registering was set only for financial remuneration and definitely for no other reason. To the fishermen the hours were a handicap for it prevented them from sleeping that night as according to the statement of the rules in the* Seattle Star, *Thursday, June 2, 1932 – "Contestants will assemble at the stated hour at Ben Paris' Recreational Parlor, there to breakfast and listen to final instructions. Contestants will proceed to Hermosa Beach at an hour set by the judges, assemble their gear and hold themselves in readiness for the call to their boats." This call was set at 4:00 A.M. allowing just two hours after 2:00 A.M. to reach Hermosa Point, approximately 45 miles away.*

"*The result of this ruling was 168 fishermen and 168 inspectors milling around in Ben Paris' spending money for tobacco, fishing tackle and food. The breakfast mentioned above cost the fishermen and inspectors exactly 25 cents each or a gross total of $84.00. Each fisherman was assessed at the time of his registration $3.00 for a boat which totaled for the 168 boats $504.00. The only compensation the fishermen received in return was the chance to listen throughout the time to a stringed orchestra made up of sailors from the fleet anchored in the harbor.*

"*Throughout the evening the political pot boiled with J. Warren Kinney boosting Initiative 62 and campaigning for Gellatly with innumerable cigars. Ben Paris also spent his spare time in behalf of the same initiative measure and in denouncing the present state administration, Ben Paris making the statement that he certainly did not want* _____, _____, *Governor Hartley reelected.* (Notes: the blanks in the text apparently represent profanities; the incumbent Governor, Ronald Hartley [R] did not run in 1932 when Clarence Martin [D] defeated John Gellatly [R].)

"*The judges for the contest were Dr. L. W. Withow, Dr. Harold A. Christoferson, Frank Hull, W. W. Connor, Dr. Everett O. Jones, Judge H. G. Sutton, J. Warren Kinney, A. W. Leonard, Samuel H. Hedges, I. F. Dix and Chas. R. Maybury. Most of these men were observed during the evening, some dropping in just a few minutes before it was necessary to leave for the fishing grounds.*

"*The excursion boat* S. S. Tacoma *was advertised frequently through the course of the evening by Ben Paris at a loud speaker, thus indicating that he*

*possibly was getting a cut out of the proceeds from the excursion. This, how-
ever, is only a surmise.*

"*On a whole, the evening was a financial success and carried out well with
the contest's idea of soaking the fishermen in every chance. This is brought out
well in the publication of the* Seattle Star *on Thursday, June 2, 1932, entitled – 'Keep on Fishing' 'You may have until August 7th at 6 P.M. to qualify.
if you are wise you will keep on fishing. A three pounder may do it but if you
are wise you will keep on fishing, display the largest fish you can for, if there
are more than 500 expected qualifiers the size of your fish displayed will have
a bearing on you entering the semi-finals.*

"*Not only 500 qualified but over 800 and instead of increasing the regulations they were weakened if anything. The second qualifying rounds were only
supposed to qualify two fishermen to a resort but this was increased to allow
three at the last minute. In other words the motto really was 'keep everybody
fishing so they can buy tackle and rent boats.'*

"*The fishermen were not required to buy special equipment for the final
contest, however, and were allowed to buy any needed tackle at any store. A
rod, reel, and gaff of any shape or size were required but it was not necessary
for them to purchase new equipment.*

"*The day of the fishing contest turned out to be exceedingly rough and
almost caused the contest to be a failure. Fish weighing 6 and 7 ounces drew
prizes and even then there were more prizes than fish. The largest fish caught
was disqualified because the man catching it was fishing with his own inspector which was very much against regulations. The fish, however, was brought
to the contest and was in reality caught before the 28th. This situation proved
to be the main topic under discussion on the beach and nothing more of
interest was noted. The failure of the fishermen due to the rough weather and
the previous below normal catches for the season makes one wonder just how
many fish each contestant would have caught if all conditions had been favorable. Would he have stopped at the poundage limit?*"

The popularity of salmon derbies quickly grew and many community
celebrations, businesses, fraternal and charitable organizations around the
Sound were sponsors. Most were held in August and September when
maturing Chinook and coho salmon were most abundant in local waters.
Notable were the early Ben Paris – *Seattle Star* contests followed by *The
Seattle Times* Salmon Derby initiated in 1940. Qualification for the finals

of the Ben Paris - *Seattle Star* Salmon Derby required renting a boat from any one of the participating establishments located throughout the sound, catching a fish from the rental boat and recording and verifying weight at the location of the rental. Each participating boathouse or resort was allocated a specific number of qualifiers so that once met, a larger entry "bumped" the smallest fish on the qualifying "ladder". At locations where year-round fishing was popular, a specific number of qualifiers were allocated to each of two periods. For example, in Elliott Bay a boathouse could have five qualifying positions from February through May, and ten from June to September with all qualifying for the finals. In this case the early qualifying fish would tend to be "blackmouth" and considerably smaller than the maturing Chinook available later on.

Periodic newspaper reports updated anglers during the qualifying period and went so far as to offer advice on where qualifying was less demanding: An 8/14/40 *Seattle Times* article reported that the 38 qualifying positions at West Seattle Boathouse were filled and it would take a twenty-pound fish to replace the smallest on that ladder; whereas, nearby Joe's Boathouse has none of its five qualifying positions filled. The rules required that the qualifying fish be put on display and salmon in iced glass-covered cases were familiar sights at sporting goods stores throughout the Seattle area. As a youngster during the 40s, I was fascinated by the fish displayed at Grayson & Brown Hardware in Rainier Valley's Columbia City, and after exiting a bus in downtown Seattle, would proceed directly to Ben Paris and the fish display case located next to the indoor trout pool.

By 1940 fame of the Ben Paris - *Seattle Star* Salmon Derby had spread. It wasn't baseball, but Seattle was apparently hosting a big-league sporting event. The derby finals were held within the confines of Elliott Bay, and attracted national radio coverage. A lengthy article in *Time* magazine described the event as: "the grand finale of the Ben Paris Salmon Derby, oldest and biggest of the Pacific Northwest's latest sport craze." *Time* reported there being at least 25 derbies in Puget Sound with 535 finalists in this one, and quoted a *"bombastic Ben Paris"* as shouting for all to hear – *"Give the salmon back to the sportsman!"* The same article indicated that Japanese anglers were barred from participating in the contest because they were too skillful, although a review of the actual rules of the Paris

Derby indicates that the bigotry was much broader and participation was limited to Caucasians. A "19-year-old girl" with a 27-pound 5-ounce fish was declared Puget Sound's champion angler and was one of five receiving a new De Soto sedan.

Figure 27. Finals of the 1952 *Seattle Times* Silver Salmon Derby at Ray's Boathouse in Ballard. Photo courtesy of the *Seattle Times*.

In addition to having qualifying for the finals, other rules differed from those of today's contests: To prevent cheating, the Paris-*Star* Derby required each angler qualifying for the finals to bring along an "inspector" who would be assigned to a different boat so that each contestant had an independent watchdog (inspectors were not required for qualifying). Motors were not allowed so fishing was limited to rental row boats assigned to each final contestant. Rods and reels were required (no hand lines – which was good for business for Paris and others). Fishing time of the finals was signaled by bombs exploding over the waterfront at 5:00 and 9:00 AM.

Not to be outdone by Paris and a competing newspaper, the *Seattle*

Times got into the act in 1940. The rules were similar but qualification for *The Seattle Times City Salmon Derby* was "open to all" but limited to boats rented from Elliott Bay and Ballard boathouses. Finals were held in Elliott Bay and Ballard on September 29th – three weeks later than the Paris finals in the same location. At the same time, qualification for a *Seattle Times Silver Salmon Derby* was in progress with the finals scheduled for November 3rd. The *Times* billed its derby as the "biggest on the coast" with a $1,000 grand prize along with five new cars (Dodges and Plymouths). It also relied on honor, rather than ride-along inspectors. As was the case with the Paris Derby, a new car was also to be awarded to the woman with the largest fish.

Big prizes combined with the depressed economy apparently overwhelmed the honor system. *Time* magazine followed up its month-old Paris Derby article with another describing the arrest of three men and a woman for driving away new cars won by fish they didn't catch, and that three men were charged with grand larceny with a woman held as a material witness. Anthony Zuanich, Jr., was described as "*a sneaky-eyed no-good ringleader from nearby Everett,* [who] *confessed that he had bought four whopping salmon from an Indian fish trapper, had hidden them at an isolated spot on the edge of the bay. On Derby morning, he and his three accomplices, to whom he had promised $300 apiece from the resale price of their prize-winning automobiles, rowed out to the spot, rowed in whooping with their dead whoppers.*"

The trap in question was located on the delta at the mouth of the Skagit River – a system hosting the largest Chinook salmon in Puget Sound. It functioned, as many others in the Sound prior to 1935, by funneling returning fish along pile-supported netting into a "pot" where the salmon remained alive until lifted from the enclosure. Since the fish were corralled, rather than entangled in webbing, they lacked tell-tale marks of net-caught fish.

The derby judges, including the Washington Department of Fisheries chief biologist and chief patrol officer, could find nothing amiss with the prize-winning fish, but the anglers were less convincing. During the awards ceremony, the major prize winners were asked to provide some details on how they caught their fish. The woman's response was that she was new to fishing and caught the fish on "a hook" in deep water.

An examination of her outfit revealed that she had on a plug and only a four-once weight – hardly what one would use for trolling deep. Zuanich didn't know what kind of plug he was using – just that it was a plug. He indicated that the fish struck at daybreak "and went 6 feet up in the air the first thing." The other two conspirators had somewhat better stories when interviewed. In addition, Zuanich, the woman, and one of the others were reported to have attempted to cheat in other salmon derbies, and in retrospect it appeared that the four had fraudulently qualified for the derby finals with fish provided by the ringleader.

The plot totally disintegrated when, after reading the newspaper account of the derby, the operator of Hope Island resort telephoned the *Times* to report that Zuanich had purchased live salmon from local Indians and that two fellow conspirators were seen watching the live pen. Later a deputy prosecutor, posing as a prospective buyer of the woman's new car, arranged a meeting with her, Zuanich showed up as well, and both were arrested. Following an hour of questioning the woman fully cooperated with the authorities and Zuanich followed up with all of the details.

Zuanich, according to the *Times*, was a fish buyer and owned a commercial gillnet boat. He ultimately confessed to masterminding the plot: After purchasing four live salmon from Swinomish Tribal members, he moved them to a live pen at Hope Island where they were kept until midnight preceding the day of the finals. He then killed the fish and drove to a spot on the shore near Joe's Boat House on the west side of Elliott Bay. At the start of the derby, Zuanich rowed from Joe's to the stash, loaded the fish into his boat, and distributed them to his accomplices at a nearby rendezvous. Plugs were hung into the jaws, a gaff wound applied, and on to the weighing station. The plan called for selling the new cars with Zuanich, who ended up doing time in prison, collecting two-thirds of the proceeds. All of the misappropriated cars were recovered and awarded to the appropriate anglers.

Fraud occasionally occurred in other salmon derbies as well. Would-be cheaters infiltrated the 1987 Port Angeles Derby when two previously frozen fish were discovered among the top entrants. The first of many derbies at Port Angeles was held in 1934 when, on September 2nd, a 27-plus-pound salmon won a new Studebaker sedan worth $1,000. Although I never chose to participate in salmon derbies, I often officiated at them including the Seattle Seafair Derbies of the 1970s which offered $10,000 as first prizes. By that time the need to qualify for the finals was long past and one merely paid an entry fee.

My job as biologist with the Department of Fisheries was to examine fish for irregularities and foster the illusion that we possessed fraud-detecting talents. My only qualifications were knowing that salmon don't normally have lead in their stomachs, that freshly killed fish are limp (pre-rigor), then stiffen (rigor), and finally are extra-limp (post-rigor), and that the three-stage process takes more time than the length of a derby day. In addition, anglers catching big fish, believing they will lose critical weight, tend to rush them in as soon as they are boated. I have often examined live salmon at derbies and most others are pre-rigor.

At one of the Seafair Derbies I was the biologist charged with maintaining honesty when two large extra-limp specimens, that I had reason to believe had been poached with a beach seine, were disqualified without complaint from the would-be contestants. The derby sponsors chose not to press charges. The Boeing Company and Bremerton Shipyard held annual employee derbies with big prizes. The latter contest had the unique rule of disallowing chum salmon since small streams near a derby weigh-in site at Seabeck on Hood Canal hosted summer-run chums that could be easily poached or legally caught. Here, I had the unpleasant task of explaining to an angler why his enormous bright "Coho"– a specimen clearly caught in saltwater – was actually a chum salmon that did not qualify for winning the new pick-up truck. However, derby cheating appears to be relatively uncommon.

During the mid-1980s, I volunteered as a consultant to an event sponsored by Schuck's Auto Supply offering a million dollars to anyone catching a tagged salmon during a two-day event held on Puget Sound. There were about five such fish involved that were acquired from a National Marine Service marine pen across from Seattle at Manchester. Each was tagged with a visible plastic label wired under its dorsal fin (Carlin tag). In addition, we arranged to have a coded wire tag implanted into the snout of each fish to verify its authenticity. Only a representative of the insurance company, wagering a million against the cost of the policy (which I believe amounted to $50 thousand) that no one would catch one of the fish, held the key to the codes inscribed on the wire tags.

The five tagged two-pound coho were released south of Seattle about two days before the event was to occur. No one collected a million dollars but a few days later one was caught off the mouth of the Puyallup River and another taken near the Vashon Island ferry dock. This may have been the first time that tagged fish were involved in such an event.

7   Puget Sound Boathouses and Resorts

In 1938 the Washington Department of Fisheries began to take a closer look at the growing recreational salmon fishery in Puget Sound. At that time it estimated that Puget Sound provided 231,000 angler days of fishing, with an average catch just over a salmon per trip. The size limit then was 12 inches and the daily bag limit was 15. Most of the activity, in those days and well into the 1950s, was fishing from boats rented from boathouses and fishing resorts located throughout Puget Sound. The most elaborate "resorts" consisted of little more than simple frame cabins grouped near a boathouse. Fishing gear was rented and sold and some resorts included a modest cafe. Urban boathouses lacked accommodations.

The Department of Fisheries reported that in 1951, Puget Sound (marine waters east of Cape Flattery) hosted 150 boathouses and fishing resorts having more than 4,000 rental boats. In that same year there were about 15,000 outboard and larger private boats registered for use and many of these were used for salmon angling. During the early years, many of these were flat- and round-bottomed row boats about 12 feet long. Some boats were a bit longer and fitted with two sets of oars so that they could be more easily rowed to more distant fishing areas. A few of these boats were still in use during the late 1950s when, as part of my job with the Washington Department of Fisheries, I was sampling sport catches and visiting boathouses throughout the Puget Sound area.

In was not uncommon, before my time, for anglers to row from Meadowdale to Possession Point on Whidbey Island. At Point Defiance Park, where strong tidal currents prevail (tending to defy passage) and where Edwin Ferris and his wife Edith built a boathouse and concession during the late 1890s, attractive round-bottomed lapstrake rental boats prevailed. Rowboats were gradually replaced by craft averaging about 16 feet that were designed for outboard motors. These boats typically carried up to three anglers.

Although outboard motors ("kickers") were also available for rent, it was very expensive to do so and most anglers transported their own 5-10 hp outboards in automobile trunks and attached them to rental boats. A number of popular boathouses existed just seaward of the busy railroad track that follows the shoreline between Edmonds and Mukilteo where speeding trains added to the difficulties of carrying outboards and other gear across the tracks. Rental boats for salmon fishing were available in essentially all of the towns and cities located on Puget Sound and were also concentrated along the shorelines near to popular fishing areas. Among these were the shorelines from Edmonds to Tulalip Bay, the southwest and eastern shores of Whidbey Island, and the west side of Camano Island.

A critical function of a Puget Sound boathouse was launching and retrieving boats at various tidal levels. Although elevators, lowering and lifting boats to the water were and continue to be used along more developed waterfronts, launching and retrieving boats on rail-mounted carts was more common. Carts, laden with anglers and gear, coasted to the water and were retrieved by cable powered by modified automobile engines. This in itself, depending upon one's experience, could be an adventure.

In addition to renting boats, outboard motors, and some boats with small inboards, fishing gear was rented or sold along with live or frozen herring and occasionally sandlance. Most boathouses maintained live-bait tanks, as well as a freshwater tank for rinsing seawater from outboards.

Figure 28. A rental boat being prepared for launching by railway during the early 1930s. University of Washington Libraries, Special Collections SOC1568.

Baitfish, preferably live and primarily herring but occasionally sandlance, was a necessary commodity for any successful boathouse.

Boathouses also served as social centers for anglers to discuss their views on fishing and related topics, places where successful anglers could be recognized for their accomplishments, and photographs of notable catches displayed. A navigational chart of local waters was invariably posted, onto which darkened marks left by soiled fingers identified local hot spots.

Puget Sound boathouses were special places for youngsters interested in fishing. The salmon and other fish brought ashore, their stomach contents exposed at the cleaning station, the stories of fish caught and lost, and the perch grazing among the anemones and life-encrusted pilings were all attractions. During the 1940s there were twelve boathouses catering to salmon anglers on Elliott and Shilshole bays and at least nine between Richmond Beach and Mukilteo. In addition to the hazards resulting from speeding trains, landslides along the steep shoreline north of Edmonds occasionally interrupted rail travel and access to these sites. Ravines, with tiny spring-fed cutthroat creeks, provided the routes for roads to local boathouses.

One such creek supplied a gravity flow of water to the boathouse at Norma Beach. The system involved collecting water of sufficient depth in wooden boxes secured in the creek bed. By dropping a worm-baited hook into a box I discovered that it also provided a haven for the trout.

From Seattle northward, being on the water early in the morning was often considered a key to success and even during the pre-dawn hours of mid-summer boathouse operators were often dealing with the rush of impatient anglers. My recollections of the previous mid-century are of anglers struggling to remove outboard motors and gas cans from trunks of cars and trips to and from the boathouse transporting gear; dipping bait, sold by the dozen, from live tanks; the smell of drying boat cushions hung from the rafters; hoisting boats onto the cart and the ride over rails into the sound. Once afloat the task was starting the outboard and, if accomplished, the underway breeze that seemed to carry a surge of pleasurable anticipation for what lay ahead.

In 1935 Carlyon's Beach near Steamboat Island at the southern end of the Sound advertised 50 rental boats, a store and modern cabins for fishermen. This location, hosting an early spring population of spawning herring, was a favorite of Eddie Bauer's – the entrepreneur and avid salmon angler whose original business was in outdoor sporting equipment. Photographs of Bauer at Steamboat Island with husky "blackmouth", once decorated the walls of his Seattle store.

Although the 1960-61 *Pacific Northwest Fishing and Hunting Guide*[50] listed 141 boathouses and resorts still catering to saltwater salmon anglers that were operating in the Puget Sound region, it was the beginning of the end of the era. Diminishing populations of resident salmon, providing a summer-long attraction, were a factor in the demise but it appears that more profitable uses of waterfront property, along with the growing popularity of private boats that could be trailered and launched at ramps and other facilities throughout the region, were also responsible. Although it had nothing to do with the quality of salmon fishing, a simultaneous decline in the numbers of lake-side resorts in the Puget Sound region appears related to similar factors.

Cama Beach was one of a dozen or so Camano Island salmon fishing resorts. Located on the Island's southwestern shore, in the 50's it advertised "*50 modern housekeeping cabins, complete modern resort, store and recreation hall. 60 boats, including 10 kickers. Blackmouth, February through April, kings and silvers through summer months; bottom fish and shellfish all year.*" My impression of Cama Beach during that period was that was that it had a bit more class than a typical hard-core Puget Sound fishing resort. The site is now included in Cama Beach State Park. As a fitting tribute to the era, a commendable effort has resulted in restoring the resort and boathouse and capturing the ambience of the past.

Figure 29. Family and friends at the remains of a Camano Island fishing resort in the summer of 1971. Chinook and anchovies massed along the nearby beach were the attraction.

8   How Good Were the Good Old Days?

There is a growing body of evidence that large Chinook salmon are far scarcer than in the past[51]. One reason for this is that very big fish get that way by spending a year or two longer feeding and growing at sea than the earlier maturing fish. However, the longer they are at sea, the more likely they are to be caught by commercial trollers and anglers alike. Over time, this could result in a heritable survival advantage for early maturity and smaller size. Gillnets, allowing a disproportionate number of small mature fish to slip through the mesh and reach the spawning grounds, may also play a significant role. Even though monster-sized fish occurred more frequently in past years it does not diminish the importance of small immature salmon in catches during the *good old days*.

Old wicker fishing baskets may provide another clue. If there were so many big trout caught back then, why were the fish slots in the creels so small? Few modern trout anglers would consider keeping a fish that would fit into one of those openings. Memories of *mostly* big salmon on Puget Sound are also not supported by facts. Early bag and size limits, and the earliest recorded data, reveals that catching small salmon was popular and they were caught in large numbers[52].

In 1921 the daily bag limit was set at 25 fish between six and fifteen inches long, with an additional three salmon over 15 inches allowed. In February, 1922 the newly appointed State Fisheries Board, whose knowledge of salmon fishing was probably limited to the commercial industry, increased the minimum legal length to 18 inches and the daily bag to just three fish. The new rule resulted in such a backlash that it lasted for only a month when the minimum length limit was promptly lowered to10 inches and a 25 bag limit, *"provided the aggregate weight of the catch did not exceed 20 pounds and one additional salmon."* Under these circumstances, two large salmon or a large and a small one would constitute a limit; whereas the unpopular short-lived rule would have allowed three large fish regardless of their weight. This clearly indicates that the public preferred the opportunity of catching small fish to the lesser chance of catching big fish.

In 1935 the minimum length was raised to 12 inches and this persisted for 23 years, with a gradual decrease in the daily bag limit.

In 1944, the questionable "*20 pound plus one*" provision was replaced by "*six salmon, over 12 inches in length, provided no more than 3 exceed 24 inches in length*", which greatly increased the potential weight of the daily bag. Even though the bag limits on small salmon had been sharply curtailed from former years, a 1951 Washington State Department of Fisheries survey found that 26% of the Chinook and 32% of the coho salmon catch on inner Puget Sound was comprised of fish less than 16 inches long.

A significant, and controversial, size and bag limit change occurred during the summer of 1958 when the minimum length was raised to 16 inches on inner Puget Sound (20 inches on the Strait of Juan de Fuca and the Pacific Ocean) with a daily bag of three. This change was fiercely resisted by many Puget Sound anglers, boathouse owners, and those with financial interests in fishing tackle that targeted small salmon. The rule change had far less impact on fishing on the Strait of Juan de Fuca and the outer coast where small salmon were less important.

Throughout this period, most anglers were believed to be incapable of identifying the various salmon species. This was verified in a survey we conducted in 1966, but it also indicated that anglers could be easily taught to identify salmon species when offered a simple clue or two[53]. Species-specific rules, along with an "educational program" involving posters and illustrations in regulations pamphlets, were initiated in 1971 and have continued since that time.

Species-specific rule differences, such as size limits, are useful for various reasons. One is the different life histories of Chinook and coho salmon. Coho in saltwater that are likely to be caught are in their final year of life. In this case, as with other salmon species that are only available to saltwater anglers as adults (pink, chum and sockeye salmon), minimum size limits have the adverse effect of selectively removing the larger individuals of a given age from the pool of potential spawners. Chinook salmon, on the other hand, are longer lived and at any one time three different age groups are vulnerable to saltwater angling. A Chinook salmon minimum size limit does protect the younger fish from harvest, although the faster-growing salmon are again more vulnerable by reaching minimum size earlier. Species-specific closures are also used to protect certain stocks, as well as to provide "bonus" bag limits in times of unanticipated abundance such as has occurred during certain pink salmon runs. Since 1976, Chinook salmon size limits have also been used to reduce sport catches so as to comply with treaty Indian catch sharing, although since the catch balance has shifted the other way, this is no longer needed.

From the very beginning of salmon management in Washington, and continuing through 1975, there were essentially no seasonal restrictions on saltwater salmon angling. The existing practice of scheduling commercial salmon fishing at times and places where recreational fishing was disallowed was unheard of in earlier days and would never have been considered by fisheries managers.

9   A Brief History of Salmon Management in Washington

In 1889, the year of statehood, a Washington Fish Commission, headed by a salaried Commissioner, was established to oversee the state's salmon resource and the commercial fishing industry. The commission existed until 1921 when the legislature created the State of Washington Department of Fisheries and Game consisting of the Division of Fisheries and the Division of Game and Game Fish. The responsibilities of Fisheries Division Director apparently were little changed from those of the Fish Commissioner; whereas, the responsibilities of the Division of Game and Game Fish constituted a new role for the state that was formerly held by the counties. However, significant county involvement in inland gamefish management continued for more than two decades. County game wardens were the primary enforcers of relevant laws, county trout hatcheries continued to operate, and due to the popularity of in-county hunting and fishing, most license revenues remained in the counties. The United States Government also had a significant role with fish in Washington prior to statehood. American shad were introduced into the territory by the U.S. Fish Commission in 1881, followed by carp in 1882 and many other non-native freshwater species in later years – some of which had a deleterious impact on our native salmon.

In 1932, the passage of Initiative 62, championed by a cadre of politically active sportsmen who were primarily interested in steelhead trout, created two separate agencies, the Department of Fisheries and the Department of Game. The Director of Fisheries was to serve at the pleasure of the Governor, while the Director of Game was eventually to be appointed by a nine-member, non-salaried commission appointed by the Governor. The Department of Fisheries, whose primary function involved commercial fishing, was to be funded through the state general fund; whereas, the Game Department would primarily rely upon the sales of fishing and hunting licenses. Species under Fisheries were legally defined as *food fish* and included salmon and important commercial marine species. These were designated, but not exclusively reserved, for commercial harvest but could also be taken for personal use (e.g., for sport) as well. Trout, and inland fishes of interest to anglers, were legally designated as *game fish* for exclusive recreational use under the Department of Game.

Apparently buoyed by the successful passage of Initiative 62, leaders in the salmon and steelhead angling communities[b] joined with commercial salmon purse seiners in support of Initiative 77, a measure directed toward outlawing salmon traps in Washington[54]. For many years most of the Puget Sound salmon catch, including disproportionate numbers of fish bound for the Fraser River, were taken in Washington traps. Most of these devices were owned by a few affluent people. The traps were constructed with small mesh netting affixed to pilings that extended from shore into migration routes. Salmon traveled along the netting until they were "led" into the "heart" of the trap where they milled about with little chance of escape.

The pro I-77campaign focused on the populist theme of returning a public resource, dominated by a few trap owners, to the people. It also raised the bogus conservation issue that the use of traps was inconsistent with salmon conservation. The fact is that in contrast to other commercial gear, properly regulated traps were capable of releasing live immature salmon and stocks in need of protection. The salmon canning industry joined with the trap owners in their unsuccessful opposition to the measure that passed by a substantial margin in 1934. Although the Department of Fisheries was required to remain "neutral", they were generally viewed as opposing the initiative.

Figure 30. A modern salmon trap on the Russian Coast in the Sea of Japan.
Photo is courtesy of Guido Rahr of the Wild Salmon Center.

In addition to eliminating the traps, the original version of I-77 changed other commercial salmon fishing practices on Puget Sound. It established a line of demarcation (Initiative 77 Line), inside of which commercial fishing was severely curtailed. This essentially encompassed the waters of inner Puget Sound, including an inshore portion of Juan de Fuca Strait east of the Elwha River, but excluded the major purse seining areas in the northern sound and San Juan Islands where Fraser River sockeye and pink salmon were normally taken. The initiative included a provision that would eventually eliminate gillnet fishing within the area, by allowing only those licensed in 1932 or 1933 to be licensed in the future ("grandfathered"). Hook-and-line fishing, including commercial salmon trolling on the inner sound was not affected by I-77.

Angling and purse-seining interests clearly drove I-77, and its passage marks the peak of political influence of sportsfishing interests on the laws of Washington. The provision to limit net fishing to the fall chum season on the inner Sound appears to be a significant concession, by the purse seiners, to sportfishing interests. The political influence of gillnet interests was apparently of little consequence, however the provision to eliminate gillnetting from inside the 77 line subsequently backfired on purse seiners and anglers when the courts determined that the grandfathering was unconstitutional. Ironically, licenses to fish in Puget Sound with gillnets continued to be issued in unlimited numbers while the provision to limit purse seining inside the I-77 line remained in effect.

The passage of I-77 was heralded by its supporters as a salmon angling panacea for Puget Sound but it appears to have fallen short of these expectations. Eliminating traps reduced the concerns of commercial interests who were modestly profiting from steelhead sales, and a year later steelhead were designated an official game fish by the Washington legislature. Unfortunately, no official sportfishing catch records are available before 1938, but there was a gradual increase in fishing activity from that time with a significant increase following WW II. It appears clear that during the 1930's, and to a lesser degree to this day, salmon sportfishing advocates have a somewhat distorted view of what is required for good fishing.

The fact that I-77 did nothing to curtail commercial trolling – fishing that directly competes with anglers for biting fish – is one example.

Before and following the I-77 campaign, the angler's purse-seine allies were creating havoc off Cape Flattery and elsewhere setting their nets on feeding schools of immature fish[55]. There remains a tendency among salmon anglers to ignore intensive out-of-sight fishing on stocks of Chinook and coho that are of potential importance to them and conservation of the resource.

The elimination of the fish traps that were intercepting most of the Fraser River fish as they passed through Washington waters, shifted the preponderance of the catch of Fraser salmon to Canada, thus motivating Washington's commercial fishing industry to seek a treaty between the United States and Canada to evenly divide the harvest of Fraser River's sockeye, and later pink salmon, between the two nations. Such a treaty was ratified in 1937. It provided for the two nations to share the costs of the resulting International Pacific Salmon Fisheries Commission, including constructing a fish ladder at Hells Canyon on the Fraser where a slide had been inhibiting salmon migrations since it occurred in 1913.

We now return to the passage of Initiative 62 in 1932 dividing game and commercial fish management between two state agencies. As should have been expected, the two new departments established by Initiative 62 were not without their jurisdictional problems. The individual responsibilities of the agencies were not separated geographically – for example at the edge of tidewater – but were based upon species defined by law as either (commercial) food fish or game fish. Fisheries clientele were essentially the commercial – fishing industry – although "personal use" (sport fishing and shellfish gathering) was recognized as a legitimate activity. Game was beholden to the state's anglers and hunters.

Problems occur when food and game fish co-mingle – as they frequently do – and then compete, eat, or even infect each other. Throughout the history of the two agencies, hatchery releases of game fish and salmon into the same waters were seldom coordinated. Game installed screens at the outlets of many lowland lakes in western Washington to keep stocked trout in with little regard for the wild salmon that would utilize the waters above the screens. Fisheries stocked salmon above natural barriers that were formerly exclusively used by trout. Largemouth bass and other non-native predatory game fish thrived in many lowland lakes that were once important for rearing juvenile coho – a situation that also existed in major salmon streams.

Each had its own police force, biological staff, vehicles, and aircraft. Commercial salmon net catches at times included significant numbers of steelhead that could not be legally sold in Washington, but were legal on the Oregon side of the Columbia, infuriating those who, without some justification, considered these fish as God's exclusive gift to anglers. Each agency had hatcheries that could have been utilized for either salmon or trout but seldom if ever were used for both. Mitigation for dam construction, such as occurred on the Cowlitz and Snake (Lyons Ferry) rivers required construction of separate facilities for each agency – ultimately at public expense – which would have been unlikely under a coordinated and cooperative hatchery program.

In 1994 the legislature merged the two departments into the Washington Department of Fish and Wildlife to be directed by an appointee of the governor. The organization maintained a lame duck commission whose role was only advisory. The following year the power of a nine-member Fish and Wildlife Commission, essentially patterned after that of the original Game Department, was restored by a vote of the people (Referendum 45). These new commissioners, appointed by the governor and confirmed by the senate, were to serve six-year terms. No two could reside in the same county and at least three must reside on each side of the Cascade Mountains. The Director of Fish and Wildlife was to serve at the pleasure of the Commission whose role was to establish the agency's policy and direction. The efficacy of this system was initially questionable but with the appointment of stronger and more qualified commissioners is, in my view, currently (2014) resulting in changes consistent with improving management of Washington's fish and wildlife resources.

10   A Career with the WDF

Following graduation from the University of Washington in 1959 (B.S. in fisheries), I was hired full-time by the Department of Fisheries to do some of the same things I was doing as a student and part-time employee. J.E. ("Al") Lasater, a WW II vet, had been my supervisor as a student and had recommended me for full-time employment as a fish biologist. Al was in the process of teaching me a great deal about fish and the natural world. He was the son of a logger and had been brought up in various western Montana lumber communities where he had fished for everything from burbot to bull trout. As crewman aboard a small tanker plying the war zones of the South Pacific, he was never without fishing tackle and was encouraged to use it by a fish-loving skipper. Al is probably the best all-around angler I have ever known. Although taking great delight in sharing his knowledge with young and old alike, he was something of a loner and delighted in doing something different or innovative – like catching a 26-pound carp on a fly. Now into his 90s, Al still zigs when others zag.

Al arranged an interview for me with Clarence Pautzke, the department's number two man and a fish biologist by profession. Pautzke had come over from the Department of Game where he had made quite a reputation with his work on steelhead. "Pautzke's Pets", an early winter stock of hatchery steelhead originating in Chambers Creek – a tributary of Puget Sound at Steilacoom – were doing very well in various river systems at that time. Pautzke, an incredibly outgoing and likeable man who epitomized the image of a good-old boy, took me to meet Milo Moore, Director of the Department of Fisheries. Moore, despite his distrust of biologists, hired me while making it clear he didn't want any more "philosophers" working for him.

The Department of Fisheries was then located at Salmon Bay in Seattle. I reported for work in new clothes, pleated trousers, a necktie; but Pautzke promptly sent me home to get my fishing tackle. I can still see the look on my wife's face at the door when she learned of the mission. He needed a good-sized blackmouth for one of his many barbeques – doubtlessly a promotional event for a fish project. It was June of 1959 and only dogfish took my mooched herring that day at Point

Defiance. A short time later Pautzke went to work for the U.S. Fish and
Wildlife Service and eventually achieved Ambassadorial status working
on international fisheries issues. At about the same time other talented
biologists, who later achieved professional prominence, were leaving
the department because of the policies of Director Moore. Soon after
retiring from federal service and looking forward to his steelhead fishing
on his home stream, the Green River, Pautzke died while undergoing hip
replacement surgery.

Since the department of Fisheries was created to take care of
the state's commercial fishing industry and the various species of
commercial importance, its recreational role was essentially limited to
monitoring and estimating salmon catches. When recreational catch
and participation estimates were initiated in 1938 for Puget Sound,
salmon sport catches anywhere else in the state were considered to
be insignificant. For years the outer coast was only closed to salmon
angling from November 1 to April 15 – when no one would be fishing
there in any event – and it was year-round fishing throughout Juan de
Fuca Strait and Puget Sound. Fishing in Puget Sound peaked during
the summer months but it was popular in these protected waters,
particularly among the more proficient anglers, throughout the year
with the highest catches per angler trip occurring during the winter
months.

During the 1930's local entrepreneurs were touting Puget Sound as
"the greatest fishing area in the world" and for a considerable time thereafter a highlight of a visit to the region included salmon fishing. The big
Puget Sound salmon fishing derbies were attracting national attention
and people were traveling there to partake in the sport. One such visitor was President Harry Truman who was frequently the guest of fellow
democrat Washington Governor Mon C. Wallgren. The Governor, at
state expense, had managed to acquire a 97-foot yacht, christened the
M.V. Olympus, for fishing and related activities under the guise of it being
a Department of Fisheries patrol vessel. An investigative reporter from
The *Seattle Post Intelligencer* caught wind of the situation and it became
a significant factor in Wallgren's defeat in the 1948 general election. His
fishing companion, however, came up with a famous upset win over
Thomas Dewey.

Figure 31. President Harry Truman, with a Puget Sound "blackmouth", and Governor Mon C. Wallgren to his right, aboard the *M.V. Olympus* in 1945.
George Skadding/the LIFE Picture Collection/Getty Images.

The new Governor, Arthur Langlie, ordered the *M.V. Olympus* sold but even he was accused of rigging the bid so a friend could buy it. The boat remains afloat and at this time it is available for charter. Wallgren is the only Washington Governor to also have served both as a Congressman and a U.S. Senator. One of his greatest accomplishments was introducing the bill that established Olympic National Park. Following his defeat for a second term as Governor, he was appointed to a position in the federal government by President Truman. In 1961 he died of injuries resulting from his stalled vehicle being hit by another on the Highway 99 Bridge crossing the Nisqually River.

During the late 1950's Washington's salmon sport fishery was growing geographically and in popularity. Entrepreneurs along Juan de Fuca Strait and the outer coast responded by providing services attracted to the angling opportunities. The typical boats used on Puget Sound were basically unsuitable for the dangerous bars and the outer coast.

Charter boats, many originally built for commercial fishing, began operating out of Westport and Ilwaco and there were soon many boats specifically designed for carrying ten or more anglers. By decade's end Puget Sound was no longer the epicenter of the state's salmon sport fishery.

From 1967 through 1979, Washington sport catches averaged well over a million fish per year, with only about 12% of the total taken in fresh water. During these years the state's salmon sport catch had exceeded the combined sport catches of California, Oregon, British Columbia and Alaska. Angler participation and catches peaked in 1976 at 1.9 million angler trips accounting for 1.7 million salmon. About 18% of these anglers were from out-of-state.

Estimating Puget Sound sport catches was my job and involved hours at a desk with a calculator. For years these estimates were heavily dependent upon mandatory reports submitted by Puget Sound boathouses. Boats rented for salmon angling were licensed by the state and boathouse owners were required to submit monthly reports listing the numbers of daily boat rentals, anglers and catches by species. These reports provided the basis for determining how many people were fishing. Fishing effort and catches from privately owned boats were estimated by counting the boats actively fishing in the various areas to establish the ratios of private and rentals. The latter were of characteristic design and painted in a manner representing the various boathouses. Catches, reported by the boathouses, were not taken at face value. Periodic catch sampling by the Department's staff provided information relating to fishing success, as well as species composition and size of the fish in the catch. In 1949 rental boats comprised more than 75% of the salmon sportfishing boats on Puget Sound, but 15 years later privately owned boats far outnumbered rentals.

The need for a new system, independent of boathouse reports, was obvious and also provided a means of escaping from the drudgery of the old system. It required that anglers maintain free "punch cards" to record dates and areas of salmon catches. A further, unenforceable, requirement was that cards were to be returned at year's end. We anticipated that only a fraction of the anglers would return their cards and that catches of these respondents would be higher than those from the overall population (e.g., *response bias*). In order to correct for this the system was designed to actively pursue data from a random selection comprising five per cent of the anglers obtaining cards. Following the initial year (1964) of the punch card, 87% of the "in sample" data was returned. Catch sampling was to remain an integral part of the system. The procedures were approved by a highly qualified University of Washington professor and statistician. In addition to catch information, the new system provided the first insight into the demographics of the salmon angling population.

Attempting to implement this obviously needed change provided a valuable learning experience in getting things done. I was instructed that the new system would only be implemented if it was approved by the Washington State Sportsmen's Council. The organization consisted of representatives from various fishing and hunting clubs scattered throughout the state and met quarterly to conduct their business which primarily consisted of debating on and ultimately voting on various resolutions. Although during my experience with the organization, little if anything appeared to result from their efforts, they did perform the important function of successfully nominating members to serve on the Washington State Game Commission.

Convincing the council that what they really needed was a salmon punch card was no easy task. The Department's reputation as an organization concerned only with the welfare of the commercial fishing industry was a problem that could only be solved by establishing a relationship with the various groups comprising the Sportsmen's Council. This involved giving many evening talks at the various clubs comprising the council. The sales pitch dwelt on reasons why salmon anglers would benefit from new information that could be used to document the importance of their sport. Opponents countered by saying that it would only lead to requiring a salmon angling license – which it eventually did. The Washington State Sportsmen's Council passed a resolution endorsing the salmon punch card. Although I doubt that he ever used it, I issued salmon punch card number 000001 to Governor Albert Rosellini for the 1964 season. I did see to it that the next three Governors of Washington put lots of holes in their cards. The experience clearly demonstrated to me the importance of establishing a constituency, outside of the agency, in order to get things done.

Figure 32. The author issuing Governor Albert Rosellini with the first Sport Salmon Catch Record ("Punch Card") in 1963 for the 1964 season.

Washington Department of Fisheries photo.

11   Saltwater Fishing in Washington

From the beginning, most of the state's saltwater anglers were after salmon and the bulk of the catch of other species was essentially "by-catch". The vast majority of anglers knew very little about the other potentially valuable recreational fishes that were available. In 1966 we conducted a survey at various important marine sportfishing landings in Puget Sound, Juan de Fuca Strait and along the outer coast[56]. Anglers were asked to identify various species of fresh fish displayed in a portable ice chest and most flunked the test. For example, only 36% correctly identified a 30-inch lingcod – perhaps the most recognizable of local "bottom fish". Chinook and coho salmon were also included in the survey and the results indicated that marine salmon angling regulations, varying by species, would be impracticable without improving general proficiency in species recognition. However, the survey also indicated that anglers were capable of improving their ability to separate the two species when provided with a simple clue: "Chinook salmon, also called blackmouth, have the teeth of their lower jaw protruding from all black gums."

The results of the survey further demonstrated a need to educate Washington's anglers. As a result, Raymond Buckley, a biologist working with me, and I wrote a guide book for saltwater anglers. We made an arrangement with our supervisors and Stan Jones, a Seattle publisher specializing in outdoor guide books, to write and provide illustrations for *Saltwater Fishing in Washington*. Since we were being paid by the State to write the book, the publishing rights were given to Jones with the understanding that he would make the book available at a reasonable price. I considered Stan to be an honorable man and believe that he fulfilled his end of the agreement very well.

Much of our work involved taking color photos of live or fresh specimens of 51 species most commonly caught by anglers. Brief descriptions of habitat preferences, life histories, preferred baits and lures and table quality were included with each fish. The book also included "how to" photos and description on filleting and cleaning fish, by fellow biologist Nick Pasquale, cutting and baiting hooks, maps of salmon fishing areas, and techniques for catching salmon.

Saltwater Fishing in Washington was a hit and it went through two or three editions. A number of years later Stan approached me about doing another but by that time I felt that the information was out of date and a major rewrite called for. At the time I was overwhelmed with other matters and Stan later died before anything could be done. However, the book appeared to play a significant role in educating Washington anglers and prophesized that the greatest potential in local saltwater fishing,

". . . lies with the fishes we have overlooked and the fact that a new era is about to begin. The salmon will still be there, but fishermen will discover the other good fishes the Washington Coast has to offer."

The prophecy was fulfilled in spades with anglers doing their part to decimate populations of rockfishes and lingcod throughout much of the Puget Sound region. The lesson to be learned is that many popular marine fishes, such as various rockfishes, grow to decent size at about the rate it takes a Douglas fir to become marketable. In addition, the many species of rockfishes, both large and small, cannot withstand the effects of an expanding swim bladder – the gas-filled organ neutralizing buoyancy – that occurs when they are hauled from the depths. This is a major source of mortality and waste – particularly in the commercial trawl fisheries, since small and otherwise unmarketable fish cannot be released alive. Lingcod, greenlings, flatfishes, and some other local species lack swim bladders and are far less impacted. Salmon and some other species with swim bladders are capable of rapidly expelling the gas as they approach the surface.

Salmon quickly reach a desirable size and are well adapted to selective fishing techniques involving "catch and release". Salmon can be efficiently produced in hatcheries; whereas, the development of techniques to artificially produce other desirable local marine fishes is, at best, in its infancy. The massive fin-clipping programs currently underway in Washington and elsewhere should eventually expand sportfishing opportunities by allowing anglers to target marked hatchery fish while protecting wild populations. Maintaining a viable saltwater sport fishery in Washington – one that we can be proud of – will primarily depend upon salmon.

Angler requirements for identifying the various species have dramatically increased over the past 50 years: the "possession limit" for an aggregated catch of marine "food fish" (excluding salmon, sturgeon and halibut) has gone from "20 pounds and one fish" to a host of species-specific rules. At the present time, in order to comply with all of Washington's angling regulations; one must now identify dozens of freshwater and marine fishes.

12 The Thirteen Point Program

At the time I went to work with the Department the position of biologist in charge of salmon sportfishing investigations was a relatively low-level position that I achieved within a few years. Although fisheries biologists tend to be reasonable although relatively introverted people, I became one of a small group of rather arrogant extroverts, and unreasonable in a sense described by George Bernard Shaw: "*The reasonable man adapts himself to the world: The unreasonable one persists in trying to adapt the world to himself. Therefore all progress depends upon the unreasonable man.*" Our group was later dubbed by a *Seattle Times* outdoor reporter as the *Young Turks*. Drs. Peter Bergman and Stephen Mathews were prominent members of the tong, along with Raymond Buckley. Lee Blankenship was a younger and upcoming participant.

Our self-imposed mission, which became known as *The Thirteen Point Sport Fishing Enhancement Program*, was to go beyond simply monitoring catches and concentrate on improving the quality of fishing. At the time, salmon fishing in Puget Sound was suffering. The conventional wisdom among our supervisors and peers was that the problem was environmental and little if anything could be done to restore the populations of Chinook and coho salmon that formerly resided within the Sound and were the mainstay of Washington's salmon sport fishery.

The initial step, during the late 1960s, toward restoring the sport fishery involved securing a grant from the U.S. Bureau of Commercial Fisheries to conduct some experiments involving hatchery coho salmon. Resident coho salmon enhancement experiments began with eggs taken from adults during the fall of 1968. The work was centered in south Puget Sound and primarily involved Minter Creek Hatchery located south of the Tacoma Narrows near the head of Carr Inlet.

Critical to success was brand-new technology, in the form of the Coded Wire Tag (CWT), enabling us to evaluate the performance of many different experimental groups in a single year. Prior to this development, the century-old technique of fin clipping was the standard method used to trace migration patterns as well as evaluate contributions and survivals of juvenile salmon. Fin excision often reduces the survival of salmon at an unpredictable rate and biases the experimental results.

In addition, the limited number of potential identifications provided by fin clipping, combined with the fact that different salmon managers were using identical marks, one could seldom be sure of the origin of a fin-clipped salmon caught at sea. Ambiguity also resulted from the fact that some clipped fins regenerated and some fins were lost from predator attacks, fin nipping among fish and abrasions in hatchery ponds, and other causes.

Pete Bergman, who was charged with managing the commercial troll fishery, had earlier become frustrated with this primitive method and, contrary to wishes of his supervisors, sought a better way. Enlisting the assistance of his friend, Bell Laboratory physicist Keith Jefferts, the coded wire tag was born. In the years that followed, CWTs, in combination with the adipose fin clip, quickly replaced fin marking on the west coast of North America and within ten years upwards of 45 million Chinook and coho salmon per year, the vast majority originating in hatcheries, were being tagged. A prestigious Canadian publication[57] stated that by 1974 the Bergman-Jefferts tag had resulted in *"More information about ocean distribution, and the numbers of fish from hatcheries in specific fisheries, was gathered in 12 months than had been gathered in previous 12 years."*

The tag codes, on the 1.1 mm lengths of surgical-grade stainless steel, originally consisted of color striping. Modern tags bear laser-inscribed numbers identifying either a specific group or an individual fish. The magnetically charged wire is injected into the snouts of juvenile salmon and has no measurable biological impact. At the time of these experiments, clipped adipose fins identified tag-bearing salmon, but electronic detection is now used. Technicians using hand-held "wands" and other electronic devices now cut the tagged snouts from sport and commercially caught fish and deliver them to laboratories where tags are excised, read under magnification, and recorded for analysis. Although in terms of numbers applied, most coded wire tagging has involved Pacific salmon, they have been successfully used throughout the world on many different species. For example, important information regarding the origins of Atlantic salmon caught on the high seas was obtained from coded wire tagging.

Collecting enough information to evaluate our experiments in the Thirteen Point Program, involving the initial major use of the new tag, was facilitated by rewarding anglers returning heads, from adipose-fin-clipped fish, to collection sites at boathouses and tackle shops. In addition to cash, participating anglers were provided with certificates and monthly up-dates on the program. Originally $1,000 a month, divided evenly among those returning tagged heads, was allocated to the program. Tag returns eventually became so numerous that individual checks were reduced to just over $1.00. Rewards were subsequently based upon a lottery system in which qualification for the drawings required returning a tagged head. Although technically illegal at the time, this was probably Washington's first state-sponsored lottery[e]. Following Washington's example, a similar collection system was soon established in Canada for recovering the tags.

Seven tagged-fish test groups were initially involved in the resident coho salmon experiments. In addition to a control representing normal hatchery production released in early April, the groups included five hatchery-reared wild stocks believed to be possible contributors to the resident population. The "lucky" seventh group was hatchery fish reared for an additional three months and released on July 2, 1970 at an average weight of 1/9 of a pound each (1/20 lb. each for the control). The basis for the extended rearing was earlier tagging work in Admiralty Inlet – the entrance to inner Puget Sound – that indicated the seaward migration of coho salmon in their second year of a three-year life span ended about the beginning of July. This being the case, we would make sure that one experimental group could not exit the sound prior to July 1.

It soon became evident that fish that were held longer in the hatchery were contributing to local sport catches at an extraordinary rate. It was estimated that over nine percent of the release of 69,000 fish tagged in the group was taken by local anglers, in contrast to less than a half of one percent of the control. All of the other groups contributed at a rate less than that of the controls. This experiment was followed-up by another involving the 1969 brood year testing three released between early May and August from Minter Creek. The results of this experiment showed a progressively greater contribution to the Puget Sound sport catch by extending the release date, but the greatest overall contribution to all Washington commercial and sport fisheries resulted from the June release. Other significant factors relating to extended rearing include the difficulty of rearing coho salmon in warm water during the summer months, additional feed costs, and an apparent reduction in adult size associated with extended hatchery rearing, although the latter condition also exists with naturally occurring resident fish.

The reason for the rapid decline in the numbers of wild resident coho salmon that occurred in the late 1950s is a question that remains unanswered. Much of the loss could have resulted from degradation of juvenile rearing that formerly existed in hundreds of ponds and lowland lakes throughout the Puget Sound basin. Although streams are normally thought of as the critical areas for juvenile coho rearing, still waters with permanent or even temporary connections to streams have been shown to also be important[58]. Such areas containing large quantities of permanent water, in contrast to low summer flows in small coho streams, could have provided the natural habitat favorable for extended rearing. All such local lakes, from the late 19th century on, were stocked with non-native fishes.

During the 1950s and 60s many such lakes were treated with rotenone to kill all of the existing fish, planted with trout, and screened in an effort to confine stocked trout to the lakes and blocking access to migratory fish. Most of these lakes and ponds contain large populations of introduced predators, the most significant being largemouth bass[59]. Juvenile coho that do rear and survive in these lakes and ponds have been shown to be larger and may rear in freshwater for an extended period. Studies in Canada have shown that juvenile coho naturally migrate far above where they were hatched to rear in lakes and ponds and these fish behave similarly here. Even in the sparsely populated areas of Western Washington, such as near my second home in the headwaters of the East Fork or of the Satsop River (Chehalis River Basin), most lowland lakes and ponds, that would have formerly reared coho, are now overpopulated with stunted largemouth bass.

The first experiments with extended rearing of Chinook salmon followed the success with coho. Researchers at the University of Washington, in cooperation with the Washington Department of Fisheries, reared fish in marine pens located at various Puget Sound locations. The fish were held about ten months beyond the normal release time for fall Chinook salmon smolts. Few of the tagged fish released from a marine pen located off Squaxin Island in the southern extremity of the Sound moved very far and an astounding 5.6 percent of the tags from the 5,400 fish released from the site were actually recovered[60]. Since recovering a tag required that it was included in a random catch sample or recognized by an angler and voluntarily returned, the total catch was obviously much higher. My boys and I once caught four of these tagged fish in one day near Johnson Point.

These experimental results were quickly transformed into major Chinook and coho salmon "delayed rearing" programs centered in south Puget Sound. Notable among these was the program at Percival Cove, an enclosed bay off Capitol Lake in Olympia. The cove, at the mouth of Percival Creek, was utilized to rear a million fall-planted fingerlings that were released, weighing about 1/10 of a pound each, during the following spring. In addition, large numbers of extended reared fish were released, in a cooperative State-Tribal program, from the Squaxin Island marine pens. During the height of the program it was estimated that 10 percent of these delayed Chinook were being caught in the local sport fishery.

The success of the resident salmon programs spawned a plethora of other ideas intended to improve salmon angling[61]. Some dealt with introducing Chinook and coho salmon stocks into local hatcheries that, in contrast to most Puget Sound hatchery fish, were known to return when they were still feeding and biting. Green River hatchery is the source of Chinook salmon brood stock throughout the Puget Sound basin. For more than a century Elliott Bay, has been the Sound's most intensively angled body of water during late summer when adult fish are present. "Non-biters" thus have had a survival advantage that is likely to be inherited. In addition, it appears that the early returning fish that were furthest from sexual maturity, and more likely to bite, have been further selected in favor of a labor-saving tendency to concentrate the egg take during the peak of the spawning period.

These feelings were reinforced in August of 1970, when I was invited to Rivers Inlet, a classic fjord located on the central coast of British Columbia, to participate in Jim Conway's television program. My job was to have Able Schiller filmed catching a big fish. Schiller, who caught his fish, was a colorful character representing the Flamingo Hotel in Las Vegas and said to have had a serious run-in with the infamous "Bugsy" Siegel. The Chinook salmon milling at the mouth of the nearby Wannock River were destined to spawn only a few miles upstream.

This large but short river, cutting through the moraine at the seaward end of glacial Owikeno Lake, discolors miles of the inlet's surface water. In some seasons the average size of Chinook salmon taken is 40 pounds, in contrast to less than 20 pounds in Puget Sound's Green River. Migration and spawning times were essentially identical. In contrast to Elliott Bay, where the "bite" lasted only for an hour or two at dawn, fishing seemed primarily limited by an annoying afternoon westerly breeze. In order to protect the fish from over-exploitation by anglers, a good portion of the upper inlet was closed to fishing. The total estimated run size was about ten percent of the contemporary return to the Green River.

One objective was to produce a superior sport salmon for Puget Sound by introducing genes from Rivers Inlet. The original intent was to capture mature males on the Wannock River spawning grounds on lures, and tether the live fish to the bank until it was time to collect sperm. The tethers, cushioned by elastic snubbers, were to be strung through the mouth, exiting the gill cover ahead of the gill arches, and secured by a knot completing a securing loop, and secured to the bank. The sperm, collected in plastic bags, was to be iced and would remain viable for only a matter of hours until it was to be used to fertilize eggs of Green River fish that would be available at Hoodsport hatchery on the shores of Hood Canal. The tethering system was similar to one used for many years by Ernie Brannon Sr., superintendent at Dungeness Hatchery, for taking Chinook spawn on the Elwha River.

State Fisheries Director Thor Tollefson went along with the idea and used his influence with the Canadian authorities to approve our request to collect the Rivers Inlet Chinook salmon sperm. He also arranged for a single-engine float plane, owned by British Columbia Packers, Ltd. for our transportation to Rivers Inlet and back to Hood Canal. Such a project had never been attempted in that area and word got back to us that the local authorities believed that we had little chance for success.

Harry Senn, a biologist and hatchery expert, and I took off from Vancouver B.C. on October 13, 1970. Flying over the mountains and snow fields on a spectacularly clear day, we landed on Owikeno Lake at a remote door-less cabin near the source of the Wannock River that was recently vacated by grizzly bear hunters. We were met there by a crew of Canadian fisheries technicians, led by Stan Hembrough, who transported us in an outboard-powered aluminum skiff to the major pool of the Wannock. Harry and I fished with big spinners and salmon egg clusters for two hours and caught one or two coho salmon, a small steelhead and a Dolly Varden. The big Chinook that were surfacing throughout the turbid pool were not interested in our offerings. We were picked up in the boat and returned to our lodging.

Our ace in the hole was a 150-foot length of eight-inch gillnet we had packed in a burlap bag. When the crew returned with the boat the next morning we returned to the "Spring Hole", ran the net out into the current, hooked it downstream and hauled the lower end toward the beach as if it were a seine. Almost immediately there was an explosion of spray and we were into big fish.

Figure 33. Director of Fisheries Donald Moos with a tethered male Wannock River Chinook salmon on a later expedition.

Apart from the lead line hanging up on boulders, the operation proceeded rather smoothly. The leashes worked perfectly and in the turbid water the fish, tethered to brush along the bank, seemed to soon settle down and hold in position. We had been tipped off that the local fisheries enforcement officer may be difficult to deal with but that he liked Hudson Bay Rum. In the midst of the operation he suddenly appeared out of the woods with the head of the local Indian band. He was totally unaware of our mission and we were fortunate in being well prepared to deal with an otherwise difficult situation.

That evening our pilot was contacted by radio and advised that we would be ready to go the next morning. Upon returning to the site, the tethered fish appeared to be doing well although one had been eaten by a grizzly. Flying weather was good and by 10:30 we had collected 28 ounces of sperm from 15 males that were released back into the river – the crew clown even suggested that a fish or two appeared to be smiling after the experience. By 4:00 p.m. that day 300,000 Green River x Rivers Inlet eggs were incubating at Hoodsport Salmon Hatchery.

The Hoh River on the outer Washington Coast was our other source of "biter genes". Hoh River Chinook, particularly the "jacks" (sexually precocious males) seemed to behave like hungry trout in their willingness to take salmon-roe-baited hooks. For two or three years during September in the 1970s, we camped about three miles above the ocean with members of the Elliott Bay Chapter of the Association of NW Steelheaders collecting blackmouth-bright jacks. Nearly all of the fish were taken on salmon roe, tethered and led back to river holding pens at camp. They were later spawned at Soleduc Hatchery or used to fertilize Green River eggs. All of these experiments included significant numbers of coded wire tagged fish for evaluation.

The importation of live sperm from Chinook at Rivers Inlet and the Hoh River are just two examples of attempts to produce superior sport fish. Only a few coded wire tags were ever recovered from these particular experiments and, although I was unaware of any professional criticism at the time, some contemporary biologists would cringe at the thought of such a thing. Some races of native fish stocks, including White River and Dungeness River spring Chinook, and their various inter-specific hybrids that were released as yearlings, demonstrated a remarkable tendency to contribute to Puget Sound sport catches. Experiments since then have demonstrated that survivals from fertile eggs native in one watershed that are transported to another for rearing and release, demonstrate a reduced survival in proportion to the distance from their native streams. It also appears that the importation of non-native sperm can reduce the fitness of local fish to survive in their native environment.

Although our attempts to artificially rear salmon that were inherently more inclined to take baited hooks and lures never paid off, years later a paper was published that described experiments with largemouth bass that supported the contention that vulnerability to angling is indeed heritable[62]. In this case the results of angling in a controlled pond, containing a population of largemouth bass, were recorded by marking individual fish each time they were caught and released. After being exposed to a season of angling with various lures, all of the bass in the pond were collected and the most and least vulnerable were stocked in separate ponds and allowed to spawn. The resulting progeny were then marked, to identify their low or high vulnerability parentage, and mixed together in a common pond and allowed to grow to catchable size. Angling and marking was resumed and it was found that the vulnerability trend continued. The experiment continued through successive generations with an increasing difference between the high and low vulnerability groups. It has also occurred to me that brown trout, which have been intensively angled for centuries longer than North American trout, appear to be more difficult to catch.

While all of this was going on we supported and implemented programs involving native stocks and managed to discourage the transfer of Green River fish to such streams as the Skagit, Elwha and Quillayute rivers. Although we worked hard to integrate local wild Chinook salmon into the hatchery populations by collecting wild adults and transporting them to hatcheries for spawning, we received little support for this work and essentially "bent our picks".

One such effort in July of 1972 was intended to capture early returning Chinook and involved spanning the Quillayute River with a "Lake Merwin Trap" – a device designed to catch northern pikeminnows in a Lewis River (Columbia River tributary) reservoir. The task of tending the trap was assigned to a brand-new biologist from the midwest.

He would call in each morning with a status report. Catches after a few days of operation consisted of a handful of sockeye salmon that gilled in short sections of mesh connecting ends of the trap to the shoreline. Since the river was low, it appeared that a freshet would move the Chinook upstream. And then it began to rain.

It was more than a freshet. The frantic morning call indicated that the trap was nowhere to be seen. Following the report I telephoned the Quillayute Coast Guard Station, located a short distance downstream in La Push, and was told that a large unidentified object had been observed floating seaward. The remains of the trap were later retrieved and disposed of. This did not end our efforts to collect early run Quillayute Chinook.

A short time later, during a helicopter survey of the Sol Duc River, the main branch of the Quillayute, I spotted a promising school of salmon in a remote pool. Prior to this we had prepared a 100-foot seine and a "john" boat for collecting fish which we managed to launch a mile or so above the targeted pool. Two young fisheries patrol officers had chosen to follow us in a canoe accompanied by a reporter/photographer from the *Port Angeles Daily News.* This river is not without its hazards, but the biologist involved in the previous adventure and I arrived at the location and managed a perfect seine set around the fish. As we drew the net onto the beach we could see that the vast majority of the fish circling in the net were ocean-bright sockeye, averaging about four pounds each, which we intended to release over the cork line. However, in flash the school panicked, hit the net and most were hopelessly gilled. At that point we chose to load the dead and dying fish into the boat and deliver them to a nearby State "honor camp" to feed the residents. However, the boat sank from the weight of the ninety-plus fish, net and occupants. By redistributing the load we managed to refloat the boat and proceed downstream. All this was being captured on film.

En route downriver our luck changed when the occupants of the canoe, after mistaking a swarm of black flies for hornets, caused it to capsize. The camera and the incriminating film were lost. The resulting newspaper article even cast a favorable light on what we were trying to accomplish. After this experience, we continued to attempt to collect the wild Chinook with only limited success.

We were fascinated by an experiment at Stanford University[63] involving the surgical castration of landlocked sockeye (kokanee). As with other Pacific salmon, kokanee die following sexual maturity. In this case the castrated fish lived twice as long as the controls and grew to be 4 to 7 times their size. We tried but were unsuccessful in attempting to apply this concept to surplus hatchery salmon. We established a technical staff to evaluate the status of Puget Sound baitfish stocks and to investigate how they might be improved. We saw to it that the net seasons on early running Chinook stocks, the fish most likely to bite, were delayed. Our coded wire tagging experiments clearly indicated that some stocks of fish contributed at higher rates to local anglers than others. For example, Cowlitz River coho lived, fed and bit off the Washington Coast; whereas, earlier returning Toutle River (a Cowlitz tributary) fish much preferred the Oregon Coast[64].

Our efforts went so far as to import live eggs of the "sixth species" of Pacific salmon from Japan – masu salmon (*O. masou*). A review of information available to us indicated they attained sizes comparable to coho salmon, did not migrate far from their streams of origin and had the feeding behavior characteristic of an excellent sport fish. A downside was that the literature indicated that most of the males remained in freshwater to compete with native fishes. Coded wire tagged smolts (17,000) were released from a south Puget Sound hatchery (Minter Creek) in 1973. Some were also released into an enclosed 26-acre lake near Olympia where they reached lengths of about twelve inches and appeared to be excellent candidates for lake angling[65]. The coded wire tag data base (Regional Mark Information System) indicates that in 1974 an estimated 39 tagged masu salmon were taken by anglers near the mouth of Minter Creek. I distinctly recall a single marine recovery in Canada but it does not appear in the data base. The program was discontinued after 1973.

During the fall of 1974 I experienced an hour or two of panic when a young biologist, who had rightfully expressed concern about the masu program, returned from a stream survey with a report that the invaders had taken over a creek in south Puget Sound. I immediately rushed off to Johns Creek and was relieved to discover that summer chum salmon, in their finest spawning colors, had returned to the stream.

These programs, along with improved fishing, created a great deal of interest in salmon and salmon angling. At personal expense and our own time we spent considerable time fishing and camping with outdoor writers and politicians. An annual trip to Neah Bay with *The Neah Bay Associates* was as important as celebrating one's wedding anniversary. Early springs at Sekiu and winter trips to Port Townsend were frequently scheduled. The simplest and perhaps the most rewarding trips of all were within a few minutes of Olympia off Anderson Island, Johnson Point or wherever else the resident salmon were congregating. Governor and later U.S. Senator Dan Evans was a frequent companion and a strong advocate for salmon, and we had some fine trips later with Governors John Spellman and Dixie Lee Ray.

On two separate occasions we spent days with U.S. Senator Henry Jackson. Perhaps the greatest champion of local salmon fishing has been Congressman Norm Dicks – a fishing companion for the past 30 years. Several governors from out-of-state fished with us during the summer of 1975 when Washington State hosted the National Governors' Conference. Because of conflicts with my normal obligations at the Department of Fisheries, I turned down a request from at least one notable angler, and his family, from the State of Georgia. A friend filled in for me and future president Jimmy Carter along with his wife and daughter enjoyed a fine late-spring day with resident Chinook salmon at Johnson Point near Olympia. Developing salmon angling advocates at lower levels of government can also be important. The person in charge of the state budget office was once a very helpful fishing companion and such relationships were very helpful in providing support for our projects.

I enjoyed guiding a number of other notable people in government at the national level. Most of these excursions were successful in terms of providing both fish and a pleasurable day on Puget Sound. However, after 30 years, I still cringe at what could have happened on a summer day in 1984 when Congressman Gillis Long (Louisiana) and his wife Catherine were guests aboard my 19-foot outdrive *Glasply*. The congressman was a member of the well-known Louisiana family and a cousin of the legendary Huey Long and we were fishing Mid Channel Bank out of Port Townsend. Although he appeared to be recovering from an illness, and his wife was correspondingly attentive, they were delightful company.

After sorting through a number of dogfish the congressman caught a nice Chinook that appeared to pretty much tax his stamina. Soon after we called it a day and headed in. After taking the passengers ashore I had the boat hoisted from the water where I pulled the plug draining the hull. Raw gasoline, from the ruptured built-in tank, poured from the opening! I don't know how many times during the trip that I had activated the starter – any of which could have sparked a disaster, but luck was with us. Although Congressman Long survived the trip he died of heart failure six months later. In the special congressional election to choose a successor to Gillis, the winner was his widow Catherine Long.

The discomforting thoughts of what could have happened with the Longs are in sharp contrast to the memories of most other trips with visiting dignitaries. A trip that I found particularly amusing occurred off Port Angeles during August of 1986. Congressman Norm Dicks had arranged to meet with Secretary of the Navy John Lehman and other top navy brass to discuss establishing an aircraft carrier base at Everett. Following a pleasant dinner the evening before, early the next morning, sans piping and other ceremony, Dicks, Lehman and a Four Star Admiral squeezed aboard my 17-foot skiff and we headed for the north side of Ediz Hook. In about two hours of motor mooching in shallow water along the spit, each hooked and landed a nice "king". Missions accomplished.

Our efforts, along with the favorable survivals of salmon throughout the region, resulted in a resurgence of the Puget Sound sport fishery and the populations of resident Chinook and coho salmon. Washington salmon sport catches peaked during the 1970s with nine consecutive years of catches exceeding a million salmon and angler trips reaching a level of nearly two million – nearly equaling the combined 1977 attendance of Seattle's three new major league sports teams.

The favorable public response to this situation and a more positive view toward recreational fishing by an agency traditionally focused upon the commercial fishing industry, resulted in some justifiable changes in angling rules. In 1971 the minimum length limits on species other than Chinook salmon were removed in inner Puget Sound from January 1 through May 31. After this date, when nearly all third-year coho had reached 16 inches, the size limit was 16 inches for all species. Daily

bag limits remained at three. Beginning in 1972, salmon anglers from
Port Angeles east to the San Juan Islands and throughout Puget Sound
were allowed to use two lines or rods per angler or two lures per line. A
justification for this was to allow anglers to experiment with different
techniques to increase their harvest of hatchery fish returning to local
waters. Earlier rules allowed only one line or lure per angler. In 1974, the
minimum length limit on all salmon species was removed from Sekiu east
throughout Puget Sound and the San Juan Islands, while the bag limit
remained at three per day. This rule, partially in response to concerns
over small salmon dying after being hooked and released, required anglers
to retain the first three salmon *brought on board,* while allowing them to
release fish brought alongside.

Our efforts to improve saltwater sport fishing were not limited to
salmon angling. Because of its historic orientation toward the commercial
industry, the Department of Fisheries had never become involved in
providing such things as marine public boat launching facilities, fishing
piers, and artificial reefs. Ray Buckley and I changed that by convincing
Director Thor Tollefson that we should be involved by competing for
funds through the Interagency Committee for Outdoor Recreation
(IAC). Soon after, Ray and I found ourselves competing one-on-one
for funds with the directors of the state departments of Parks, Natural
Resources, and Game. We did remarkably well and the fact that I took
the IAC Director fishing on Puget Sound may have helped.

Due to high survivals and hatchery programs designed to enhance
resident salmon stocks, Puget Sound catches were at record levels. Ocean
productivity was also high and fishing from the Columbia River to Neah
Bay and throughout the Strait of Juan de Fuca was excellent. However,
the fair winds that had driven the salmon sport fishery for a decade were
about to shift.

The so-called Boldt Decision in 1974, requiring a 50-50 split of
salmon taken by Treaty Indians and others, triggered a double-barreled
impact on Washington's salmon sport fishery. Due to the relatively high
recreational catches of salmon, particularly Puget Sound Chinook, there
followed a rush to restrict the recreational fishery in order to comply with
the ruling. In addition to angling restrictions and closures, our efforts
to improve recreational fishing abruptly ended under the new mandate.

No attempts will be made here to detail the confusing, inconsistent and bewildering array of restrictions that followed and continue to this day. The initial assault restricted anglers to a single line and lure and increased the Chinook salmon minimum size on the Sound and Strait to 22 inches. Other restrictions, some of which were desirable in any case, required use of barbless hooks; established various minimum *and* maximum length limits, many time and area closures and eventually, to protect weak wild stocks, the "selective" harvest of fin-clipped hatchery salmon.

In 1978 the Pacific Fisheries Management Council began to take a far more active role in regulating Washington's coastal salmon sport fishery. Seasons, for the four coastal regions (Canadian border south to Cape Alava, Cape Alava to the Queets River, Queets River to Leadbetter Point, Leadbetter Point to Cape Falcon, Oregon) were established on a catch quota basis by species. Since the method and timetable for establishing coastal regulations occurred a relatively short time before the seasons were to occur, and well after rules were established for State waters (Strait of Juan de Fuca and Puget Sound), the "outside" regulations could not be incorporated into the State's regulation pamphlet. In addition, rules in both regions were frequently changed during the season. This added even more confusion and increased the difficulty for residents and visitors alike to adequately plan for a fishing trip. The popularity of Washington State as a salmon angling destination plummeted and to make matters worse an increasing number of Washington's resident salmon anglers were spending their money for salmon fishing in British Columbia and Alaska, often after paying dearly for a fish originating in Washington! Washington was no longer an "exporter" of salmon angling benefits – it suddenly became an "importer" with a significant "trade deficit".

The days of free salmon punch cards ended in 1978 when a $3.00 fee was imposed on anglers between 16 and 69 years of age. The charge made the State eligible for funds collected from federal taxes on fishing tackle and related purchases. We saw to it that the original fee, in recognition of the federal contribution to salmon management and importance of tourism, made no distinction between Washington resident and non-resident anglers. License fees have gradually increased since then and non-residents are currently charged a much higher fee for salmon angling for more than two days.

13   The Boldt Decision

In 1854-55, in order to clear the way for settlement, Washington Territorial Governor Isaac Stevens executed several nearly identical treaties with specific Indian Tribes in what is now western Washington State. Among other provisions, the treaties stated: "*The right of taking fish at usual and accustomed grounds and stations is further secured to said Indians in common with all citizens of the Territory. . .*" As riparian land was developed and became privately owned, conflicts arose over Indian access to traditional tribal fishing sites. The state and federal courts intervened in these conflicts and eventually upheld access rights of Indians, over and on private land, to fishing sites. But, in addition to access, there followed a seemingly endless series of confusing and conflicting federal and state court decisions regarding the overall meaning of tribal treaty fishing rights. Although the state courts consistently upheld the state's authority to regulate off-reservation tribal fishing, the federal court rulings gradually limited the state's authority over tribal treaty fishing. For example, in 1905 the U.S. Supreme Court, in referring to the state's management authority in respect to treaty fishing rights, indicated: "*Nor* (does the treaty right) *restrain the State unreasonably, if at all, in the regulation of the right*". Subsequent rulings of the high court, although ill-defined, were increasingly limiting to the state's control over treaty Indian fishing.

Consistent with other social upheavals of the 1960s, state and tribal fishing conflicts became a common occurrence in the Puyallup and Nisqually rivers that flow into Puget Sound at Tacoma and near Olympia, respectively. These confrontations involving marginally trained officers, tribal fishermen and their supporters, often reflected poorly on the state officials. Few if any of the Fisheries and Game officers at the time had any formal law enforcement or other training to deal with these situations and it was well into the 80s before it was required. It did not help that various high-profile personalities found it fashionable to descend on the area in order to be arrested and photographed fishing with Indians in violation of state regulations.

A cowboy and Indian incident, that never made television or the newspapers, is indicative of the level of the state's preparedness in dealing with the chaos. It occurred on the bank of the Nisqually River when a crew of Fisheries officers, led by a sergeant, destined to head the agency's enforcement branch, encountered a group of Indians fishing in violation of state rules. Since they were outnumbered, the sergeant decided that the best way to handle the situation was to challenge the leader of the group to a fist-fight and that the Indians would avoid arrest if their champion won. The parties agreed and the sergeant was quickly knocked to the ground. At that moment another officer, unaware of the agreement, emerged from a thicket and tackled and cuffed the winner. True to the code of the West, the order was given that the Indians were not to be charged.

Prior to Judge Boldt's ruling in 1974, there were significant differences between the legal positions of the departments of Fisheries and Game. For many years the Washington Game Commission was a group of citizens essentially chosen from a list provided to the Governor by the Washington State Sportsmen's Council. Delegates to the quarterly meetings of the council, primarily white males, represented fishing and hunting organizations across the state. The relationship between the Department of Game and the council appeared to be almost symbiotic in that each appeared to support and praise the accomplishments of the other. Despite the growing number of federal court cases to the contrary, the prevailing view within Game and its constituents was that, apart from acknowledging the rights of Indians to fishing without state interference on reservations; fishing "*in common*" clearly means that off the reservations everyone fishes and hunts under the State's rules.

Fisheries, under the direct control of Governor Dan Evans, viewed things differently and concluded that there was some sort of a treaty right that extended beyond reservation boundaries, and had gone so far as to sanction some off-reservation salmon fishing. Fellow Republican Slade Gorton, the independently elected State Attorney General, clearly supported the Department of Game's position and somehow these contrasting views largely escaped public notice. In December, 1973, these differences were blatantly made public at the banquet and quarterly meeting of the Washington State Sportsmen's Council in Tacoma. I was there representing the Department of Fisheries. The banquet gathering included representatives of fishing and hunting organizations across the state and their spouses – all dressed in their finest holiday attire.

The scheduled banquet speaker had failed to appear and the attorney representing Game in U.S. v Washington (the Boldt Case) was asked to fill in. Unfortunately, he had way too much to drink and upon reaching the podium immediately went into a tirade against the Director of Fisheries Thor Tollefson and Governor Evans, referring to them as "assholes". Although preceding Boldt's 1974 ruling by about two months, the incident appears to have coincided with a federal court ruling requiring Game to establish a tribal fishery for steelhead – a precedent that Fisheries had previously established for salmon. Despite their sympathy with the views of the speaker, the audience, as well as the Director of Game, was appalled by the presentation and the attorney was quickly removed from the case.

More than three years of preparation involving the submission of briefs and testimony and questioning of witnesses preceded the trial. In 1969 U.S. District (Oregon) Court Judge Robert C. Belloni had set the stage for Judge Boldt by ruling that Columbia River treaty tribes were entitled to a "fair and equitable share" of the harvest that originated above Bonneville Dam. It was then up to Boldt to quantify the share. During this period Judge Boldt provided both State agencies (Fisheries and Game) to suggest what the catch shares should be. Fisheries proposed a third each to recreational, commercial and Indian tribes; Game proposed no off-reservation share other than what may be taken as a licensed angler[f]. Separate attorneys represented the two state agencies' positions in the three- week trial. Leading up to the trial the state courts had made what I believed a politically motivated ruling that the departments of Fisheries and Game lacked the statutory authority to allocate the harvest among different user groups as directed by Boldt, despite the fact that they had been forever allocating harvests among non-tribal fishers and hunters.

The long-simmering controversy over the interpretation of treaty Indian fishing rights came to a boil in 1974 with the U.S. District Court George C. Boldt's ruling that fishing *"in common"* means equal sharing of the salmon and steelhead harvest throughout the Puget Sound and Washington coastal region as far south as Grays Harbor. Fish that originated outside of the "usual and accustomed fishing areas" of tribes with recognized treaties were exempt from the court rulings. This exemption included fish from watersheds (including hatcheries) tributary to the Columbia below Bonneville and the Washington coast south of Grays Harbor. Later rulings expanded the sharing principals to essentially all economically valuable species of fish and shellfish within the Boldt Case area.

Both Fisheries and Game were thunderstruck by Judge George Boldt's 50:50 decision in what had become known as U.S. v. Washington. To quote Dr. Richard R. Whitney, Technical Fisheries Advisor to Judge Boldt, "... *the 50:50 formula was from a Webster's Dictionary dating from the time of the treaties, reasoning that it might be what Governor Stevens had in mind – never mind what the Indians thought.*"[8] The ruling was later appealed and upheld in its entirety in 1975 by the U.S. Ninth Circuit Court, which in doing so, slammed our officials comparing the "... *machinations of Washington state authorities, in avoiding recognition of treaty fishing rights, to the bigotry that had characterized reactions to public school integration in the Deep South.*"

In 1975, after serving 18 years in Congress and later as Governor Evans' Director of Fisheries, Thor Tollefson retired. The Governor appointed Donald Moos, former State Representative and Director of Agriculture, then working in the Governor's Office on natural resource issues, as the new Director of Fisheries. I may have been about the only one in the Department that Don knew at the time. He was among those that I had taken fishing in order to demonstrate the job we had done with the resident-salmon program. Our first trip was to the Johnson Point herring pens located ten miles from my home next to the local boathouse and launching ramp. Hungry and frustrated Chinook and coho were attracted to the perimeter of the pens used to hold herring before being processed and sold for bait. To make things even more interesting, we would rig up a fly rod, a bit of lead to get a plug-cut herring beneath the surface, and slowly troll the perimeter of the pen. It was important that our inexpensive freshwater fly reels were well lubricated and oily spray would soak our wrists and hands as the hooked fish raced through the shallows for deeper water. It turned out to be an interesting day and Don and I have fished many times together since then and remained good friends until his death in 2014.

Because of my association with Don and the success of the salmon angling program, I was promoted from my relatively low but otherwise rewarding position to Deputy Director of Fisheries. My close colleague, the co-inventor of the coded wire tag, Dr. Peter Bergman, was placed in charge of the salmon program – which constituted most of the agency's staff and budget. Pete was on loan to work on an United Nations FAO project, involving coded wire tagging Atlantic salmon in Iceland, when we telephoned him about his new job. These were to be interesting and challenging times.

Don was originally a wheat farmer from a tiny Eastern Washington town in Lincoln County. He had previously served in the State Legislature and as Director of Agriculture and was determined that his stewardship would be consistent with wise use and the overall public interest. He believed that favors from the commercial industry were offered in expectation of something in return, and were to be avoided. During the late spring of 1976, our nation's bicentennial year, Don was approached by Ralph Munro, a member of Governor's staff and later to become Washington's Secretary of State. Our state was to host a day's celebration in Washington D.C. to be organized by Ralph. He asked Don to get a donation of 700 pounds of salmon from the industry for the celebration. Don said he couldn't do it since it was inappropriate to seek such favors from the industry he was charged with regulating and soon after discussed it with me. I suggested that he get back to Ralph and tell him that we could catch the fish for the celebration. Nearly all of the 700 pounds we donated to the cause were large Chinook taken on mooching gear out of Neah Bay in the vicinity of Cape Flattery by three or four of us in accordance with sportfishing regulations and at our personal expense. Fishing was good that year and apart from one troublesome incident, collecting the fish was great fun.

Pete Bergman and I each fished from our 16-foot open aluminum outboards and on this occasion we went out early and returned about mid-day to the dock with limits (3 fish each) of "kings". There, as we unloaded our catch, we were greeted by two or three small-boat commercial salmon trollers ("kelpers") who recognized us and were apparently waiting for fishing to improve before they ventured out. Later in the day we were visited by three or four VIPs that we had arranged to take fishing. They too did very well but as they boated the last of their impressive catch near Mushroom Rock a stiff breeze had arisen from the east. By that time our two-boat fleet was joined by a companion operating a much larger, more comfortable vessel and to avoid loosening their teeth and compressing vertebral discs through the seven miles of chop, we transferred our passengers to the larger boat. Unfortunately, we left the fish in our boats and when we were again greeted at the dock by the kelpers we appeared to have exceeded the bag limit. Our explanation was to no avail and almost immediately the news had spread by radio along the entire the length of the coast. We should have done what we already knew – avoid even the appearance of wrong doing.

The Department of Fisheries did not wait for the Supreme Court affirmation before implementing the Boldt decision and this was not a popular undertaking for an agency with a constituency comprised largely of non-Indian fishermen. In addition, the staff appeared largely sympathetic with a state assistant attorney general, assigned to represent the agency, who had labeled the ruling as "*morally reprehensible and unconstitutional*". The controversy was worsened by politically motivated elected officials who went so far as to advocate ignoring the federal court ruling. Responsible politicians risked damaging their careers by advocating more sensible courses of action. Congressman Lloyd Meeds, whose district was well represented by commercial fishermen, was one such person who took the risk who suffered politically.

The turmoil peaked during the fall of 1976. A strong run of chum salmon, many of which originated at the state hatchery on Hood Canal, was returning and prices paid for "brights" were at an all-time high. Chum salmon values rapidly decline as the fish take on their spawning colors – so much, in fact, that only the eggs, made into "red caviar" for Asian markets, are often saleable. In years of abundance, tons of chum salmon carcasses, sans the valuable roe, have been discarded by tribal fishers into the waters of southern Hood Canal contributing to the anoxic conditions common in the region. However the silvery-sided chums passing through northern Hood Canal were worth $10 each.

Port Townsend and Port Ludlow near the entrance to the Canal, were home ports to a sizeable gillnet fleet that were outspoken critics of the court ruling and of anyone willing to implement it. Gillnets were fished at night. The 1800-foot-long nets, buoyed by fist-sized oval floats, drift with wind and tide as a wall of mesh held in place by a "lead line" extending along the bottom the length of the net. The size of the mesh utilized is based upon the species sought. Escape from the net is prevented by the web catching under the gill covers and onto other head and body parts. It is usually difficult to remove a salmon from the net without injuring it. Purse seining, involving larger vessels and crews, is the other method used for chum salmon fishing but this activity occurs during daylight hours. Enforcing laws regulating to this nighttime gill net-fishing had always been difficult but now became a Herculean task.

The federal court ruling required putting a larger share of the allowable harvest into the Indian catch, which required limiting the times and areas where "non-Indians" were allowed to fish. The first significant regulations designed to accomplish the task were promulgated during the fall of 1976. Anarchy, under the guise of "protest fishing" which included selling the catch, reigned in the Sound and particularly at night at the entrance to Hood Canal. State fisheries patrol officers, ill-prepared and poorly equipped to deal with the unprecedented situation, and somewhat sympathetic to the violators, were charged with the overwhelming task of enforcing the law. In a normal situation violators would be cited and their catches would be confiscated and perhaps their vessels as well. Enforcement was now limited to attempting to issue citations and the fishermen became increasingly threatening and aggressive during the process. Some apparently took pleasure in harassing the officers. Fisheries Patrol Officer Jim Tuggle describes events on the night of October 6, 1976[66]:

". . . initiated by a few hotheaded gillnetters, multiple assaults against officers occurred as small patrol boats were rammed repeatedly by much larger and heavier gillnet boats. Shouts from enraged fishermen could be heard on the radio urging their cohorts to sink the patrol boats and kill the officers. Patrol boats were maneuvered quickly to avoid sinking and certain disaster. Despite attempts to avoid collisions, gillnet boats still managed to ram the much smaller patrol vessels. The confrontation became so violent that the U.S. Coast Guard dispatched a cutter, and the commander of that vessel, Chief Bob La Francis, ordered the bow-mounted 50-caliber machine gun uncovered, loaded and manned. The gillnetters quickly dispersed, threatened by the Coast Guard's presence, but feeling vindicated by their overpowering intimidation of the Fisheries officers. No closed season gillnet fishing arrests took place that night, but if it were not for Chief LaFrancis's

decisive actions, several Fisheries Patrol Officers might have died that might – and perhaps some gillnetters as well."

Two weeks later the officers managed to put together a "fleet" of two 23-foot Glasplys – essentially pleasure boats – along with an ancient steel-hulled ex-Coast Guard vessel, and proceeded to the north end of Hood Canal. Officer Tuggle again describes the events that followed:

"Dozens, perhaps even 50 or 60 gillnetters were fishing in a closed season. As our patrol boat began to approach one of the outermost gillnet boats from the armada, other gillnetters untied themselves from their nets and began making runs at the patrol boats standing by while officers attempted to issue a citation to the operators of the first boat they came to that was fishing in defiance of state regulations and court orders. Heavy wakes rocked the patrol boats as gillnet vessels of various sizes made pass after pass right at the vulnerable patrol boats standing by. Still, officers were directed to only write citations, and not make any physical arrests. The enforcement effort was called off. The few citations that were issued were generally not aggressively pursued by elected county prosecutors and judges."

Despite the dangers, and lack of federal assistance to enforce Federal Law, Patrol Officers returned to northern Hood Canal on the night of October 24, 1976 with a 32-foot Roberts-built boat on loan from the Department's Shellfish Division, along with the fore-mentioned ex-Coast Guard vessel. Tuggle continues:

"Just before dark . . . (we) . . . left the confines of the Ballard Locks and headed in a northerly direction to enforce the closed commercial salmon season near Foul Weather Bluff. Since the Roberts built boat was new to us, we had to make certain how some of its equipment worked, where lifejackets and fire-extinguishers were stowed, and also checked out the high pressure fire hose and pump that we might use to thwart the high speed passes of some of the gillnet boats. We reveled in the mental images that we each envisioned of hosing down one of the reckless boat operators that had successfully kept us from completing our last patrol. Yes, the pump and fire hose worked! I also located a high power hand-held spotlight that likely would come in handy once darkness set in. Too soon darkness came. And with it the sight of lights of the gillnet boats that were once again fishing in violation of state regulations and federal mandate. Here we were at Foul Weather Bluff.

As per our practice, the first vessel fishing in violation that we came to was

also the first to be cited. As Glen Corliss pulled our boat alongside the Sandy
Girl, *Joe Salte and Pat Heenan prepared to do the boarding. Heenan – only
as his sense of humor would allow – had secretly put a false set of vampire-
like teeth into his mouth that night . . . but if you knew Pat Heenan it was
consistent with his character. Pat helped keep some of us sane in those days,
but drove his bosses to the edge of insanity. It was all part of being young, and
how we reacted to troubled times.*

Glen moved our boat away from the Sandy Girl *a few yards so that
we could stand-by while Heenan and Salte issued the citation. A group of
gillnetters gathered in the near distance in sort of a huddle. It looked to me
as if they were holding a meeting there on the calm black waters of northern
Hood Canal. Other, more seemingly hostile, gillnetters soon began the all too
familiar pattern of making high speed passes at our boat as we stood by* Sandy
Girl. *The high speed passes didn't seem quite as menacing in the larger boat
and although we were rocked by wakes, we were steadfast in our resolve to
complete the issuance of the citation and then continue on to other vessels fishing in violation.*

*As boat after boat headed for us, I could see a pattern. They seemed to turn
their steering wheels in a sort of tangent-like curve. We could predict that they
would likely not collide with us, but would come intimidatingly close. Their
near-miss-passes were still very unnerving.*

*I held the powerful spotlight in my hand to continue to illuminate the aft
deck of the* Sandy Girl *where Pat and Joe were completing their official tasks.
I also shined the light on the gillnet vessels as they sped past us to make sure
that no one on their back decks threw anything at us. No foreign objects or
missiles of any sort were hurled at us, and no firearms came into view even
though we knew every boat out there had them aboard.*

*The huddle of gillnet boats in the distance appeared to break up, and out
of it emerged a very large vessel named the* Alaska Revenge. *My attention was
drawn to it because of its size and the direction of its course: It was head-
ing at full speed right at the side of our boat! We were now on a much larger
boat than on previous nights, but the* Alaska Revenge *dwarfed the* Roberts. *As boats grow in length they gain in beam and draft, so that their weight
increases exponentially. The* Alaska Revenge *appeared to be huge as it bore
down on us. Its mission was clear to me. My mind raced as I realized that the
subject of that meeting of the gillnet boats was the selection of a large boat to*

ram us, and either sink us, kill us, or disable us from completing our enforcement tasks. Our boat was considerably smaller than the old 40 footer that was 100 yards or so away from us – a boat large enough to be viewed as unwise to attempt to ram and sink, at least by a boat the size of the Alaska Revenge.

But now, here came the Alaska Revenge *on a certain collision course with a boatload of Fisheries Patrol Officers. Others aboard the Roberts had also focused their attention to the approaching disaster. Frightened shouts of the impending crash were acted on by Glen Corliss as he quickly put the engine of our vessel into gear in an attempt to avoid disaster. The* Alaska Revenge *never wavered from its course as the other gillnetters had, and as I screamed 'lookout!' and as I dove for the opposite side of the deck away from the impact area, I heard two quick gunshots. As I scrambled to my feet, Glen maneuvered our boat so that the* Alaska Revenge *seemed to pass through the would-be watery grave where our aft deck had been two seconds before, narrowly missing our boat. The* Alaska Revenge *had missed us!*

The engine of the Alaska Revenge *could be heard to drop in RPMs as I stood and looked around at my fellow officers to see what exactly had happened. Officer Howard Oliver had been the one to fire the two quick buckshot blasts that had saved our lives. Now the* Alaska Revenge *was in reverse, backing away from our position, and apparently not under command or control."*

Buckshot penetrated the windshield of the pilot house and the vessel operator, William Carlson, was seriously wounded in the head and neck. First aid was quickly administered by the officers and he was transported by helicopter to Seattle's Harborview Hospital. A young woman who had been warned of trouble by Carlson, and a dog, were also aboard the vessel.

The news media had a field day and the gillnetters gained a martyr. Their portrayal was that a gillnet fisherman had been wounded while attempting to protect his sole livelihood. A never publicized fact was that, even though he had a short length of gillnet and a few chum salmon aboard, the unfortunate young man was not a licensed gillnet fisherman at all. At any other time gillnetters would have considered him an outright poacher. Nevertheless he was, as far as they were concerned, a member of their fraternity and has remained so ever since.

The shooting precipitated a march on Olympia that was organized by the aggrieved fishermen and families. Busses and caravans arrived carrying hundreds of protesters. Don Moos and I were not invited to the rally but

I suggested that we make an appearance anyway. We stood alongside Phil Sutherland, a gillnetter activist from Port Townsend, on a balcony above the throng on the floor of the capitol rotunda. Don made a brief statement relating to responsibility, treaties and the laws which obviously did not go over very well. I don't recall what Phil had to say but it was something that the people wanted to hear. Soon afterwards, while the rally was still underway, the State Patrol whisked us out through a back door.

I felt good about what we had done in facing the crowd at the rally. However soon afterwards we were told that James Johnson, our attorney, had followed us onto balcony of the rotunda and had made his own speech, to tumulus cheers, regarding the "*morally reprehensible*" federal court ruling and his unrelenting efforts to overturn it – brave and confident words from a man associated with an unbroken string of federal courts losses. I learned later that Governor Evans shared our displeasure over Johnson's speech and I suspect that it resulted in a conversation with Johnson's boss, Attorney General Slade Gorton.

An investigation of the shooting of the purported gillnetter was conducted by the Kitsap County Prosecutor. As I recall, the major question addressed was if the *Alaska Revenge* was in forward or reverse gear when the shots were fired. The threatened officers were convinced that the impact of the shotgun blasts had resulted in Carlson pulling back on the throttle to throw the vessel into reverse. The Prosecutor saw it differently and the matter was settled out of court with a relatively modest award to the seriously injured boat operator.

Adding to the problems confronting the new administrators of the Department was a fisheries management system that was largely out of control: there were thousands of licensed commercial salmon fishermen, many of whom sold few if any fish and primarily benefited from tax write-off; the state lacked authority to control mixed-stock fishing off its own coast; most of the Chinook and coho salmon stocks that originated in Washington streams and hatcheries migrated northward where they were primarily harvested in Canada and South East Alaska. Steps were immediately taken to correct these problems.

The department successfully supported legislation to limit the sales of commercial fishing licenses and retire those that had no record of catches. Legislation was adopted to eliminate sales of new commercial fishing licenses and a federally-funded vessel and license "buy back " program was implemented to reduce the size of the fleet. Salmon net fisheries operating in areas where abundant stocks of hatchery fish were intermixed with wild fish were greatly curtailed and shifted to "terminal areas" where harvestable surpluses clearly existed and impacts to wild stocks were reduced.

Although fraught with administrative difficulties and criticism, the vessel and license buy-back program was the only one of these programs that could be considered the least bit popular. At least once, and probably more often, a "fisherman" sold his boat and license and immediately purchased another boat and license from another fisherman participating in the program. We later discovered that this same buyer was a member of a board appointed by us to review applicants for the program! The fact that purchased boats, that were later auctioned off for far less than their cost, could later be used for fishing by treaty Indians was a bitter pill for some to swallow.

Cramming non-Indian net fishermen into small terminal areas where hatchery fish were concentrated was anything but popular. Up until that time, a major pseudo-scandal resulted from the Department's practice of selling hatchery-surplus salmon for human consumption. These were years of high survivals of hatchery salmon and thousands of adult fish, far more than could be utilized at the hatcheries were returning to these facilities each year. The agency was under constant pressure by commercial interests to expand fishing opportunities in traditional open-water fishing areas containing intermixed wild and hatchery fish. Yielding to this pressure would further impact wild stocks that were already over-fished. The department sold the surplus salmon to the highest bidders and used the funds to support the hatchery program. Some commercial fishermen interpreted this as a plot to eliminate them or as a means of supplementing the income of our employees. Fishermen's wives were common visitors to the Department where they spent many fruitless days searching the files for evidence of corruption.

I was convinced that the State's legal strategy to overturn Judge Boldt's ruling included demonstrating that it could not possibly work. At the time, Chinook salmon sport fishing in Puget Sound, primarily for resident fish, had been very good and these catches far exceeded those of south Puget Sound tribes. In order to balance the catch, sport salmon fishing was on the verge of being shut down. At the same time large numbers of hatchery Chinook, primarily "jacks" (two- and three-year-old sexually precocious males) were entering the State's trap at the mouth of the Deschutes River in Olympia. These fish were surplus to spawning needs and had already passed through the Sound's fisheries.

I saw this as an opportunity to reduce the imbalance in the catch and reduce the impact on the sport catch, providing that the Squaxin Tribe would take the fish from the trap and count them as part of their treaty share. They agreed to do just that and the shit hit the fan. I was first threatened with "resign or else" by "our" attorney, who was to become a State Supreme Court Justice, and then asked to resign by State Senator Jack Metcalf, a former gillnetter and member of congress to be, on the far-fetched basis that trap fishing is illegal in Washington.

My problems with our legal representation had begun earlier in dealings with treaty Indian fishing. In 1977, during my tenure as Acting Director of Fisheries, I brokered an agreement between Billy Frank, Jr. and Governor Dixy Lee Ray that supported the construction of a tribal salmon hatchery on the Nisqually River. Later, I arranged for the return of Billy's old dugout canoe, confiscated years before as evidence of illegal fishing, on his birthday. None of these and other such events went unnoticed.

In a July 26, 1979 letter to Washington Deputy Attorney General Edward B. Mackie, Director of Fisheries Gordon Sandison minces no words in expressing dissatisfaction with their "petition for reconsideration" of the Boldt Decision to the U.S. Supreme Court that was filed without knowledge of the Department of Fisheries. Sandison viewed the continuation of the State's extraordinary machinations and recalcitrance in dealing adequately with tribal fishing rights as a threat to the State's future involvement in salmon management.

We will never know what would have occurred if serious attempts had been made to negotiate a settlement of the treaty prior to Judge Boldt's ruling in 1974. Such a timely effort to reach a settlement, recognizing a significant treaty right, would have required a leader with an uncommon level of political courage, but it would have had an excellent chance of mitigating the final outcome. It is also clear that any person responsible for a successful settlement would have been forever maligned for having done so. A settlement attempt during the late 1970s, by a federally appointed Task Force, occurred after the Ninth Circuit Court of Appeals affirmed Boldt's initial and earlier ruling – reminiscent of an adage involving a horse and a barn door. The fact that the compromise was rejected by the tribes came as no surprise to anyone closely associated with the issue.

The U.S. Supreme Court initially refused to review the fishing case, but many associated with commercial and recreational fishing, as well as their elected representatives, including Washington State Attorney General Slade Gorton, were unwilling to accept defeat. In 1979, by a 6 to 3 vote, the Supreme Court upheld the main elements of the Boldt decision. However, it did significantly disagree with Boldt by including reservation, ceremonial and subsistence catches to be counted as part of the tribes' share of the catch.

The U.S. Supreme Court decision did not end the controversy over treaty Indian fishing in Washington nor, apparently, sway the opinion of Washington voters. Four years after the Supreme Court ruling, Initiative 456 qualified for the 1984 general election. The intent of the measure was to overturn the treaties between the tribes and the United States and return fisheries management to the State of Washington. Although the measure was, from the very beginning, fruitless, it was approved by state voters and remains ignored among the statues relating to fisheries management (Chapter 77.110 RCW).

In 2000, twenty-one years after the Supreme Court ruling, following many years of public service culminating in two terms as a U.S. Senator, Slade Gorton suffered a razor-thin loss for reelection. His defeat could be attributed to the lasting bitterness of Indian tribes, made wealthy from gambling interests rather than fishing, who contributed to Gorton's democratic opponent. The same could be said for thwarting Jim Johnson's initial bid for election to the Washington State Supreme Court in 2002. Johnson, during his career as a Washington assistant attorney general and in private practice, was viewed by the tribes as the reincarnation of George Custer. However in 2004, in focusing on their successful effort to defeat a measure (I-892) that would have increased opportunities for non-Indians to share in tribal gambling revenues, Johnson apparently passed under the tribes' radar and was elected to the State Supreme Court where he remained until his retirement in 2014.

Just what kind of a guy was George Boldt? As a representative
of the Department of Fisheries, I traveled with the judge to various
reservations and rivers on the Olympic Peninsula to observe and discuss
environmental impacts in preparation for "Phase II" – an issue of major
consequence that apparently "remains in the wings of the stage". I found
the judge to be a very personable man who was dedicated to the task
before him. In my dealings with him, and his appointed fisheries expert/
advisor, conservation of the resource was always of prime importance.
Although it currently appears that treaty Indian fishing rights are
considered more important than conservation by the National Marine
Fisheries Service, under Boldt and his chosen expert advisor this was
never the case. On many occasions, both treaty and non-treaty fisheries
were curtailed for conservation purposes.

14 Co-Management: A Fish War Truce

Following the U.S. Supreme Court's ruling in 1979 the State's attorneys and fisheries managers, along with others associated with commercial and recreational fishing, conceded that 50:50 was real and here to stay. Achieving this requires competent technicians and scientists to collect and analyze data in order to properly forecast run sizes, determine fishing mortalities and harvest rates under the variety of circumstances. It also requires a level of trust and cooperation between the state and tribal technical staffs that was lacking in 1975. As a result, Judge Boldt created the Fisheries Advisory Board (FAB). Its purpose was to efficiently and fairly resolve the never-ending technical disputes between the tribes and state agencies in day-to-day salmon and steelhead management.

Dr. Richard Whitney, who was then leader of the U.S. Fish and Wildlife Service Cooperative Fishery Research Unit at the University of Washington (UW), was appointed as the fisheries expert representing the Federal Court. His appointment was significantly influenced by a recommendation from Guy McMinds, a Quinault Indian with a UW degree in fisheries, to the tribes who then supported Whitney. The FAB Chairman recalls that the first FAB meeting in the fall of 1975, dealing with sharing the steelhead harvest in Puget Sound streams, was a "total disaster"[67]. It was erroneously perceived initially that FAB meetings were subject to the Open Meetings Act. The Department of Game set up Whitney by encouraging steelhead anglers to attend. The tribes responded by seeing to it that they also were well represented. Although nothing was accomplished, an outright riot was somehow avoided.

Later meetings were arranged that usually involved one representative from a side and Dr. Whitney the non-voting chairman. By 1976 the FAB caught on as a way to quickly resolve issues and from then through 1979 there were 352 such meetings conducted at mutually acceptable locations or by telephone conference calls. In most cases the disputes were trivial and the parties were able to reach agreements by simply getting together and talking things over. Attorneys were not allowed to speak unless all representatives agreed that they could. If there was no agreement, the Chairman could make a recommendation which, with a single exception, was accepted by the Judge if it went to court. In my opinion, Whitney did a masterful job of facilitating agreements and resolving disputes in a timely manner. The State's position appeared to prevail whenever it was supported by relevant data. The level of disagreement between the parties emphasized the need for such things as establishing agreed-upon spawning escapement goals, to get serious about watershed planning and learn more about the stock compositions and numbers of the salmon intercepted at sea.

To assist in this latter task, the State, with the able assistance of Dr. Fred Johnson, an expert from the U.S. Bureau of Standards, had developed a complex computerized model which played a prominent role in managing the coastal fisheries for Chinook and coho salmon. Much of the information in the model resulted from recoveries of coded wire tags, although it included assumptions and educated guesses relating to unknowns such as natural mortality rates at specific life stages, kill rates of undersized fish released from hooks or from salmon dropping from gill nets. Since the tribes depended heavily upon fish that escaped the ocean fisheries, they were intensely interested in learning more about the fish caught at sea that would otherwise have returned to their "usual and accustomed fishing areas".

Even though there were now equal partners in salmon management, the State was reluctant to share the computer model, used to determine the allowable catches of both parties, with the tribes. The State's technicians feared that their counterparts were likely to manipulate the model to their advantage. Against his better judgment, Director of Fisheries Bill Wilkerson, went along with the technical staff and permitted the matter to go before the Federal District Court. The State was embarrassed by the proceedings and the ruling. The true motivations for restricting access to the model never were expressed and the best that the state's attorney could do was to argue that unlimited tribal access to the model could result in someone selling or stealing its secrets for use in some unrelated endeavor.

The constant reliance on the FAB to resolve disputes, the mutual distrust between the State and Tribal fisheries managers, as exemplified by the fisheries model fiasco in court, convinced Wilkerson that it was time to foster a new relationship with the tribes based upon cooperation, trust and respect – attributes that had been obviously lacking in the technical arena of "harvest management". The new era began with a meeting of "Boldt Case

Area" tribal leaders and Department officials at Port Ludlow in March of 1984, heralding a significant improvement in the State-Tribal relationship. The salmon resource was to be co-managed. Consensus building, rather than the federal courts, would provide the basis for resolving problems, and tribal and state interactions would shift from divvying up fish to more important issues of common interest. From then on consensus would be required for all fisheries management issues and dispute resolution was to become a thing of the past. Later that year, following 26 years of service, I left the Department of Fisheries and joined Northwest Marine Technology, the firm that developed the coded-wire-tagging system.

In 1991, seven years after retiring from the Department of Fisheries, Dr. Whitney and I, in response to a request from Canadian officials involved with native affairs in the Ministry of Environment, traveled to Vancouver Island where we lectured fisheries managers. The issue of native fishing rights was coming to a head there as well and our advice was essentially to contact the key leaders in the communities, deal with it in a conciliatory manner, and attempt to work out catch-sharing agreements.

Management of the Washington's salmon resources has become much more sophisticated following implementation of the Boldt Decision. But there is a significant downside to the existing relationship between the state and tribes that impacts Washington's salmon sport fishery. The tribal attitude toward sport fishing is often less than sympathetic. Some of this results from the many unfortunate incidents that occurred in the 60s and 70s during the heat of the treaty fishing conflict. "We don't play with our food" is a common tribal retort.

As a result, the tribes maintain a careful, if not suspicious, eye on the rules governing salmon angling. When they do approve of a state proposal designed to increase angling opportunity, they are prone to require new, redundant and expensive monitoring programs to evaluate the results that the state can ill afford.

The State, on the other hand, essentially maintains a "hands off" policy relating to tribal fishing. For example, during the winter of 2004-05 Makah Indian trollers, operating primarily in the western portion of Juan de Fuca Strait, harvested 17,000 more Chinook salmon than had been projected[68] – a number several times greater than the corresponding annual Juan de Fuca Strait sport catch. The State, far less concerned with alienating anglers than the Makahs, did its utmost to minimize the significance of the overage, going so far as falsely claiming that the catch consisted almost entirely of hatchery fish. The Juan de Fuca Strait sport catch, on the other hand, is closely scrutinized by the tribes and requires expensive catch-monitoring programs.

Following almost 30 years of co-management there is no consensus on basic management questions. There is no agreed-upon spawning escapement goal for some stocks, and no consensus regarding the desirability of hatchery-origin fish spawning naturally with wild fish. Although there are notable exceptions to the generalization, tribal managers tend to maintain that *a fish is a fish* regardless of its origin. The failure to recognize a difference between hatchery strays and wild salmon on the spawning grounds flies in the face of ESA recovery requiring the establishment of viable self-perpetuating populations. The science also shows that natural spawning is far more productive if hatchery straying is minimized. The state acknowledges this difference and so do the federal fisheries agencies. Despite this, there is no agreement between the co-managers.

My many discussions with State fisheries managers and the results of their efforts leave me with the impression that they feel powerless in dealing with the tribes. There is neither an institutional memory of the many issues that were resolved to the State's satisfaction through the proceedings of the Fisheries Advisory Board during the 1970s, nor an awareness of provisions in The Boldt Decision that would enable them to do a better job for their constituents and the resource. In his review of this manuscript, Dr. Whitney has cited a number of quotations from Boldt that appeared to be ignored or forgotten, including one he considers of particular significance (U.S. v. Washington 384 F. Supp. 312 p. 339): *In the opinion of this court, judicial integrity also requires this court to hold that the tribes' contention that the state does not have legal authority to regulate the exercise of their off-reservation treaty right fishing must be and is hereby denied by this court.* I must leave it to others to judge the significance of this and other provisions.

Some critical issues cannot be solved by consensus between the state and tribes. A fair and efficient system of dispute resolution is essential for leveling the playing field and facilitating progressive management. Co-management, as it currently exists, is neither in the best interest of the public nor of the salmon resource.

15 Whatever Happened to 50:50?

Accurate catch statistics and other assessments of fishing mortality are a basic requirement for optimizing spawning escapements, evaluating hatchery production, and allocating the harvest in accordance with the Boldt Decision. Immediately following the Supreme Court ruling, the tribes placed great emphasis on achieving the 50:50 split and receiving "pay-back" for shortfalls in their catches for the period following Boldt's original decision. At that time, largely due to high sport catches throughout Puget Sound and the Strait of Juan de Fuca, Chinook salmon catches were grossly imbalanced. However, the deficit was less than believed by the tribes who distrusted the system utilizing angler catch records ("punch-cards").

As a result, an expensive four-year study, including two years of preliminary field work, was conducted to assess the accuracy of the sport catch estimate system[69]. The work involved contacting anglers throughout the Puget Sound region, both on the water and on shore, at the completion of a trip, as well as aerial boat counts from flights throughout the region. Skilled statisticians, representing both tribal and state interests, eventually produced a detailed report concluding that the method, if conducted properly, was basically sound although due to "response bias" tended to *overestimate* the catch – not what the tribes expected! Response bias was first documented when the system was initiated in 1964, and results from the tendency of successful anglers to be more conscientious than the less successful in returning their catch records. A similar evaluation of the reporting accuracy of commercial and tribal catches has never been conducted. Every indication is that the impacts of commercial and tribal fishing are significantly underestimated.

There is more than suspicion to support this conclusion. Tribal, as well as non-Indian commercial catches, are required to be documented on "fish tickets" that are eventually returned to the state for compilation. Despite the obvious fact that many Indian fish, and some non-Indian catches, are sold directly to consumers "over-the-bank" and not properly recorded, an investigation has never been conducted to assess or correct the problem. A worst case example may be what has occurred with reporting of catches by members of the Skokomish Tribe fishing in the

Hood Canal where the small fraction of the coho catch examined for biological purposes often exceeded the total reported catch. Thousands of chum salmon carcasses, stripped of valuable roe, were unrecorded and discarded into the Canal. State officials have in the past observed, in random observations, more salmon in Skokomish-set gillnets than were obviously being reported but, apparently to avoid offending the tribe, no corrective action was ever taken and the state officials reporting the problems were, in no uncertain terms, directed by administrators to back off and keep quiet.

Although tribal catches appear to be higher than the official numbers, these figures indicate that treaty Indian catches in the Boldt Case area are grossly higher than mandated in the U.S. Supreme Court's 50:50 ruling. For example, according to the Pacific Management Council documents from 1996 through 2000, treaty Indians caught 54% of the Chinook on Puget Sound (water east of Cape Flattery) and 65% of the coho salmon. During the following ten years their Chinook catch frequently approached 70% and tribal coho catches were significantly higher. Despite this apparent discrepancy the tribes are frequently able to thwart the efforts of the state to increase recreational fishing opportunities since agreements on rules require consensus between the parties.

The Department of Fish and Wildlife's willingness to conceal the extent of the allocation discrepancy surfaced during the 2009 Washington State Legislative Session before the Senate Natural Resource Committee when the agency Director presented graphs indicating that the Puget Sound Chinook allocation had essentially achieved 50:50 by 2007 and the coho catch was not that far off. As a witness to the presentation, I could hardly believe what was occurring and due to my intervention the record was eventually, but quietly, corrected. In 2007 the Puget Sound tribes had harvested 66% and 72%, respectively, of the allowable catch of Chinook and coho salmon in the Boldt Case Area.

Having been subjected to the wrath accompanying implementation of the Boldt decision, it was, to say the least, surprising to me that this catch imbalance could have occurred with so little if any notice or reaction. During the mid-1980s, the state fisheries management agency had quietly and unilaterally decided that its constituents were not fully entitled to their full share of harvestable salmon and, in contrast to earlier times

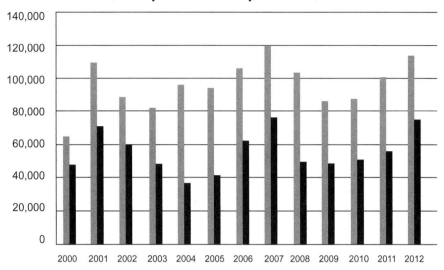

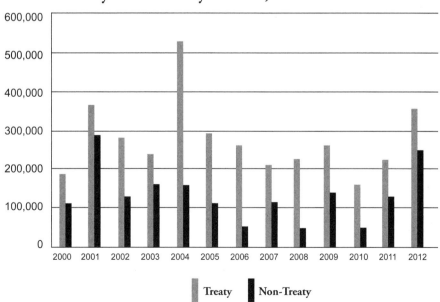

Figure 34. WDFW charts showing Puget Sound Tribal (gray) and Non-Tribal (black) catches of chinook and coho salmon for the years 2000 through 2012. Catch sharing has not varied significantly through 2013.

when a primary function of the Washington Department of Fisheries was publishing annual catch figures, there is no convenient way to access the catch numbers. The pendulum has swung even further in favor of tribal influence over harvest management. The relatively minor process of altering a recreational bag, size limit, or any other fishing rule involves tribal approval, public notification and a formal hearing.

When I asked about this catch imbalance, Director Phil Anderson responded by indicating that within the Puget Sound area the State's policy is to utilize the non-treaty share of Chinook and coho to maximize recreational fishing activity, and that even though he had the authority to do so, 50:50 catch sharing could only be achieved by increasing Puget Sound harvests in non-Indian commercial net fisheries. In a remarkable gesture of conciliation, the Washington Department of Fish and Wildlife apparently agreed to give up a significant portion of its constituency's fish without any public notice.

Although the Director's rationale could be viewed favorably by most Puget Sound salmon anglers it appears to fail a litmus test for providing non-Indian fishers with their fair share of benefits, and avoiding major wastages of hatchery fish paid for by the citizens of the state. The State has the authority to allow limited non-tribal commercial fisheries (e.g., seines) in hatchery stream estuaries that selectively targeted marked hatchery fish and healthy wild stocks. Presented with this choice, or adopting a more conciliatory approach to recreational fisheries, it appears that the tribes would favor the latter.

Although frequently overestimated, the harvestable portion of a living resource is that which can be taken without diminishing the level of future benefits. Determining the appropriate level of harvest of a population of fish that disappears for all but a fraction of its life is fraught with pitfalls, but once estimated it is up to the managers of the harvest to determine who gets to catch the fish. Briefly, using Chinook and coho as an example, the process to determine overall abundance during a fishing season involves analyzing hatchery releases and expected return rates, and returns of wild fish based upon the strength of the parent stocks and the abundance of the resulting juveniles. Varying ocean productivity further complicates the process. The available information is fed into a computer model which provides an initial estimate of abundance. Numbers of fish needed for spawning are subtracted, leaving the portion available for harvest. Harvest rates are monitored during the fishing season, to compare with previous years of known abundance, to determine if adjustments in the fishing regulations are required to achieve management goals.

A major cause of restricting saltwater sport fishing results from its reliance on mixed populations or stocks of fish from many different streams and hatcheries. The proportions of the various populations comprising the mixture, in specific areas, are determined from CWT recoveries in catches through the years. Managers curtail sport fishing when the estimated impact on the weakest population, in the mix, reaches a pre-determined critical level. While "weak stock management" appears to be a sensible approach, it fails if an inappropriate population is identified to be in need of protection.

For example, The National Oceanic and Atmospheric Administration (NOAA) Fisheries has determined that Puget Sound Chinook ESA listing requires recovering at least two river populations in each of several areas, including Hood Canal. The Skokomish River is one such population and the other, lacking a reasonable choice, is "Mid Hood Canal" (consisting of the Hamma Hamma, Dosewallips and Duckabush rivers). Despite the relatively pristine condition of these streams and their estuaries, they are insignificant producers of Chinook salmon and unlikely to ever be anything else. The few Chinook returning to these streams most likely result from hatchery straying. Nevertheless, when recreational fishing impacts on Mid Hood Canal Chinook salmon reach a critical level, sport fishing throughout Puget Sound is at risk of being curtailed. The impacts of weak stock management have been significantly mitigated by mass-marking (adipose fin clipping) hatchery salmon and often requiring anglers to release wild salmon that are unmarked. However, release and drop-off mortality is assessed under these circumstances.

In contrast, tribal net fisheries tend to focus on mature stocks returning to rivers and estuaries and can avoid impacting some of the weak stocks, intermingled with others, that chronically curtail saltwater sport fishing. Tribal "mixed stock fishing" occurs when it fails to recognize the difference between wild and fin-clipped hatchery-origin salmon intermixed in their catches. As a result, both the wild and hatchery components of the catch tend to be harvested in proportion to their overall abundance. This often results in killing too many wild fish and too few hatchery fish. This could only be corrected by abandoning the use of gillnets in favor of gear appropriate for releasing the various species encountered that are in need of protection.

Even if all landed salmon are accurately reported, the resulting kill from fishing is always higher than documented. This includes salmon that are released, or escape, from hook-and-lines and later die from the resulting trauma (hooking mortality); or die from injuries inflicted by nets but fall from the mesh before being boated ("drop-out"). Other unrecorded kills result from entanglement in the derelict "ghost nets" that festoon reefs and snags as well as the fish plucked from nets, or rendered un-saleable, by seals and sea lions.

Fisheries managers only partially account for some of these impacts by adding factors to arrive at the total kill. In most cases, these are no more than negotiated guesses. Currently, in addition to the salmon that they catch and retain, anglers are charged with killing from 7% to 14% (depending upon species and area) of the salmon they catch and release, and an additional 5% of fish that they are estimated to hook

Figure 35. Entangled seal pups attracted to salmon in a tribal Puget Sound river gillnet. Losses of salmon from such nets are not accounted for.
Photo is courtesy of the Washington Department of Fish and Wildlife.

and lose that they may never see. Drop-off lacks factual basis. On the other hand, although fisheries managers know better, no drop-out or other non-landed loss is accounted for in tribal freshwater gillnets, and there is only a 3% add-on to gillnets fished in marine waters, which is supposed to include both drop-out and fish taken from nets by marine mammals. It is worth repeating that these assessments are largely the results of negotiation rather than investigation, and the State fisheries managers have done a poor job of representing their recreational constituents in the process.

16   Initiative 640

Washington is one of the states allowing citizens to become directly involved in the law-making process. As previously noted, Washington's steelhead and salmon anglers were successful in convincing voters to pass two significant initiatives during the 1930's. I-62 created two separate agencies – the Department of Fisheries and the Department of Game and I-77, co-championed by Puget Sound anglers and purse seiners, which eliminated fish traps and certain other fishing gear in state waters. Anglers also played a key role in passing I-25 (1960) that, if not having been subsequently ruled illegal in that it circumvented federal law, would have prevented the completion of Tacoma's high dams on the Cowlitz River.

Chinook and coho salmon are important recreational and commercial fish so that both non-indian user groups are seeking the same fish. The separate fishing regulations, promulgated by the State, allocate the catch between the recreational and commercial sectors. The value of the catch to the citizens of the state will vary significantly with use. Commercial salmon caught before or after they are in their prime[b] condition reduces market value. Nets that "corral" rather than entangle and damage fish tend to provide products of higher quality. There may be gross differences between the economic values of commercial and recreational fisheries competing for the same fish. Washington's statutes provide no clear guidelines for allocating the harvest.

It therefore appears logical that allocation should be based upon maximizing overall benefits to the citizens of the state, but this has not been the case. The only semi-relevant statutes that provide little if any assistance in resolving the matter: RCW 77.04.0912 , in part, states: *"(t)he department shall conserve the wildlife and food fish, game fish, and shellfish resources in a manner that does not impair the resource. In a manner consistent with this goal, the department shall seek to maintain the economic well-being and stability of the fishing industry in the state. The department shall promote orderly fisheries and shall enhance and improve recreational and commercial fishing in this state."* RCW 77.65.160 declares that *"(t) he legislature, recognizing that anadromous salmon within the waters of the state are fished for both recreational and commercial purposes and that the recreational anadromous salmon fishery is a major recreational and economic asset to the state and improves the quality of life for all residents of the state, declares that it is the policy of the state to enhance and improve recreational anadromous salmon fishing in the state."*

In 1995, eleven years after retiring from the Washington Department of Fisheries and having been urged on by some friends and acquaintances to do so, I got into the act and helped draft an initiative. None of its provisions impacted treaty Indian fishing since state law was incapable of doing so. It intended to do a number of things – too many, as it turned out: (1) It required that harvestable food fish and shellfish be managed in a manner providing the greatest value to the citizens of the state. It recognized Chinook and coho salmon, unless proven otherwise, as being most valuable in the recreational catch and the other three salmon species as more valuable commercially. (2) It reduced levels of "by-catch" by requiring the use of gear that complied with specific standards, set the stage for selective fishing by curbing the use of some existing gear, such as gillnets, and requiring the modification of others. (4) It directed the department and the governor to work to minimize Canadian and other foreign interceptions of Washington salmon, by reducing our interceptions of Canadian fish if necessary. (3) It established a hatchery policy requiring that operations are consistent with the protection and rehabilitation of natural stocks

The "non-Indian" commercial fishing industry obviously, and vehemently, opposed the initiative. They were not interested in changing fishing methods, backing off on Canadian interceptions, or allocating the non-treaty catch in a manner that was best for the State. At considerable expense they were successful in convincing voters that the initiative was simply a means of depriving thousands of working families from their livelihoods while turning over the major part of the fisheries resource to sport fishermen.

Since the number of ESA listings and over-fished stocks were increasing by leaps and bounds, and reforming fishing practices was clearly a best buy, opposition from some sources was unanticipated. The environmental community, unable to admit that habitat issues were not the only problem, was unwilling to support fishery reform. Even though the initiative would not have impacted treaty Indian fishing, the Chairman of the Northwest

Indian Fisheries Commission opposed the measure and suggested it was initiated by bigots. Although a study had just shown that local gillnets were killing thousands of sea birds, the Audubon Society objected as well.

Although the leaders of the environmental community certainly recognize the need for fishery reform, why are they not advocates for it? The reasons appear to be that they fear alienating the tribes and losing their most powerful ally on habitat issues and the associated funding support, and they are intimidated by potential accusations of racism.

Voters rejected I-640 by a substantial margin.

17   Piracy at Sea and the Pacific Salmon Treaty

For many years, until 1933 when fish traps were made illegal by Initiative 77, the bulk of the commercial catch of British Columbia's Fraser River salmon was harvested by Washington fishermen as the runs passed through Washington waters en route to the Canadian river. During construction of a railroad through the Fraser Canyon in 1914 a slide at Hells Gate transformed the site from a swift-flowing river into a narrow torrent that, depending on flow, was often a barrier to adult salmon. Fish stocks and catches plummeted. This ultimately resulted in the two nations joining in *The Fraser River Convention* in 1937 and established the *International Pacific Salmon Fisheries Commission*[70]. The expense for building a "fish ladder" past Hells Gate was to be shared, including the cost and responsibility of managing the fishery. The treaty also called for providing for adequate spawning escapements and equal sharing of the catch. The ladder was completed in 1946 and was successful in greatly increasing returns of the valuable sockeye.

A problem, which was not addressed until years later, was that most of the Chinook salmon that originate in Washington and the Columbia River system, as well as much of the Oregon Coast, migrate into Canada and as far as South East Alaska where many are caught in ocean fisheries. Puget Sound and Washington's north coastal coho stocks, while not migrating as far, also congregate in Canadian waters where they are heavily exploited. Prior to the seaward extension of Canada's territorial waters in 1970 and their establishment of 200-mile *Exclusive Economic Zones* in 1977, the Washington commercial troll fleet had access to these waters where most of its catch occurred.

Washington's sport fishery was also suffered a significant loss when the line defining the EEZ, rather than continuing in the Northwest course of the international boundary in Juan de Fuca Strait, angled Southwest at the Strait's entrance. This limited Washington's access to the prime salmon, halibut and other fishing available on Swiftshure Bank – a loss to become even more significant with the subsequent increase in off-shore capability of the sportfishing fleet.

Canada eventually tired of joint management and sharing the bounties of their most productive salmon river. Unlike what had occurred with hydro development on the Columbia, they had protected Fraser salmon by foregoing the temptations offered by dams and cheap power. They also had ambitions for further enhancing the fish runs, benefits they did not wish to share, and justifiably believed that past U.S investments in Fraser River recovery had been repaid many times over. Their leverage for securing an agreement more to their liking was to increase their interceptions of northmigrating Chinook and coho salmon produced in the lower 48. A further complication was that Alaska benefited from the status quo since few of "their" fish migrate in a southerly direction, in contrast to the large numbers of Canadian and "lower 48" fish traveling to Alaskan coastal waters. For example, less than five percent of the oceancaught Chinook salmon in Alaska originate in that state[71].

By 1970, 65% of the total catch of Chinook salmon produced in Puget Sound and 60% of the coho were harvested in Canada[72]. Interception rates of other Washington and Columbia River Chinook salmon stocks were at a similar level. Most of these Chinook and coho salmon were taken by commercial trollers, although a significant number of coho were taken by Canadian nets in Juan de Fuca Strait.

During the mid-1970s, for the first time in the State's history, the hierarchy of the Department of Fisheries was questioning the wisdom of the existing policies relating to the interceptions of Washington-produced fish by Canada and vice versa. It seemed obvious that the best thing for the fish and regional economy was a system that benefited the people propagating and otherwise caring for the fish. It is more difficult to protect a salmon stream or less attractive to invest in salmon enhancement if most of the fish are caught elsewhere.

The Moos administration, with the concurrence of Governor Evans, adopted the position that the country/region that produces the fish should be the principal beneficiary of the investment. This concept, previously espoused by the United States and other Nations, was somehow viewed with less importance in these negotiations. Backing off on Fraser fish was not what the industry wanted since it was the State's most valuable commercial salmon fishery. Even the Treaty Indian Tribes, who were more dependent upon salmon produced in and returning to their "usual and accustomed" fishing areas, were reluctant to agree to reduce catches of Fraser River fish, while north sound tribes, dependent upon Fraser salmon, were adamantly opposed to it. Nevertheless, the only solution to reducing the interceptions of Washington salmon involved backing off on Fraser River salmon.

The series of meetings between the two governments seemed to go on forever and involved the Federal Governments and representatives from the Washington Department of Fisheries, Treaty Indian Tribes, and the State of Alaska. Catch figures, interception rates, and economic values of the interceptions were argued ad nauseam. Science was a casualty of the process. Presented with agreed-upon data "scientists" dexterously spun the facts in a manner favorable to their constituencies. These negotiations for The Pacific Salmon Treaty (PST) were completed in 1985. The principles of the treaty were to prevent overfishing and provide for each party to receive benefits equivalent to the production of salmon originating in its waters – the "equity principal". The Treaty also called for cooperation in management, research and enhancement; the desirability in most cases of reducing interceptions; avoiding undue disruption of existing fisheries; and that the parties should take into account the annual variations in abundance of the stocks.

But by the early 1990s, it was clear that, to the detriment of the salmon stocks, the PST had failed. For it to have worked would have required a level of cooperation and objectivity that simply did not exist. Satisfying the equity principal was the most contentious issue. Although Peter Bergman and I had retired from the Washington Department of Fisheries in the early 1980s, personal interests and our new jobs with Northwest Marine Technology (NMT) kept us informed on issues relating to the PST. The coded-wire-tagging system relied upon to evaluate Chinook and coho catches interceptions by both the U.S. and Canada was an NMT product and Pete was the co-inventor of the tag.

It appeared to us that Canada was getting seriously short-changed on equity – that is getting far less in catch value than she produced. Canada was responding by overexploiting Chinook and coho salmon originating in the lower 48, while over-harvesting their own intermixed stocks. Apart from the outstanding efforts of Jerry Paveltich, West Coast Director of Trout Unlimited, and a few others, the general public remained woefully ignorant of the fact that excessive U.S. commercial net catches of Canadian sockeye was occurring at the expense of sport fishing and threatening the very existence of Washington's Chinook and coho salmon stocks.

Another flaw in the treaty required consensus on the U.S. side in decision making – unanimity (that bane of sensibility) between Alaska, the Treaty Tribes, and Washington (who also represented Oregon). By August, 1997 it was clear that higher levels of government were required to end the controversy. William Ruckelshaus (U.S) and Dr. David Strangway (Canada) were appointed to investigate the controversy and recommend a solution that would result in the two nations benefiting in proportion to what they were producing.

Pete Bergman and I reviewed the available data and estimated that equity could be achieved at a cost to U.S. fishermen of about $10 million per year. Most of this would be in lost revenue resulting from catching fewer Canadian sockeye. At the same time U.S. citizens were paying about $1 billion per year in an up-hill battle to maintain our Chinook and coho salmon, stocks while foregoing untold millions of dollars in recreational and other benefits resulting from northern interceptions. In July, 1998 we sent our critique of the fundamental problems in implementing the PST, and resulting consequences, to President Clinton. Copies were also provided to key officials in the governments of the U.S. and Canada, including Ruckelshaus and Strangway, as well as to Washington's congressional delegation. At serious risk of exaggerating our role, following is my version of subsequent events.

The Canadians loved our analysis and many of their newspapers covered the story. *"Canada getting short-changed in salmon treaty, 2 U.S. experts say"*, read an August headline in the *Vancouver Sun*[73]. We were even invited, but declined, to appear on Canadian television. U.S. treaty participants at the state and tribal level were less complimentary. The Northwest Indian Fisheries Commission, chaired by Billy Frank, referred to our letter and analysis as a *"diatribe"*. A spokesman for the Alaska Department of Fish and Game saw it as *"a very simplistic view of the process and issues."* Jeff Koenings, a scientist and special assistant to the Alaska Commissioner of Fish and Game, and later to become Director of the Washington Department of Fish and Wildlife, took exception to our charge that Alaska has not lived up to terms of the treaty.

At higher levels of government our views were taken more seriously as summarized in an official Canadian news release[74]:

"In July, American fisheries biologists Peter Bergman and Frank Haw wrote to President Clinton about the link between ESA listings and failure to implement the Pacific Salmon Treaty. They argue that the U.S. has been taking more than its fair share of West Coast salmon, violating the equity principle in the Treaty. Canada, in response, has been overfishing U.S. coho and Chinook. The result according to Bergman and Haw has been ESA listing in the Pacific Northwest.

"They continue, noting that: 'Recovery efforts will cost [the U.S.] at least hundreds of millions of dollars annually imposed on non-fishing interests and the public generally. The cost to achieve [a U.S. – Canada] equity balance in the fisheries is only about ten million dollars annually.' If the equity imbalance was addressed, so too could overfishing of U.S. northwest fish. This could help avoid further ESA listings and the 'enormous unnecessary costs' they would entail.

"Ruckelshaus/Strangway and Bergman/Haw agree that the Pacific Salmon Treaty is the key policy tool for managing serious declines in shared salmon stocks. Moreover, they agree that a key element of any agreement would be a mutually acceptable reduction of interceptions – that is, a reduction of Canadian interceptions of Pacific Northwest salmon stocks, in return for reduced interceptions of Canadian stocks in Alaska and the Pacific Northwest."

In June of 1999 the U.S. and Canada signed an agreement to resolve PST related disputes[75]. The U.S. share of Fraser sockeye would be reduced to just 16.5% of the total catch and the agreement recognized that U.S. fishermen had, for years, taken more than their fair share of salmon. "Abundance-based management" was also implemented. This common-sense principle simply means that rather than establishing fixed catch and interception levels, they should vary with the projected run size. The agreement also contained a highly significant note that, in our view, was the crux of the problem with implementing the PST: *"In the past, scientists related to the PST and salmon management appeared, with rare exception, unable to reach objective conclusions, with analyses uniformly supporting their parent agency's desires. **This lack of objectivity was apparent when scientists working with identical data uniformly reached self-serving, different conclusions.**"* (Emphasis added.)

The 1999 agreement got things moving. It did not solve all of the problems and interceptions of Washington's Chinook and coho salmon stocks are still too high. Much of the problem results from the continuing difficulties in dealing with Alaska and its then powerful congressional delegation. Southeastern Alaska's troll-caught Chinook salmon are indeed a prime commercial product. However, since fewer than 5% of these fish originate in Alaska and are merely visiting from British Columbia and the lower 48, Chinook listed under the Endangered Species Act comprise a portion of the Alaskan and other troll and sport catches that occur here and southward along the Canadian and lower 48 coasts.

Alaska-origin Chinook salmon are essentially absent from the Canadian ocean commercial troll and sport catch. A recent 25-year average indicates that about 48 percent of the Canadian coastal troll and sport catch originates in the lower 48 and includes Puget Sound and Columbia River ESA-listed fish. Chinook sport and troll catches in Georgia Strait are primarily of Canadian origin (70%) although significant portions of the catch originate in Puget Sound (25%)[76]. The Georgia Strait Chinook fishery once the jewel in the crown of the Canadian salmon sport fishery has undergone a catastrophic decline with average annual catches of more than 300,000 from 1975 to 1984 and free-falling to 19,000 fifteen years later. Coho catches have experienced a similar decline.

Negotiations between the U.S. and Canada relating to salmon interceptions will doubtlessly continue. Alaska is the world's richest area in valuable fish stocks that can be justifiably harvested without impacting returns to other jurisdictions. Alaska appears to have done an excellent job of managing its own salmon stocks, but takes a different view when exploiting those of others. The lower 48 suffers from Alaska's transgressions on Canadian stocks since they can only retaliate in kind by taking fish originating in the south. Establishing reasonable limitations on the interceptions of Canadian and lower 48 salmon off Alaska, something that state can easily afford, is a basic requirement for rationalizing Chinook salmon management in the Pacific Northwest.

18   The ESA: Isolation, Variation and Adaption

*T*he *Endangered Species Act of 1973*, the Nation's most significant environmental law, was enacted to protect imperiled fish, wildlife and plants from the ". . . *consequences of economic growth and development untendered by adequate concern and conservation."* Although there are many exceptions with fish, a *biological/taxonomic species* is usually defined as a group of organisms capable of interbreeding resulting in reproductively viable offspring. An oft-given example is that a donkey and horse are different species since their offspring are sterile; whereas dogs, regardless of size and shape, are all *Canis lupus familiaris*. Animals and plants with identical two-part scientific names (genus followed by species) are recognized as the same taxonomic species. Differing heritable characteristics within a species, resulting from prolonged reproductive isolation, may result in use of a third scientific name designating a *subspecies*. Thus, *familiaris*, the third term in the scientific name of dogs, designates them as a subspecies of the grey wolf.

Coastal cutthroat trout (*Oncorhynchus clarki clarki*) are native to western Washington; whereas, westslope (referring to the Rocky Mountains) cutthroat (*Oncorhynchus clarki lewisi*), with markedly different spotting and coloration, are native east of Washington's Cascade Mountains. Offspring of the two subspecies would be fertile with intermediate visual characteristics. Although there are many recognized inland subspecies of trout and char, reproductive isolation in North American anadromous Pacific salmon apparently does not occur to the extent required to result in any subspecies designations.

Taxonomy, the science of classifying plants and animals, is not an exact science and it is not unusual for scientific names to change, as occurred when some Dolly Varden became bull trout, and rainbow and cutthroat trout were determined to be more closely related to Pacific salmon than Atlantic salmon.

The ESA departs from the taxonomic definition and redefines "species" in a manner allowing various *distinct population segments* (DPS's) *within* a species, to qualify for listing: "*The term 'species' includes any subspecies of fish or wildlife or plants, and any distinct population segment (DPS) of any species or vertebrate fish or wildlife which interbreeds when mature."* Thus, regardless of the overall abundance of a taxonomic species, population segments that are to various degrees reproductively isolated and considered *evolutionarily significant* qualify for listing – there's the rub.

Sockeye salmon are generally abundant throughout most of their natural range. However, Snake River sockeye, originating in lake systems 6500 feet high in the Rockies, above nine major dams, and at the very edge of their natural range, are listed as endangered. In this case, large sums are being expended to perpetuate a population that may, at best, become a naturally sustaining curiosity. Successful listings, initiated either by the U.S. Fish and Wildlife Service (freshwater fishes) or by NOAA Fisheries (marine and anadromous species) trigger a series of events to recover the listed organism that typically focuses on habitat issues but includes protective enforcement, penalties and mandatory recovery plans. There are currently over 1,300 threatened and endangered animal and plant ESA listings in the United States.

The focus of the Act is to restore *self-sustaining* viable populations. Hatchery fish alone cannot satisfy these provisions even if they appear genetically identical to the listed wild population. Examples of listed Chinook salmon include Snake River spring- and summer-run fish, Snake River fall-runs, upper Columbia springs, and lower river falls, and Puget Sound Chinook salmon. ESA listing can result in extraordinary levels of protection and expenditures. Although all costs are not attributable to listing, in 2006 alone expenditures on salmon recovery were in excess of 394 million dollars[77]. In addition, many other public and private activities that impact stream flows and habitat are subject to costly restrictions and mitigation under the Act.

The Puget Sound Chinook salmon ESA listing includes 22 populations. Some are in reasonable condition while others barely exist. All are subject to varying levels of fishing. The independent scientists comprising the Hatchery Scientific Review Group have concluded that one of the most serious problems in restoring wild Chinook and coho salmon populations results from the disproportionately high fraction of hatchery origin salmon spawning with wild fish[78]. The scientists conclude that the productivity of the wild fish could double if hatchery strays were reduced to a small fraction of the natural spawning population. With current levels of hatchery production, this could only occur by selectively harvesting fin-clipped hatchery fish while live releasing or otherwise avoiding catching wild fish.

Some question the validity of a problem with hatchery straying since these salmon often originate from local wild populations and can be observed naturally spawning like any other salmon. The problem lies in what is referred to as *domestication*. Various hatchery practices facilitate domestication, but short-circuiting the freshwater rearing process, key to the success of hatcheries, appears to be the most significant of these. In nature, the rigors associated with surviving from egg to seaward migrant, eliminates the vast majority of the young. In contrast, in the spoon-fed protected environment of a hatchery, survival from egg to smolt typically exceeds 90%. Although returning hatchery adult salmon have demonstrated an ability to survive downstream migration and life at sea, they have not passed nature's most difficult early test. The mating of a hatchery fish with a wild-origin fish could result in offspring with reduced chances for pre-smolt survival. The vast majority of hatchery salmon are produced to be caught and this appears to be their wisest and best use.

This is not to say, as implied by some, that such fish are incapable of surviving and reproducing under natural conditions. There are many examples of hatchery salmon and trout establishing viable populations beyond their natural range. Through the process of natural selection, in the absence of continuing hatchery influence, they have adapted to their colonized waters. Chinook salmon, coho salmon, and steelhead originating in Washington hatcheries have established viable natural populations throughout the Great Lakes. These Chinook originated in our Green River (Duwamish system) and the coho probably have similar ties to local hatcheries[79]. Chinook salmon in New Zealand, first introduced in 1870, have long supported a popular river sport fishery on fish that have diverged into separate stocks adapted to unique conditions in different streams[80]. Chinook salmon, again Green River stock, likely resulting from escapees from fish farms, recently colonized a Patagonian river flowing into the Atlantic Ocean[81]. Steelhead trout, with hatchery ancestors, are now also included among the local sea-run fishes[82].

In contrast to these range extensions of Pacific salmon, the many attempts to establish wild populations of Atlantic salmon (*Salmo salar*) beyond their natural range have failed. Included, was a Washington

Department of Fisheries release from a south Puget Sound Hatchery (Minter Creek) during the mid-1970s. Even though many farmed Atlantic salmon escapees from saltwater pens in both Puget Sound and British Columbia have ascended local rivers, they have failed to effectively reproduce.

Some of the world's finest wild trout fishing results from releases of hatchery fish that have developed wild populations in the southern hemisphere – far removed from the natural range of any member of family Salmonidae. Closer to home, streams originally too warm for trout, cooled by tail-water flows from the depths of reservoirs, provide some of the finest trout fishing in North America[i]. Huge sea-run brown trout, originating in fresh-water stocks from European hatcheries, attract anglers from far and wide to Patagonia at the southern tip of South America. Elsewhere in the Southern hemisphere anadromous brown trout populations have been established on remote islands in the southern regions of the Atlantic (Falkland) and Indian oceans (Kerguelen).

If used properly, so as to avoid problems associated with domestication and inbreeding, hatcheries can be useful to maintain and eventually restore unique populations of wild fish. In most cases this would involve restoring critical freshwater habitat. The most significant project of this kind is occurring on Washington's Elwha River and requires removing two dams that have blocked passage to existing pristine habitat in Olympic National Park since 1912. At this writing (2014) this $350 million project is well underway with mind-boggling quantities of century-old sediments pouring into Juan de Fuca Strait.

For many years a hatchery on the lower Elwha River below the dams was charged with preserving the native Chinook salmon that are rightfully noted for their large size. However, at the risk of being labeled an iconoclast, I challenge the popular notion that 100-pound fish were once common there since authentic records of such fish appear lacking. Bruce Brown's *Mountain in the Clouds*[83] has been used to authenticate the 100-pounders. He cited a translation of a 1790 entry in the journal of the Spanish explorer Manuel Quimper regarding observations made at Neah Bay where Columbia River fish would have been far more common than those from the Elwha[84]. Jim Lichatowich, an otherwise highly qualified biologist, but citing Brown as a source, goes so far to write that the Elwha was home to "many over 100 pounds."[85] However, late 19th century ichthyologists, who appeared fascinated by the trout of nearby lakes Crescent and Sutherland, made no mention of the giants of the Elwha. *The Fishes of Puget Sound*[86], published in 1895 and co-authored by the famous ichthyologist David Starr Jordan, had this to say about the size of local Chinook: "*It commonly weighs about 17 (11 to 20) pounds, but specimens weighing 70 pounds are on record.*" Regardless, the mythical giants have played an important role in convincing the public that the dams must be removed – and that is good.

The Elwha salmon hatchery, once mislabeled by road signs as a "spawning channel", located below the two dams, is the logical source of Chinook salmon for restocking the upper river and letting nature take its course. In addition to preventing the upstream migration of salmon, the dams have blocked the downstream flow of gravel required for natural spawning and the finer sediments that built nearby Ediz Hook – the protective barrier for Port Angeles that is currently artificially maintained. Hopefully, these remaining Chinook salmon will be up to the task of restoring wild progeny to the upper river, and the other of four species of salmon as well as anadromous trout and char will again find this pristine upstream habitat to their liking.

Physical barriers in the western states such as mountain ranges and impassible waterfalls have isolated cutthroat trout into clearly different subspecies. Few anglers would fail to differentiate coastal from westslope cutthroat trout while none, including biologists, can visually identify different populations of Chinook salmon. The reason for this is that populations of Pacific salmon and steelhead are not really isolated. The Pacific Ocean and the connected waterways provide an open route to all streams hosting these fish. All stray to some extent, which tends to homogenize the various stocks comprising a species. Straying also allows the fish to colonize healing watersheds previously devastated by massive floods, advancing glaciers, or volcanic eruptions and without it there would be no salmon. There are very important genetic differences between the stocks comprising a salmon species but they tend to be less significant than those among totally isolated populations.

The fossil remains of million-year-old adult sockeye salmon, so detailed that scales can be read, were recently discovered by an angler far up the South Fork of the Skokomish River that now drains into southern Hood Canal[87]. Standing there on the bank at the head of a canyon, it is difficult to imagine the lake that reared the smolts and preserved the remains of the adult fish. The lake existed at a time when the Puget Sound region was covered by a glacial ice field that dammed the stream that eventually flowed into the Pacific in the region which is now Grays Harbor. The fossils are located at the head of this ancient lake where spawned-out carcasses would accumulate. As the glacier receded, the lake became a flowing stream and new and different habitat was created that was eventually colonized by straying salmon. If salmon invariably return to spawn where they originated they would no longer exist.

A modern example of straying, colonization and adaptation is provided by the previously mentioned introduction of Chinook salmon into New Zealand[88]. The introduction involved a single race of fish from a Sacramento River system hatchery into the Waitaki River during the early 20th Century. Within ten years the fish had colonized the Waitaki and established self-sustaining populations in other major rivers as far as 140 miles away. The results of studies, published in 1993, concluded that these New Zealand salmon, shaped through natural selection by varying conditions, now *"differed in all life history traits examined among rivers"*. Had the adults resulting from these releases not been subject to natural selection, in the absence of the overwhelming influence of cultured fish, it appears doubtful that these rivers would now sustain unique runs of wild Chinook salmon.

The ESA is doing much to stimulate actions to restore Pacific salmon. However, in contrast to the situation with Pacific salmon, total reproductive isolation occurs among many native species of inland fishes. Land barriers and seawater, lethal to most freshwater fishes, that separates watersheds, have totally isolated many populations of a given species for many thousands of years. Significant genetic differences are far more likely in such populations than with anadromous salmon and steelhead. Pigmy whitefish, for example, occur in only a few deep Washington lakes and each population is totally isolated from the other; mountain whitefish populations in watersheds separated by saltwater are isolated, along with most of the other native species similarly intolerant. Although Washington has only about 40 native inland fish species[89], there is likely to be many populations of each that are far more genetically unique than those established for salmon and steelhead. The Olympic mudminnow, endemic to some lowlands of western Washington, is one such species that has been genetically analyzed and variation between populations was found to be high[90].

The many creeks and rivers flowing directly into just Puget Sound are home to about 15 *true* species of native fishes that are intolerant of sea-water. Thus, such fish in each watershed are reproductively isolated from other watersheds. According to the criteria established for salmon, each of these species in these watersheds appears to qualify as a distinct population segment (DPS). The total DPS number in this example alone would exceed 100. The redside shiners in Mason County's Sherwood Creek would lose a popularity contest with the Chinook salmon in the Skokomish River but they appear to be a more significant DPS since the ESA has nothing to do with popularity. I believe that the criteria for establishing DPSs needs reviewing and that to fail to do so exposes the ESA to inappropriate and disingenuous applications.

One of most questionable local ESA listings involves three species of Puget Sound rockfishes that have somehow been identified as distinct from cohorts residing west of the barely discernible sill at the eastern end of Juan de Fuca Strait. It appears there is little if any genetic information currently available to support these listings. Well after listing occurred, NOAA Fisheries sought assistance from the angling public to collect genetic material to determine if, in fact, Puget Sound represents a distinct population segment (DPS) for yelloweye and canary rockfish. Collecting this information should have preceded listing.

The existing policies of ESA listing populations has, at least in one case, *reduced* the abundance of wild Chinook salmon returning to south Puget Sound. The Deschutes River (not to be confused with Oregon's Deschutes) tumbles over an 80-foot natural barrier to upstream salmon migration into what was originally a tide flat at the upper end of Budd Inlet in the southern extremity of Puget Sound. The power of the falls was a primary influence in establishing Tumwater – the oldest permanent American settlement on Puget Sound. Since 1951 a low dam three kilometers below the falls transformed the tide flat into Capitol Lake. A three-phased fishway, allowing salmon to ascend the falls to utilize the spawning and freshwater rearing habitat was begun in 1952 and completed in 1954 at a total cost of $300,000.

In 1950, 203,000 marked Chinook salmon fingerlings from Green River Hatchery were released below the barrier falls. A year later significant numbers of these marked fish appeared in Puget Sound sport catches and 3,200 of the resulting adults entered the completed lower unit of the new fishway in 1953[91]. For the following 30 years, Chinook released into the Deschutes system were a major contributor to the Puget Sound sport Chinook catch.

Although significant returns of hatchery-origin Chinook salmon still ascend the Deschutes fishways, they are trapped at the head of the falls and not allowed to progress upstream to utilize the available habitat – the very intent of constructing the fishways. The reason for not allowing natural production to occur is that Tribal and State co-managers fear that ESA listing would result from allowing a natural-origin population to develop and that this would interfere with management of the harvest.

19   Hatchery Reform

The simple process of stripping ripe eggs from salmon or trout into a bucket and adding a squirt or two of sperm was performed as early as the fourteenth century by a French monk[92]. A series of papers published in 1763-64 describes experiments conducted in Germany on methods of taking eggs of salmon and trout and fertilizing them artificially by mixing the eggs and sperm in water. Here in the Pacific Northwest, salmon and trout culture has been going on for about 130 years. Conventional wisdom of the day concluded that the natural process of salmon reproduction was grossly inefficient and releasing millions of newly hatched fry would reverse the impacts of overfishing that was decimating prime stocks of Columbia River and other Chinook salmon stocks during the 1880s. Since it was far easier to dump untold millions of salmon fry into the rivers than control commercial fishing or protect salmon streams, more and more hatcheries were built. Lacking means to evaluate the results of the early salmon hatcheries, advances in technology were slow in coming and for much of their existence hatcheries did little, if anything, to reverse declines in salmon abundance.

Evaluation of hatchery production requires calculating the relevant costs and benefits involved in the process. Negative factors such as impacts on wild fish and other environmental issues must also be considered. Potential benefits include the value of the harvested fish, economic activity resulting from fishing, and consumer surplus – a concept discussed in the Allocation chapter that follows. Although the level of participation in recreational fishing is a more appropriate measure of its value than the magnitude of the catch, participation is directly related to the catch rate and ease of access.

An evaluation of hatchery contributions requires that a representative number of the fish that are released are marked or tagged so that they can be identified in catches and as surviving adults. For many years, clipping various combinations of fins from juvenile fish was the method used to identify and evaluate the performance of hatchery salmon. Perhaps the most significant resulting discovery was that the survivals were highly dependent upon releasing "smolts" – fish with the fitness and urge to migrate to sea. This required rearing fish for as long as a year. Other experiments led to improvements in disease control, diets and other options available to fish culturists. It was not until the 1970s that the coded wire tagging system provided the means to objectively evaluate the production from the hundreds of hatcheries and artificial rearing facilities existing from northern California to Alaska's Cook Inlet.

Unfortunately, the best science has not been included in the development of hatchery technology since those involved with artificial salmon culture tended to work independently from those involved with fish in the natural world. Furthermore, there was a tendency for the latter to look askance at artificial salmon culture since hatcheries were often offered as inadequate substitutes for habitat losses resulting from dams and other development. Why should they participate in improving hatcheries if this would only justify the destruction of even more natural salmon habitat?

Recent books and other technical articles have focused on the plight of wild salmon while aptly, and even eloquently, describing the problems with salmon hatcheries. These authors have become known in the trade as "hatchery bashers". Poor science, failure to achieve production goals, destruction of wild stocks from interbreeding, competition, spreading disease, and stimulating mixed stock fisheries were foremost among the criticisms. Apart from implying that hatcheries should be eliminated and that river systems should be restored to their pristine condition, few if any practical solutions were being offered. The State, Federal and Tribal hatchery managers, on the other hand, appeared to ignore the valid criticism and continued to do business as usual. Nevertheless, local salmon hatcheries have produced some very large numbers of Chinook and coho salmon. According to the Washington Department of Fish and Wildlife website (4/16/14) an estimated 75% of the "salmon" currently caught in Puget Sound and 90% in the Columbia River originate in hatcheries. Although not indicated, this estimate includes only Chinook and coho salmon and not the large catches of wild chum, pink and sockeye salmon taken in Puget Sound.

I confess that as a top official in the Washington Department of Fisheries during the mid-70s, when survivals of salmon released from Washington hatcheries was much higher than today, and in response to the Boldt Decision, I was an outspoken advocate for doubling the state catch primarily by increasing hatchery production. Several years later, fish geneticists published papers describing how domesticated hatchery fish spawning in the wild were a threat to wild populations and eliminating hatcheries was receiving serious consideration.

Pete Bergman and I at Northwest Marine Technology were in frequent contact with Lee Blankenship (Washington Fish and Wildlife) and less often with Dr. Conrad Mahnken (NOAA Fisheries) with whom Lee shared a common interest in aquaculture. Together, we recognized the important role of hatcheries and believed that hatchery practices could be altered to provide fish to catch while being compatible with, or even supportive to, wild salmon populations.

We expressed these views to Kay Gabriel and Gary Smith, advisors to U.S. Senator Slade Gorton, who told the senator that they supported the concept. The Senator agreed and appointed us to a Science Advisory Team to recommend a process for hatchery reform in the Puget Sound and Washington Coastal area. The Columbia River basin was purposely left out because of the jurisdictional morass in the region. We were correct in believing that the concept would eventually spread to the Columbia if it first proved successful elsewhere.

Senator Gorton understood the need to appoint representatives from the various agencies managing hatcheries, but he chose his own Science Team so as to ensure independence and circumvent the ingrained provincialism of the fisheries agencies. In 1999, a bipartisan group including Senator Gorton, U.S. Senator Patty Murray, U.S., Congressman Norm Dicks, and Washington Governor Gary Locke reviewed the Science Team's conclusions and approved a process and budgets for the purpose of reforming hatcheries to support wild stock recovery and sustainable fisheries. Following Senator Gorton's departure from congress, Congressman Norm Dicks became the uncontested champion of Hatchery Reform and salmon recovery.

The process, incorporating recommendations from a committee of past presidents of the American Fisheries Society, resulted in the appointment of a Hatchery Scientific Review Group (HSRG) consisting of five Independent Scientists, including two from Alaska, a Canadian, a retiree, and a private consultant. Four scientists chosen by their agencies represented the tribes, the Washington Department of Fish and Wildlife, the

U.S. Fish and Wildlife Service, and the National Marine Fisheries Service. Expertise in the nine-member group included genetics, fish diseases, biometrics, computer modeling, and fish culture.

The group completed its review of all the salmon hatcheries in the Puget Sound and Washington Coastal[93] region and the concept has indeed spread to the Columbia River basin. In addition, a modified version of salmon hatchery reform is being implemented in California. Foremost among the science group's recommendations is the need to evaluate and establish goals based upon the production of fish and impacts on wild stocks. Past goals were often based upon the numbers or pounds of fish released, which appears analogous to evaluating farm production on the amount of planted seed; or a ball player's productivity with his times at bat.

Another recommendation is having only integrated or segregated hatchery stocks. An integrated hatchery stock is one that remains closely related to the native fish in the watershed. The ties are maintained by including prescribed fractions of wild fish in the spawning operations while greatly reducing the number of hatchery-origin fish that stray to spawn with the native stocks. A segregated stock is one that is separated in time or space from spawning with a wild population thus posing no significant threat to the genetic integrity of wild stocks.

Marking all hatchery-origin salmon that are intended for harvest is the cornerstone of hatchery and fishery reform. Since hatchery salmon are visually indistinguishable from their wild counterparts, implementing the concepts of integration and segregation requires marking hatchery fish so that they can be readily identified as harvestable hatchery fish wherever they occur. Selective fishing will reduce the existing waste of surplus hatchery fish by getting more of them in the catch and reducing the numbers of hatchery "strays" spawning with wild fish, and thus facilitate the process of natural selection and local adaptation that is required to optimize productivity. In most cases selective fishing will require sorting and releasing wild fish. This requires the use of fishing gear that minimizes injuries during the sorting process. Until recently, anglers were essentially alone in participating in large-scale mark selective salmon and steelhead fisheries although there have always been unused practical options for commercial harvesting as well.

Adipose fin clips are ideally suited for marking salmon and trout for these purposes. The small fleshy tabs are located behind the dorsal fin of all members of the salmon family. The function of this fin has been a puzzle to ichthyologists[94]. It may provide some hydrodynamic swimming advantage, and enlarged adipose fins are a secondary sexual characteristic of mature male Pacific salmon and some other trout and char. In contrast to experiments involving the excision of the more functional fins, removing the adipose fin has proven to have little if any effect on growth or survival[95].

The first major hurdle to implementing hatchery reform was in getting the various management agencies to adipose fin clip all of the hatchery salmon that were "intended for harvest". The state of Washington had already embarked upon an ambitious program to mark hatchery Chinook and coho salmon for the purpose of providing selective fishing opportunities for anglers. Years before this, the Washington Department of Game had initiated a program to fin-clip hatchery steelhead and sea-run cutthroat trout for selective fishing. State legislation had been passed in 1995 mandating that all hatchery-produced Chinook and coho salmon were to be externally recognizable.

However, the State's perception is that Washington's treaty Indian tribes are not subject to state laws[j] and as "co-managers" of the resource were able to prevent the full implementation of the statute even at hatcheries fully funded by the state. Due to pressure from an influential state senator/gillnet fisherman, mass marking was even delayed in the Willapa Bay basin despite the fact that federal funding was specifically provided to accomplish the task. I believe that tribal objections to mass marking result from concerns that it would lead to altering tribal fishing methods and, as to the non-Indian gillnet fishery, this was also the source of the State Senator's objection. Although, an equally important use of the mark is separating wild and hatchery origin salmon in the hatchery and spawning grounds, the prevailing view among tribal authorities is that separation is of no consequence. Although this is clearly inconsistent with the ESA the state and NOAA Fisheries have not, as yet, seriously challenged tribal adherence to this concept.

The U.S. Congress came to the rescue in 2003 with mass marking when Sec. 129 of H.R. 2691-29 was passed into law: *"The United States Fish and Wildlife Service shall, in carrying out its responsibilities to protect threatened and endangered species of salmon, implemented a system of mass marking of salmonid stocks, intended for harvest, that are released from Federally operated or Federally financed hatcheries including but not limited to fish releases of coho, chinook, and steelhead species. Marked fish must have a visible mark that can be readily identified by commercial and recreational fishers."*

Since most Columbia River hatcheries, some others, along with tribal hatcheries are financed to at least some degree by the Federal Government, this law became the savior of hatchery reform. It came about quietly through the efforts of Congressman Dicks. It also facilitated implementation of the existing state laws requiring marking the hatchery fish in State facilities that were not being marked due to objections from the tribal co-managers. It is noteworthy that despite the fact that hatchery operations were costing taxpayers many millions of dollars annually, none of the state or federal agencies responsible for salmon management had chosen to recommend legislation mandating the marking of fish or for hatchery reform.

Another kind of hatchery reform, dealing with costs and benefits, is sorely needed. In 2009 the Washington Department of Fish and Wildlife took the commendable first step of calculating the costs of producing an adult steelhead and salmon at each of the state's Puget Sound and coastal salmon and steelhead hatcheries. (A vast improvement over assessments based upon numbers/pounds of salmon released.) Cost per adult was calculated by dividing the annual operational costs by the number of adults produced – defined as the sum of (1) total catch (regardless of where it occurred), (2) hatchery spawning needs, (3) hatchery surplus and (4) "strays". Dollar costs of producing an adult at the facilities were found to range (and average) as follows: Chinook 5 – 105 ($35), coho 3 – 64 ($12), steelhead 18 – 288 ($95) and chum 0.2 – 0.6 ($0.40).

Calculating the cost of an adult produced was a good start but only an initial step in measuring the productivity of hatcheries paid for by the citizens of the state. A large fraction of the adults produced in these facilities are caught in Canada, caught by nobody (hatchery surplus) or stray into natural spawning areas. A more logical measure of success would emphasize value in the Washington catch and the impact on wild stocks. For example, the below average cost for an adult Chinook produced at Forks

Creek Hatchery (Willapa River) is listed at $26. However, only about 25% of these fish enter the Washington catch, so that the operational cost of providing a Chinook to, what should be, the targeted catch is about 4 x $26 or $104.

Such an analysis would provide fisheries managers with a basis for prioritizing hatchery funding and facilitate funneling harvests into fisheries with the highest economic yields. In view of the low interception rate and cost of chum salmon, one would also be amiss in ignoring the advantages of producing more of them for the commercial industry.

A short time ago I watched a film called *Moneyball.* It was the true story of how a low budget baseball team managed to compete with the likes of the Yankees by taking a fresh and more objective look at data relating to performance and costs – it paid off for the Oakland Athletics. It is clearly time to play *Moneyfish* and we will do things far more differently when the game is underway.

Forty-some years ago, when the CWT system was in its infancy, Pete Bergman and I envisioned its most important function as a tool for evaluating options for increasing hatchery survivals and contributions to targeted fisheries. This would be accomplished by comparing tag returns of test groups with controls representing normal hatchery production fish.

During the ensuing years the numbers of fish coded wire tagged increased from tens of thousands in 1968 to 50 million annually by 2008. Over this period a total of 1.4 billion Pacific Coast salmon and steelhead were coded wire tagged (90% being Chinook and coho) resulting in 5.6 million recoveries[96]. However, the overwhelming purpose of all this was monitoring catches and the status of the various stocks comprising the harvest. Although this is of critical importance in managing the fisheries and complying with catch sharing in accordance with Indian fishing rights and the Pacific Salmon Treaty, there is much to gain by utilizing this technology to evaluate options designed to improve fishing. Experiments relating to diets, immunization, conditioning, straying, contribution to targeted fisheries, and other things are bound to pay off if properly conducted.

20   Fishery Reform

Throughout the years, irrational fisheries have devastated many of the world's stocks of fish, including the marvelously productive Grand Banks cod fishery that played such an important role in European and American history[97]. The April 2007 issue of *National Geographic Magazine* is primarily devoted to "The Global Fish Crisis" resulting from fishing. Closer to home, coastal rockfish and groundfish stocks have been devastated by inappropriate fishing methods and management practices. Despite the ESA listing of various local stocks of Chinook salmon, harvest rates of these fish commonly result in spawning escapements lower than those established for recovery.

State and Tribal fisheries managers justified these seemingly irrational impacts by claiming that the existing freshwater habitat is the limiting factor and that allowing more wild fish to escape would be a waste of fish that should be harvested. In addition to the active fisheries, unaccounted losses of fish, birds, crabs, shellfish, and sea mammals continue to occur from entanglements in the derelict fishing gear that festoons and litters the most productive waters and migratory pathways of Puget Sound. The Northwest Strait Commission/Foundation (NWSC) estimates *"that fishermen lost on average the equivalent of from 150 to 300 gillnets (1,800 ft. long by 100 ft. deep) per year over the 30-year period. There are likely several thousand derelict gillnets remaining in Puget Sound."*[98] The synthetic mesh of modern nets is relatively impervious to rot and is capable of killing fish and other wildlife for many years. Another passage from a NWSC report reveals how damaging these nets appear to be: *"Recently 46 derelict gillnets were removed from Lopez Island. The nets contained 43 dead seabirds, two salmonids, rockfish, lingcod, crab and one marine mammal, probably a harbor seal. However, beneath the nets divers found literally piles of dead seabird and fish bones."*

An assessment of the impact on sturgeon of derelict tribal gillnets in the Columbia River above Bonneville Dam revealed that they were a significant source of mortality. The estimated kill was based on the unrealistic assumptions that all lost nets were reported by tribal fishers, though no reporting requirement existed – and that none of the live, dead and rotting fish fell from the nets as they were grappled and dragged to the surface[99].

Selective fishing means different things to different people. In this context we mean fishing with gear capable of catching specific fish while minimizing damage to other fish and animals. Targeted fish include fin-marked hatchery fish and healthy stocks of wild fish including pink, sockeye and chum salmon – three species which in the foreseeable future will/should be primarily commercial fish.

Reef nets, used by northern Puget Sound Indians prior to the arrival of Europeans on the Pacific Coast, are outstanding examples of commercial fishing gear well adapted for selective fishing. However, use of the gear is restricted to a few specific sites among the San Juan Islands. Ropes laced with plastic streamers are arranged in a funnel shape leading migrating salmon toward the surface and over a small-mesh scoop net suspended below the surface. When fishermen in towers observe salmon swimming into the net, it is quickly pulled to the surface. The catch, trapped into a submerged pocket in the net, can be quickly slid into a live box for sorting.

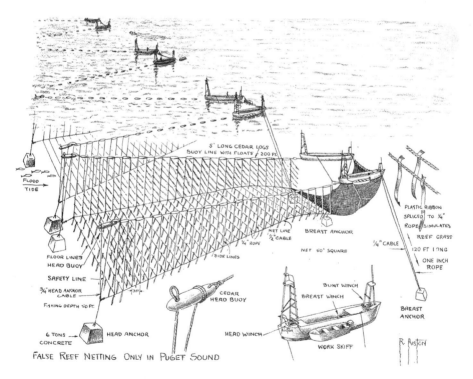

Figure 36. Diagram of a reef net.
Courtesy of the Puget Sound Reef Netters Association.

Untargeted fish are easily released unharmed. Marketed fish undergo little if any bruising and the overall quality of the product commands a much higher price than fish taken by other methods.

Despite its advantages, the use of reef nets remains restricted to a few specific sites. Even though reef netting may be superior to other fishing methods, practitioners are limited to the fishing periods for other commercial gears. They are, in fact, more restricted since they are often required to release non-targeted fish that other gears are allowed to keep, since they alone can do it successfully.

Reef nets would only work in areas where tidal currents and fish behavior was favorable. Other suitable sites in Puget Sound, in addition to where they are currently allowed, doubtlessly exist. Throughout the 1950s, during periods of adult salmon migrations, the Department of Fisheries utilized a reef net at Bush Point on Whidbey Island to tag large numbers of coho, pink and chum salmon. This gear was chosen for the project because it did little harm to the mature salmon that were caught and tagged. We have had recent conversations with a Lummi Island reef-net fisherman who was interested in testing a potential site near the bridge in Hood Canal.

Beach seining, offering a similar advantage, is another technique used by biologists to collect adult salmon for tagging. The relatively small mesh and heavy twine prevents fish from becoming entangled. One end of the net is typically run out from shore and hooked around the fish and back to the shallows, in the form of a rough semi-circle, where fish can be dealt with or released. Horse-drawn beach seines were used extensively on the sandy banks of the Lower Columbia in the heydays of the modern fishery.

Recognizing the need for fishing selectively and after reviewing results achieved in British Columbia, Washington and Oregon began evaluating "tangle nets" in the lower Columbia River in 2001. Gillnets, depending upon mesh size, are designed to catch fish of a specific size range[100]. Chinook nets, measuring eight inches or more (stretch-measured diagonally across the square from knot to knot) have the largest mesh, followed by those for chum and coho, sockeye and pink salmon. Mesh size allows the targeted fish to enter the net beyond its gill covers and no further due to the increasing body size. Withdrawal from the net is stymied by the gill covers and other parts catching in the web. Tangle nets

Figure 37. Lifting a San Juan Island reef net.
Photo courtesy of Kathi Melville.

are simply small-mesh gillnets that catch onto jaws and other mouth parts in a less damaging manner. A primary convenience to fishermen is that it is not all that different from traditional gillnetting.

Gillnets/tangle nets are designed to represent an invisible drifting curtain made more effective by modern developments with finer, less visible synthetic mesh. They are most commonly fished at night to reduce visibility. Gillnet lengths are limited to 1800 feet in Puget Sound and Coastal Bays and to 1500 feet in the Columbia River. Tangle nets are much shorter because successfully releasing non-targeted fish requires promptly tending the entire net. Floats support the length of the nets at the surface and a "lead line" along the bottom maintains the vertical configuration of the "curtain". Puget Sound nets are typically 100 feet or more in depth whereas those used in rivers and coastal bays are designed to drift over much shallower water. Tribal fishers commonly use gillnets that are anchored or fixed to the shore ("set nets") in bays and rivers.

The original tests with 4.5-inch mesh tangle nets were promising if they were tended within 45 minutes of being set and non-target wild fish were revived and then released after being allowed to recover in a water-filled "recovery box". Fisheries managers decided, without further tests, that 5.25-inch mesh, that many fishermen already owned, should be allowed. Unfortunately, this mesh size was near perfect for killing thousands of steelhead, including ESA-listed fish. Successful use of tangle nets also requires a high degree of responsibility among the practitioners – perhaps more than can be expected while fishing under the cover of darkness when gillnetting typically occurs. One of the fishermen recently arrested while participating in the tangle net season was cited for "soaking" his net for 79 minutes, rather than the prescribed 45, and failing to have any water in his recovery box. He was president of Salmon for All – a prominent organization purporting to advocate conservation and wild salmon recovery[101].

Proponents of fishery reform were further upset in 2007 when the Washington Department of Fish and Wildlife withdrew its proposal to test alternative methods of selectively harvesting salmon commercially because of criticism from gillnet fishermen. The agency stood to receive $445,000 from the Northwest Power Planning and Conservation Council for the badly needed project that would lead to the use of gear that could selectively harvest hatchery salmon while protecting ESA listed stocks[102].

Seining for salmon in the Pacific Northwest probably occurred soon after the arrival of humans. A seine is typically a long net with relatively small mesh, rigged with floats at the top and weights dragging the bottom that is hauled around fish and then drawn in so that the catch is concentrated in a short section, or "pocket" of the net. In late July of 1811, in the lower Columbia on his trip upstream from Astoria, the explorer David Thompson observed Indians seining salmon with a 30-fathom (180-foot) net rigged with 60 feet of line for hauling at either end of the net[103]. They were apparently taking about ten fish in each set of the net. A few days later near the mouth of the John Day River, Thompson measured a seined salmon at four feet four inches in length with a girth of 28 inches. Chipped-stone net weights used on such seines are among the most common artifacts collected along the river. South Puget Sound tribal fishermen currently use beach seines to catch salmon. Such nets are well suited for selectively harvesting marked hatchery fish, while releasing others, if they choose to do so. *Nets that corral fish, rather than entangle them, are obviously superior for live sorting.*

Indian dip nets, such as those shown in old photographs of the now inundated Celilo Falls, are still used at certain locations in the Columbia Basin. Similar to large landing nets used by anglers, they are also suitable for sorting fish. A promising new site for dip netting is located in Seattle in the fish-way/ladder at the Ballard Locks (the outlet to Lake Washington). Chinook, coho and sockeye salmon all pass into the lake through the fish-way and locks. Both wild and hatchery Chinook and coho salmon occur in the lake system. There is an existing problem with managing the returning Chinook because there is typically a harvestable surplus of hatchery Chinook along with a wild stock (primarily Cedar River fish) that is chronically weak. A tribal dip-net fishery for marked Chinook has been proposed but has been rejected in favor of gillnetting.

In view of tribal dependence on gillnetting, a relaxation of the grip on the method came from a surprising source. The Colville Indian Tribes were not party to the Stevens Treaties and their fishing rights are limited to their reservation in north central Washington. The Okanogan River, flows through the reservation into the Columbia River below that river's up-stream fish barrier at Chief Joseph Dam. Prior to the completion of

Figure 38. Squaxin Island tribal fisherman beach seining for coho salmon near Olympia.

Chief Joseph Dam in the 1950s, upstream migration of salmon had been entirely blocked by Grand Coulee Dam in the 1930s. The Okanogan still has runs of hatchery-augmented Chinook and steelhead, as well as the Columbia's largest run of wild sockeye salmon that originate in lake systems across the border in British Columbia. However, the most important historical Colville fishing sites, such as Kettle Falls, were above Chief Joseph and Grand Coulee dams.

In 2006, in anticipation of the need to protect the remaining wild salmon and steelhead populations while harvesting anticipated hatchery returns, the tribe began experimenting with seines. The tests were highly successful, resulting in efficient fishing and low mortality rates on releases of wild salmon. A new $51 million salmon hatchery, located on the Columbia below Chief Joseph Dam, was dedicated in 2013.

After rejecting the concept two years earlier, Washington began testing seines and traps in the lower Columbia River in 2009. Although inadequate efforts to install a suitable fish trap initially failed, it was not at all surprising that both beach and small purse seines were found to be effective both at catching and in releasing fish with minimal impact. Later that year, Washington's Fish and Wildlife Commission adopted a landmark Hatchery and Fishery Reform Policy recognizing the need to *"develop, promote and implement alternative fishing gear to maximize catch of hatchery-origin fish with minimal mortality to native salmon and steelhead."*

The Coastal Conservation Association (CCA) is a non-profit organization currently comprised of 17 coastal state chapters. CCA originated in Texas in 1977 and spread to other Gulf Coast and Eastern Seaboard states. Although it has been involved in many issues, particularly those relating to fishing and catch allocation, CCA is best known for spearheading successful efforts to curtail inshore gillnet fishing. In 2007, due largely to the efforts of Gary Loomis, a well-known manufacturer of fishing rods, CCA chapters were established in Washington and Oregon.

CCA in the Northwest soon became involved in many different issues, but from the very beginning the major target was the Columbia River gillnet fishery that occurs in the lower river below Bonneville Dam. Although the lower river separates the two states, which had historically co-managed the fishery, the official border crowds the Washington shore so that the vast majority of the river and fishing is in Oregon. A CCA-sponsored Oregon Initiative outlawing gillnets while allowing for more sustainable selective commercial fishing garnered the signatures required to qualify it for the 2012 general fall election.

During the pre-election fray, Oregon Governor John Kitzhaber, then enjoying widespread popularity in the midst of his third term, stepped forward with a compromise that was acceptable to the initiative sponsors but strongly opposed by the commercial-fishing communities. Kitzhaber would phase in the commercial selective fishing reforms in the main-stem Columbia but allow gillnetting in off-channel bays and other areas that were frequented by few wild fish but heavily stocked with hatchery fish in these so-called "safe areas". In addition, the proposal allocated a higher fraction of the allowable catch to the recreational fishery.

Although CCA's initiative remained on the ballot, the sponsors abandoned their campaign for the initiative measure, shifted their support to Kitzhaber's proposal and urged others to do the same. Nevertheless, the measure remained on the ballot and, as could be expected, was rejected by a significant margin. Although commercial and tribal fishing interests attempted to characterize the defeat as overwhelming public support for the continuation of gillnet fishing, the contention was effectively mitigated by the circumstances leading up to the election[104].

Native American tribal leaders have been critical of state actions that would curtail gillnet fishing by non-tribal members. In a 9/6/12 news release, The Columbia River Inter-Tribal Fish Commission opposed the 2012 Oregon Measure outlawing non-tribal gillnets in the lower Columbia. The Northwest Indian Fisheries Commission had done the same in response to I-640 in 1996 also doing away with non-Indian gillnets. It appears that the unspoken reason for this is that the tribes would prefer not to be identified as the only users of irrational gear. Ironically, although documentation resulting from early "European" contacts with Northwest Indians includes many descriptions of fishing methods suitable for selective fishing (seines, weirs, traps, reef nets, dip nets, etc.), one would be hard pressed to locate a reference to gillnets in these early references.

During the 2012 gubernatorial campaign in Washington, CCA polled both ultimate winner Jay Inslee and runner-up republican Rob McKenna and both had favored Columbia River fishery reform. This, and Washington's 2009 fishery reform policy, set the stage for working with Oregon to develop a plan and time table to implement Kitzhaber's proposal. Lawsuits by gillnet interests in both states to derail the process have thus far failed, and foot dragging among important members of the fisheries agencies have frustrated proponents for change. However, it appears that we may finally be turning the corner for fishery reform.

21   Salmon Habitat: the Ninth Life of the Green River

Environmental depredations to the productivity of our waters
began during the middle of the nineteenth century following the
migrations of Europeans into the Pacific Northwest. Even before, the
westward pursuit and over-exploitation of beavers to satisfy European
sartorial tastes in hats doubtlessly impacted stream ecology and native
trout populations[105]. Subsequent activities were so wantonly destructive
that it is difficult to understand how they were ever tolerated. The timber
industry's widespread use of splash dams epitomizes the disregard for
salmon habitat that persisted well into the twentieth century.

Lacking railways and roads, logs from the hinterlands were moved by
flowing water. Wooden splash dams were designed to store enough water
to create flash floods of a magnitude sufficient to wash giant logs cut from
the ancient forests to staging sites where they could be rafted or otherwise
transported to mills. In Grays Harbor County alone there were more than
200 such dams and some of them were as high as 45 feet[106]. One can only
imagine the damage to salmon and habitat resulting from the periodic
drying followed by flash floods and huge logs tearing through spawning
gravel. Lowland farmers were also impacted by the rampaging floods that
tore huge chunks from pastures and drowned livestock. Cheaper ways of
transporting logs by rail and road, rather than concerns for the salmon,
finally eliminated the use of splash dams although some continued to
operate well into the 1930s.

As splash dams faded from the scene they were being replaced with
infinitely more imposing concrete barriers to satisfy growing demands for
power, irrigation, and to curtail flooding that threatened developments
in natural flood plains; where natural rivers meander and provide critical
habitat for salmon and other wildlife. Much has been written on the
effect of dams on salmon and the costly attempts to mitigate the damage
with hatcheries and, apart from applauding current projects removing
obsolete fish-blocking dams, I need say no more[107].

The fact that viable stocks of wild Chinook, coho and chum salmon,
and steelhead still exist in many urban Washington streams is more a
tribute to the resilience of the fish than to responsible stewardship. This
may be most dramatically demonstrated in the state's most populous

and highly developed region – the Duwamish basin – a river and bay receiving its waters that have much to do with the development of salmon angling in the Pacific Northwest.

My first memories of the river valley were from atop Beacon Hill, during World War II at a time when barrage balloons floated above the city, searchlights crisscrossed the sky over the blacked-out neighborhoods, and occasional test bursts of anti-aircraft fire punctuated the ambience of wartime Seattle. It was an exciting time for young boys far removed from significant discomforts of war and buoyed by propaganda fueling enthusiasm for the conflict. Jack Armstrong, Little Orphan Annie, Captain Midnight, and the other stars of the 15-minute after-school radio serials had joined with comic book super heroes to do their best to win the war.

Boys are particularly fascinated with war planes, and just over the crest of Beacon Hill, amid the Duwamish flood plain, is the birthplace of the B-17 Flying Fortress and B-29 Super Fort. From atop the hill the factory and hangers would have dominated the view if not for the cleverly camouflaged structures made to appear as innocent farm buildings and pasture. In spite of my obsession with water and fish, the dark waters of the languid river located beyond the airfield, with its constricted banks and ugly surroundings was of little interest.

Boeing is only one of many industries located on the Duwamish flood plain. Early in the Twentieth Century, using fill from regrades of nearby hills, the river's multi-channeled estuary and tide flats were replaced by what was then, at 350 acres, the world's largest artificial island. Harbor Island, surrounded by the East and West Channels of the Duwamish and Elliott Bay on the north, held this title until 1938. My father worked in a ship yard and my maternal grandfather in a mill that were both located on Harbor Island. Dozens of other heavy and light industries had taken over the former estuary of the Duwamish.

As a boy I was puzzled over why the lower river was the Duwamish while the same river, above Tukwila, was the Green River. It wasn't until years later that I learned that the distinction results from a series of man-made diversions of three tributaries named according to the color of their waters: the clear Green, the glacial White, and the tannin-tinged Black draining Lake Washington. Cedar River originally joined the Black, near present-day Renton, to flow for a short distance into the north side of the Duwamish at what is now Tukwila.

In 1912, in order to alleviate flooding in Renton, the Cedar was diverted into the south end of Lake Washington and from there, joined with lake water, flowed into the Black. Upstream at Auburn, the White River and Green joined creating the Duwamish. But the White, a naturally wayward and troublesome stream, split in its lower reaches and the southern branch, the Stuck, flowed into the Puyallup and on to Tacoma's Commencement Bay. Following a natural flood diverting the entire White into the Puyallup, a dam was completed in 1916 that permanently diverted the White's entire flow into the Puyallup.

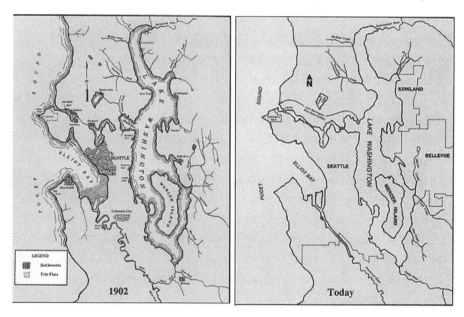

Figure 39. The lower Duwamish and Lake Washington systems before (left) and after (right) watershed diversions. The White River at its junction with the Green River is south of the depicted area. The figure on the left is inaccurate in not reflecting the greater surface area of the lake before it was lowered in 1916. From Lake Washington Ship Canal – Wikipedia, the free encyclopedia.

The construction of the Lake Washington Ship Canal lowered the level of Lake Washington by nine feet in 1916 and dried up the Black River so that flows of the remaining tributaries of the lake, including Cedar River, entered Puget Sound through the Ballard Locks at Shilshole Bay. The official origin of the Duwamish River is now considered to be below the historic mouth of the Black River and above that it is the Green. These former Duwamish tributaries, comprising 70% of the river's original drainage, were all important salmon streams and the flow from the Green is all that remains of today's Duwamish. It was then left entirely to the returning salmon and steelhead to decide where they belonged.

In 1911, 61 miles above tide-water, a significant portion of the Green was diverted to Tacoma for municipal and industrial use. The diverting structure blocked thousands of upstream-migrating fish from access to many miles of suitable habitat and also resulted in low downstream summer flows that were detrimental to wild salmon and steelhead. The Washington State Department of Fish and Game attempted to mitigate the loss at the cul-de-sac by trapping and taking all of the available spawn. The egg-taking records at the site provide the best information on the magnitude of the salmon and steelhead runs eliminated by the diversion[108]. Due to diminishing returns the effort was discontinued in 1920.

From April, 1912 through the end of the following March, more than 14 million eggs were taken at the barrier. From 1912 through 1920 peak counts of mature females (males were not counted) were 280 Chinook (1917), 3117 coho (1912) and 1308 steelhead (1912). The relatively low numbers of Chinook that were trapped at the diversion were influenced by a weir spanning the lower Green at the mouth of Soos Creek that was erected annually between 1904 and 1924 to capture Chinook salmon for the local hatchery. A weir is similar to a "picket fence" across a stream with pickets spaced to prevent the passage of fish of specific size.

The prevailing belief at the time was that natural spawning was wasteful in comparison to artificial production and efforts were made to maximize interception of Chinook at the weir. But during fall freshet, along with the associated debris, weirs are subject to failure and this allowed some Chinook to reach the upper river. The weir would have had little if any impact on upstream returns of coho salmon or steelhead which occurred at different times and during even higher flows.

In 1962, about 5 miles above the Tacoma diversion, 235-foot- high Howard Hansen Dam was completed to contain flood water in the lower valley. Since fish were already blocked at the Tacoma diversion, the dam had no facilities for either up- or downstream fish passage, thus further complicating access to the pristine salmon and steelhead habitat that still exists upstream. The resulting flood control accelerated the transfer of lower valley land from agricultural to industrial use along with the attendant increase in environmental consequences. However, the dam's storage capacity was also beneficial to fish by augmenting flows during periods of low water and reducing flood-related scouring of naturally spawned eggs in the river below.

In 2001, because of the extraordinarily high level of toxic sediments in the much maligned estuary – the health of which is considered a key component of juvenile salmon survival – the U.S. Environmental Protection Agency listed the waters as a federal Superfund site. Among other problems, it was determined that juvenile salmon from the lower Duwamish exhibited reduced growth and immune system function relative to salmon from uncontaminated areas.

Given these facts and nothing else, who would have ever guessed that the Green River, until well into the Twenty-first Century, would host Puget Sound's most stable population of Chinook salmon? Even though higher fractions of Green River Chinook salmon are typically harvested, than from the larger and relatively pristine streams to the north, the numbers of natural spawners, consisting of both hatchery strays and natural origin fish, consistently rivaled the numbers escaping to the Skagit and Snohomish river systems[109]. Although many of the adult Chinook naturally spawning in the Green originated in the hatchery, located on a tributary (Soos Creek) near Auburn, indications are that wild-origin fish comprised a significant portion of the run.

These adverse conditions, through a process akin to natural selection, may have played a role in creating a tough and adaptable stock of Chinook salmon. Most of state and tribal hatcheries in Puget Sound depend upon transplanted Green River Chinook. The Chinook salmon successfully stocked into the Great Lakes during the 1960s are Green River fish and they have since established many natural spawning populations throughout the region. South America even has wild Chinook salmon after Green River fish, apparent fugitives from fish-farming ventures, became established in Patagonian streams.

Since the ESA listing of Puget Sound Chinook, NOAA Fisheries[110] has determined that wild populations in specific rivers throughout the region must be restored before official overall recovery can be achieved. At least three of these identified populations are Green River Chinook that have been transplanted into other rivers (Nisqually, Skokomish, as well one or more of the so-called mid Hood Canal streams: Hamma Hamma, Duckabush and/or Dosewallips). Although the native population in the Green itself was originally identified in the ESA recovery plan as a "category *1 population*" deserving the highest priority for recovery, it has since been quietly given lesser status by NOAA Fisheries, with consent of the co-managers, who are apparently willing to relegate it to perpetual domesticity in its native waters. There are two reasons for this – one said and the other unspoken.

Maintaining a viable wild population of Chinook salmon, shaped by natural selection and the resulting ability to adapt to a changing environment, will require fishing selectively so that wild-origin fish are afforded the protection required for recovery and hatchery fish provide the harvest. This could be accomplished without reducing the catch by taking full advantage of fish surplus to hatchery needs. More wild-origin fish, and a corresponding reduction of natural-spawning hatchery fish, would also increase natural productivity and facilitate integration of wild fish into the hatchery brood stock in conformation with hatchery reform recommendations. However, the Muckleshoot Tribe is not interested in fishing selectively and, lacking a viable dispute resolution system, there is no way of effectively addressing the issue.

The other reason given by state and federal fisheries authorities for giving up on Green River wild Chinook is that conditions in the river are viewed as being on an irreversible downward trend for wild-fish production. This potentially self-fulfilling prophecy is inconsistent with ongoing public expenditures to restore the Duwamish basin. The projected cost of the Superfund alone, to clean up the lower river, is $300 million and enormous environmental expenditures have been made elsewhere in the basin. These investments appear at odds with any gloomy assessment of the future.

The on-going surge in wild pink salmon production in the Green River also flies in the face of the assessment of the existing habitat. In recent cycle years, hundreds of thousands of these fish, far more than in the past – when the highest recorded count was 13 fish – have returned to the river. Prior to this phenomenon, the biological consensus would have been that here, at the southern extremity of the range of pink salmon, wild Chinook are far better adapted to the Green than pink salmon. Could it be that wild Chinook have not been given the chance?

It appears that Seattle, and the citizens of King County, would be proud to have a viable population of wild Chinook salmon that migrated through the heart of the city and spawned in the last remaining tributary of the Duwamish. The fact that this is indeed a legacy population of native fish that played an important role in the development of the city and the salmon sport fishery, would be frosting on the cake.

22 A Cleaner, More Productive Puget Sound

The productivity of Puget Sound has suffered. Changes are most profound south of the Tacoma Narrows where survivals of hatchery Chinook and coho have plummeted from some of the state's highest to the lowest. Annual sport catches of south sound resident Chinook and coho salmon there have decreased from tens of thousands during the 70s and 80s to only a few hundred currently. I don't know of anyone who has seen a herring ball here in recent years. Elsewhere in the sound, populations of resident salmon are depressed and formerly common, if not abundant, species (e.g., various members of the codfish family, sablefish and others) no longer find these waters to their liking.

In addition to the decrease in survivals of Chinook, coho and steelhead originating in the Puget Sound basin, there appear to be significant shifts in the composition and numbers of marine species encountered by the angler. In the surfperch family (all live-bearers), clouds of miniature shiners have replaced the larger pile and striped seaperch that once could be viewed grazing on life-encrusted pilings anywhere in the Sound. The once abundant members of the codfish family – Pacific cod, tomcod, walleye pollock, and hake – have all but disappeared. Tomcod and pollock were often a nuisance to salmon anglers as far south as Anderson Island. During the 1970s pollock were even targeted by a small fleet of charter boats operating out of the Tacoma Narrows. Juvenile sablefish that once competed with salmon for surface-trolled baits or lures in the summer tide rips of the northern sound are gone. Rock sole that appeared to be the dominant flatfishes seem to have given way to the smaller, but no less abundant, sand dabs. While fishing pressure may have contributed to the demise of cod and hake, as it certainly has to local rockfishes, environmental changes appear to be heavily involved in the shifts in abundance of the other species.

The Puget Sound Partnership, established in 2007, is charged with achieving lofty goals for cleaning up the Sound by 2020. In more than half of the allotted time, little if any progress is being made to improve conditions for fish in Puget Sound, nor have listed Chinook and steelhead shown signs of recovery. Our stewardship has failed to protect this jewel in the crown of the Northwest. A new and more aggressive approach is sorely needed to do the job.

Hopefully, even with the retirement of Congressman Norm Dicks, the strongest proponent of clean-up, someone will step into the breach to restore Puget Sound to its former health and productivity. A successful effort in this direction could be highly beneficial to salmon and other species and would significantly improve the quality of life within the region. Not that long ago, obituaries were being written on Lake Erie. Its subsequent resurrection now provides quality angling for most of the important North American fresh-water game fishes, including our "own" relocated salmon and steelhead.

A current New York State Department of Environmental Conservation website describes the outstanding fishing in Lake Erie and tributaries for steelhead recognized as originating in Washington. Elsewhere the agency touts its fishery for salmon originating in our Green River. In view of the enormous size of Lake Erie, it's relatively slow flushing rate, the surrounding industry and population density, it appears that repairing Puget Sound is within our reach if we have the will to do so.

The phenomenal increase in south sound pink salmon is the glaring exception to this discouraging trend. In addition, south Puget Sound chum salmon and cutthroat trout appear to be holding their own. Reduced competition from juvenile coho could be increasing stream survivals of cutthroat which have also benefited from catch-and-release rules.

23   Allocation – Or Who Should Get the Fish?

From the perspective of a Washington State fisheries manager, distributing the allowable catch is the most contentious part of the job. But first of all, harvest levels that do not impair future yields must be determined along with provisions that satisfy treaty Indian fishing rights. Although pressure from fishing interests and miscalculations may result in over-fishing, a great deal of attention is given to determining appropriate harvest levels. As indicated in a previous chapter, much less attention is given to achieving the treaty-mandated catch allocations – with non-Indian Chinook and coho salmon fishers in the Boldt Case Area being the losers. This loss is worsened by failing to optimize the value of what the public is allowed to catch.

For example, salmon fishing off the outer Washington Coast is limited to hook-and-line fishing by commercial trollers[k] using a multitude of lines and lures, and recreational anglers. Ocean salmon fishing is controlled by the Pacific Fisheries Management Council (PFMC) comprised of members from Washington, Oregon, California and Idaho, operating under the Federal Magnuson-Stevens Act. Prior to the opening of the salmon sportfishing season off the outer Washington coast, commercial trollers exercise a privilege granted by the PFMC of taking "half" of the allowable *landed* non-Indian ocean Chinook catch – the same "biting" fish that could otherwise be caught by anglers. Commercial troll-caught salmon are known for their quality and command a high price. In recent years about 80 vessels participated in this fishery with only 20 or so accounting for a major portion of the catch.

Among its other responsibilities, the PFMC collects economic information, indicating that in recent years, in terms of "value to coastal communities and state incomes", Washington's coastal salmon sport fishery is worth five times that of its commercial counterpart. In view of the differences in value, it appears logical that managers might consider shifting a higher fraction of the allowable Chinook catch to the sport fishery. But even if the Council somehow concludes that evenly dividing the catch makes sense, the method of doing so by counting numbers in the landed catch appears even more obviously flawed.

Coastal salmon catches are limited by their impact on the weakest stock[1] in the mixture of available fish and/or to satisfy treaty Indian catch sharing. Impacts include fish landed and counted as well as the estimated uncounted waste resulting from the specific fishing method. As a result, in order to land half of the catch, the troll fishery kills for more fish do due a higher rate of by-catch mortality. In this case, catch division clearly flies in the face of economics and biological sensibility. Catch division only makes sense if it considers total fishing mortality. Doing so encourages the use and development of less wasteful fishing methods. Washington has yet to bring this issue to the PFMC for rectification.

Since these Chinook are primarily north-migrating stocks they are exposed to a more intensive commercial harvest in the Canadian and Alaskan troll fisheries and will subsequently be taken in commercial inshore and river nets as well. The elimination of the non-Indian portion of the Washington troll fishery, leaving half of the ocean harvest in the commercial tribal catch, would have a negligible impact on the availability of fish to local markets. It would increase the value of the non-tribal catch, and reduce the existing level of waste. Since the sport catch is, with few exceptions, locally consumed – rather than sold to the highest bidder and often exported – transferring the catch to the sport fishery would virtually ensure that the catch is used within the region.

Reallocating the 45,000 or so Chinook salmon currently taken annually by the troll fleet into the sport fishery could result in an additional 100,000 angler trips per year that would be worth millions to coastal communities and the state. Washington anglers currently lay out many hundreds of dollars to fly to Alaska for two or three days of fishing for a chance of bringing home one or two Chinook salmon – fish and dollars that could otherwise be available at home.

Between 1976 and 2003, due in large part to competition from farmed salmon, the inflation-adjusted value of troll-caught Chinook salmon plummeted by about 75%, but has since rebounded. The recovery was facilitated by a vigorous federally funded campaign promoting *wild* salmon; the implication was obvious – don't buy farmed fish. These expenditures went so far as to provide $0.5 million to paint a giant "wild" Chinook salmon onto an *Alaska Airlines* passenger plane. However, there now appears to be more objective comparisons of farmed and wild salmon[m] coming to light that may again negatively impact prices paid for troll-caught fish. In addition, salmon farmers appear to be effectively addressing environmental problems associated with their industry. The fact is that if the price to the consumer of a Pacific Northwest "wild" Chinook salmon included the cost of management and production, only the richest could ever afford one.

During the last 150 years of our Nation's history there has been a gradual shift from hunting and fishing for the market to doing it for pleasure and personal use. The trend is a consequence of an ever increasing population and limited resources. Sustainable commercial use of most of our marine fishes remains the best and wisest use, but it appears that in our State we have passed the time when the non-tribal catch of Chinook and coho salmon should be designated primarily for recreational use. Such is not the case with pink, sockeye and chum salmon. It is also noteworthy that Treaty Indian fishing rights essentially guarantee that a large fraction of Washington's Chinook and coho catch will remain commercially available.

Fishing guides, like gill-netters and commercial trollers, are professional fishermen. Guides, however, generally require killing fewer fish to make a living. There is even an increasing trend among anglers, particularly those willing to pay for the most expensive guides, to release their entire catch. For various reasons, including the sporadic and unpredictable open seasons, and unlike what has occurred in British Columbia and Alaska, services that feature high-quality saltwater fishing experiences are not readily available in Washington.

The charter boats operating out of the various coastal ports, specializing in large groups of anglers using heavy tackle, provide a valuable service. But this is not the kind of experience that results from close contact with a knowledgeable guide who is an expert in catching fish in a manner most pleasing to the angler. Clearing the way for this service to expand, which includes reallocating the commercial troll catch of Chinook salmon to the recreational fishery and open seasons that one can depend upon, could result in a new corps of professional fishermen-guides with a future.

Evaluating the true value of Washington's recreational salmon fishing is complicated. Studies, involving travel, other expenditures and interviews are used to arrive at estimates that even then, although uniformly high, appear questionable. Such estimates usually neglect the concept of consumer surplus, which is the value of the fishing experience minus the cost of participating. This concept can be applied to any recreational activity and is a significant factor in determining where we choose to live and work. There are doubtlessly many living in the Puget Sound region who have foregone opportunities for significantly higher salaries elsewhere in favor of maintaining access to fishing or some other recreational activity. I and no doubt others, view consumer surplus from angling as a significant portion of overall wealth. Economists have attempted to place dollar values on consumer surplus with surveys asking participants how much they would be willing to pay if the particular activity was no longer free. My experience with such surveys[111] dealing with anglers is that for various reasons it is difficult to get reliable responses – one being that an honest answer could be used to justify a substantial new fee.

I leave it to others to provide methods of measuring consumer surplus. At the present time, since anglers are drawn to good and inexpensive fishing, levels of participation may be its best measure. Participation should also be an important factor in evaluating how well our recreational fisheries are being managed. By this measure alone we are not doing well. Although Washington's population doubled from 1976 to 2009, participation in saltwater salmon angling decreased by two thirds.

In other parts of the world an economic evaluation of salmon angling is far less complicated. In Iceland and northern Europe, the fishing rights on specific waters are sold at the market price. Although netting the fish for the market is an option, selling angling privileges is the overwhelming choice of successful entrepreneurs. The cost to an angler for a day's fishing on a salmon stream can be thousands of dollars. This is indicative of consumer surplus values of salmon angling in Washington where, when fishing is good, we spend relatively little to participate.

More than once, the Icelandic Director of Freshwater Fisheries has visited Washington and fished for Chinook salmon at less expense, including travel, than he would have paid for Atlantic salmon fishing at home. Considering what people elsewhere are willing to pay for angling of no greater, and often lesser, value than what was available here is a clear indication of the contribution of salmon angling to our quality of life.

24   Restoring Washington's Salmon Sport Fishery

On the eve of my 82nd year, with memories of the Sound and its fish spanning all but a few of those years, we headed for Kingston. But the usual pleasure and excitement associated with going fishing was lacking. It was the traffic. In the pre-dawn darkness of a mid-winter work day, we faced an unending river of south-bound headlights and nothing but tail lights ahead. Joining the two-way flow on the Narrows Bridge, already appearing in need of more expansion, a nostalgic glimpse toward Point Evans and Defiance provided only momentary relief.

Passing turn-offs to fishing areas of former years – Hale Pass, Purdy, Manchester, Agate Pass, and Hansville – the congestion continued. Everywhere there were cars, lights, houses, and new developments. Where did all these people come from, where are they going, when did it happen and why hadn't I noticed it before? It was much the same all the way to our destination where a large marina had sprung from the ground. It was as if I had awoken from a 50-year nap. The optimism that I had maintained for half a century was suddenly shaken, along with any remaining pride in what had occurred during my stewardship.

The most difficult task in restoring our sport fishery to a semblance of the past will be repairing damage inflicted upon the Puget Sound Basin by development and population increase. In order to fill the breach left by retired Congressman Norm Dicks, a new champion with stature and commitment for the cause is sorely needed. Our strongest ally in this effort should be the Treaty Indian Tribes. Utilizing the second (environmental) edge of their Treaty sword they should be a powerful force. Other tasks, summarized below, appear to be almost "low hanging fruit" by comparison.

Federal and state fisheries management often behaves as though they believe that treaty Indian fishing rights supersede conservation and the Endangered Species Act. This is inconsistent with my experience with Judge George Boldt and his expert Fisheries Advisor, when conservation was *the* foremost consideration in resolving disputes. A clear definition of the relationship between conservation and Indian treaty fishing rights is necessary to proceed with rational management and salmon recovery.

State-Tribal fisheries co-management is not functioning well and the depleted stocks of mutually important salmon are showing no signs of recovery. Significant changes in management strategy are necessary to do the job. The consensus required for significant change is seldom forthcoming. Efficient, science-based dispute resolution is desperately needed to get the process on track.

The State has failed to adequately represent the interests of recreational salmon anglers in dealing with the Treaty Indian Tribes. In my opinion, the state is negligent in failing to exercise the authority granted by the federal courts. The chronic shortfalls in the non-treaty share of Chinook and coho salmon in the Boldt Case Area result from this problem. A fresh new approach by the State in dealing with the tribes is sorely needed.

A large fraction of the catch of Chinook and coho salmon originating in Washington hatcheries and rivers is taken north of the border, while our catches include relatively few Chinook and coho originating elsewhere. Washington must continue to seek agreements and policies that return the fruits of its waters and investments to the citizens of the State.

An international authority on fish conservation once said, to the effect, that a primary role of fisheries managers is writing obituaries on formerly important stocks of fish. This assessment is not without merit. Although fisheries managers are limited in what they can do regarding impacts resulting from population increase and the associated developments, there is much to be done within their own bailiwick to make fishing less wasteful, sustainable harvest more valuable, natural spawning more productive and hatcheries more cost effective. In doing so, the public will become more aware of the value of the resource and willing to provide the support needed. Our experience during implementation of the Thirteen Point Program demonstrated that citizens of the state and their political representatives are eager to support efforts that improve local fishing.

It appears that salmon anglers alone could derive significantly more enjoyment from their sport by redefining their goals and expectations. Remarkable attitudinal changes focusing on the joys of fishing, rather than killing fish, have occurred elsewhere in the recreational fishing community. Examples in freshwater include bass and wild-trout fishing; billfish and other species in saltwater. These shifts have resulted in increasing the overall value and sustainability of these resources. Salmon anglers appear to remain focused on bringing home the bacon to the extent that a frequently heard boast is how quickly it took to kill a limit. Rather than derive pleasure and satisfaction from catching and carefully releasing a wild salmon, the requirement is often perceived as troublesome in interfering with one's overall objective.

Salmon are somewhat different in that the wisest and best use of healthy stocks does involve killing and eating them. Hatchery fish are produced specifically for this purpose and it is often a disservice to wild salmon to kill too few of the former. Despite this, much can be gained by altering the views prevalent among Washington's salmon anglers.

Acknowledgements

Dr. Keith Jefferts, founder of Northwest Marine Technology and an unfailing proponent of rational fisheries management, is primarily responsible for providing me with the time and resources to complete this project. NMT's biological staff: Victoria Heath, Geraldine Vander Haegen and Dave Knutzen have never hesitated to assist me in this and other endeavors on innumerable occasions. Many of the references to salmon derbies and Puget Sound during the good old days resulted from the records of Don Edge who maintains an excellent website on the topic.

My good friend Pete Bergman has been an inspiration to me throughout my professional career, and our fifty-plus-year association has led to many of the views herein expressed. Special tribute is due to our colleague Lee Blankenship who has eagerly taken up the baton and in doing so has done more than any other person I know of to implement the reforms needed to rationalize salmon management in Washington.

I am most appreciative of Dr. Richard Whitney for his exhaustive review and many suggestions. Most of which have been incorporated into this book.

Particular recognition is due to Angela my wife of 60 years, who has made the best of our relatively modest lifestyle, withstood countless days alone while I have pursued my interests, and done her best to enjoy our thinly disguised vacations that invariably involved fishing. Thanks also for her care that added quality years to my life, without which I could never have written this document. And most of all, for the care, love and example she has provided for our offspring.

Finally, as a proud father, I dedicate this effort to Michael, Gregory and Mary Gwendoline who willingly accepted the fact that a trip to Disneyland could never compete with the natural wonders of Washington and the Pacific Northwest.

List of Figures

Figure 1: Chinook salmon: Photo courtesy of the Washington Department of Fish and Game.

Figure 2: Coho salmon: Photo courtesy of the Washington Department of Fish and Game.

Figure 3: Pink salmon: Photo courtesy of the Washington Department of Fish and Game.

Figure 4: Chum salmon: Photo courtesy of the Washington Department of Fish and Game.

Figure 5: Sockeye salmon: Photo is courtesy of the Washington Department of Fish and Game.

Figure 6: A miniature cutthroat trout from a small western Washington creek. Author photo.

Figure 7: Sea-run cutthroat trout (*Oncorhynchus clarki*) from Case Inlet, Puget Sound. Author photo.

Figure 8: Author's concept of how a Makah fish hook may have been baited with herring.

Figure 9: Lummi men trolling for salmon. University of Washington Libraries, Special Collections NA689.

Figure 10: This photograph of another form of hook-and-line fishing by the Makah was taken from a 1938 U.S. Bureau of Fisheries Bulletin with the following caption: "Modified floating hook-and-line gear used for coho salmon by the natives at Neah Bay before white fishermen operated in that district. The bone hook was baited with a whole herring." The text of the accompanying article further describes the gear as consisting of "... a bladder float to which is attached a line of twisted sinew suspending a stone weight. A second line is fastened to the weight, and the free end is attached to a shank of whalebone bearing a double hook of bone lashed with bark. As many as thirty of these units were attached together, each hook was baited with a whole herring, and the string was drifted from a canoe. Both types of gear were fished close to the surface, and the principal catch was coho salmon, preferred by the natives because of its suitability for drying."

Figure 11: Yelm Jim's weir on the Puyallup River (C.A. 1885). Courtesy of the Washington State Museum. These remarkable structures for capturing salmon were among the many devices widely used by Indians throughout the Pacific Northwest.

Figure 12: Trolling gear: 1940's era rod and reel, ("jigger") spoons, plugs, rotating flasher and herring dodger (below). Author photo.

Figure 13: Harry Dunagan's Seattle waterfront (ca. 1911). University of Washington Libraries, Special Collections SEA2170.31

Figure 30: A modern salmon trap on the Russian Coast in the Sea of Japan. Photo is courtesy of Guido Rahr of the Wild Salmon Center.

Figure 31: President Harry Truman, with a Puget Sound "blackmouth", and Governor Mon C. Wallgren to his right, aboard the *M. V. Olympus* in 1945. George Skadding/the LIFE Picture Collection/Getty Images.

Figure 32: The author issuing Governor Albert Rosellini with the first Sport Salmon Catch Record ("Punch Card") in 1963 for the 1964 season. Washington Department of Fisheries photo.

Figure 33: Director of Fisheries Donald Moos with a tethered male Wannock River Chinook salmon on a later expedition.

Figure 34: Corrected charts, from WDFW, showing Puget Sound Tribal (black) and Non-Tribal (gray) catches of Chinook and coho salmon for the years 2000 through 2007. Catch sharing has not varied significantly through 2013.

Figure 35: Entangled seal pups attracted to salmon in a tribal Puget Soundriver gillnet. Losses of salmon from such nets are not accounted for. Photo is courtesy of the Washington Department of Fish and Wildlife.

Figure 36: Diagram of a reef net. Courtesy of the Puget Sound Reef Netters Association.

Figure 37: Lifting a San Juan Island reef net. Photo courtesy of Kathi Melville.

Figure 38: Squaxin Island tribal fisherman beach seining for coho salmon near Olympia. Author photo.

Figure 39: The lower Duwamish and Lake Washington systems before (left) and after (right) watershed diversions. The White River at its junction with the Green River is south of the depicted area. The figure on the left is inaccurate in not reflecting the greater surface area of the lake before it was lowered in 1916. From Lake Washington Ship Canal – Wikipedia, the free encyclopedia.

End Notes

1. Haig-Brown, R. 1943. A *River Never Sleeps*. 364 pages.

2. Haw, Frank, H. O. Wendler and Gene Deschamps. 1967. "Development of Washington State Salmon Sport Fishery through 1964." State of WA Dept. of Fish., Res. Bull. No. 7.

3. Washington State Sport Catch Reports 1967-2000. Washington Department of Fisheries 1967-1991. Washington Department of Fish and Wildlife 1992 – 2000.

4. Bagley, Clarence B. 1929. *History of King County Washington*. 1929. S. J. Clarke Publishing Company.

5. Wilkes, Charles. 1845. "Narrative of the United States exploring expeditions during the years 1838, 1839, 1840, 1841, 1842." Volume 4. Lea and Blanchard, Philadelphia.

6. Collins, J. W. 1892. "Report of the fisheries of the Pacific Coast of the U.S." Rep. U.S. Comm. Fish 1888, App. 1:269.

7. Rathbun, Richard. 1893. "A review of the fisheries in the contiguous waters of the State of Washington and British Columbia." Report U.S. Fish Commission for 1899, pp. 254-350, plates. Washington.

8. Swan, James G. 1868. "The Indians of Cape Flattery: at the entrance to the Strait of Fuca, Washington Territory." Smithsonian contributions to knowledge; XVI (8).

9. Heizer, Robert F. (Editor). 1820. "Narrative of the adventures and sufferings of John R. Jewitt while held as a captive of the Nootka Indians of Vancouver Island, 1803 to 1805."

10. Croes, Dale R. 1995. "The Hoko River archaeological site complex." The wet/dry site (45CA213), 3,000-1,700 B.P.

11. Stewart, Hilary. 1977. *Indian fishing: Early Methods on the Northwest Coast.* Douglas & McIntyre – Vancouver/Toronto. University of Washington Press – Seattle.

12. Craig, J. A. and R. L Hacker. 1940. "The history and development of the fisheries of the Columbia River." U.S. Department of the Interior, Bureau of Fisheries, Bulletin 32.

13. Rounsefell, G. A. and G. B. Kelez. 1938. "The salmon and salmon fisheries of Swiftshure Bank, Puget Sound, and the Fraser River." U.S. Department of Commerce Bureau of Fisheries, Bulletin No. 27.

14. Pressey, Richard T. 1953. "The sport fishery for salmon on Puget Sound." Washington Dept. of Fisheries, Fisheries Research Papers (1) l:33-49.

15. Craig, Joseph A. and Robert L. Hacker. 1940. "History and development of the fisheries of the Columbia River." U.S. Bureau of Fisheries Bulletin 32(49).

16. Holder, Charles F. 1908. :Sport fishing in California and Florida." Bulletin of the Bureau of Fisheries, Vol. XXVIII, Part I.

17. Christianson, Russell R. 2011, Tacoma Tackle. Manufacturers and their fishing tackle from Tacoma, Washington. Russell R. Christianson, PO Box 791, Freeland, WA 98249.

18. Lone, Jim and Mark Spogen. 2005. Salmon Plugs of the Northwest. Lone&Spogen, PO Box 17577, Seattle, WA 98127.

19. Bradner, Enos. 1969. *Northwest Angling.* Binfords & Mort, Publishers. Second Edition.

20 Wing, Robert C., with Newell, Gordon. 1979. *Peter Puget.* Gray Beard Publishing, Seattle, WA.

21. Wilkes, Charles. 1845. "Narrative of the United States exploring expeditions during the years 1838, 1839, 1840, 1841, 1842." Volume 4. Lea and Blanchard, Philadelphia.

22. Scofield, W. L. 1956. "Trolling gear in California." California Dept. of Fish and Game. Marine Fisheries Branch Fish Bulletin No. 103.

23. Reichert, Milton S. (Editor) 1935. *Fishing Guide to the Northwest.* General Publishing Corp., Seattle, WA.

24. Bradner, Enos. 1969. *Northwest Angling.* Binfords & Mort, Publishers. Second Edition.

25. Haig-Brown, Roderick L. 1964. *Fisherman's Fall.* Lyons and Burford, Publishers.

26. Williams, Walter R. 1959. "The fishery for herring (*Clupea pallasi*) on Puget Sound. Fisheries Research Papers, Washington Dept. of Fisheries 2(2):5-29.

27. Pruter, Alonzo T. 1959. "Tagging experiments at Holme's Harbor, Washington." Fisheries Research Papers, Washington Dept. of Fisheries 2(2):66-70.

28. Pasquale, Nicholas. 1964. "Notable migrations of sablefish tagged in Puget Sound." Fish. Res. Pap. Washington Dept. of Fisheries 2 (3):68.

29. Rounsefell, G. A. and G. B. Kelez. 1938. "The salmon and salmon fisheries of Swiftshure Bank, Puget Sound, and the Fraser River." U.S. Department of Commerce Bureau of Fisheries, Bulletin No. 27.

30. Ferguson, Bruce, Johnson, Les, and Pat Trotter. 1985. *Fly Fishing for Pacific Salmon.* Frank Amato Publications.

31. Pressy, Richard T. 1953. "The sport fishery for salmon on Puget Sound." Washington Dept. of Fisheries, Fisheries Research Papers (1)1:33-49.

32. Haw, Frank, H. O. Wendler and Gene Deschamps. 1967. "Development of Washington State salmon sport fishery through 1964." State of Washington Dept. of Fisheries, research bulletin no. 7.

33. Kirkness, Walter. 1948. "Sport fishery on Puget Sound, and Food of the Chinook and silver salmon of Puget Sound." Two articles included in the 1948 Annual Report, State of Washington Department of Fisheries. 27-32.

34. Smith, Victor E. 1921. "The taking of immature salmon in the waters of the State of Washington." Thirtieth annual report of the State Fish Commission (Washington). Olympia.

35. Kirkness, Walter. 1948. "Sport fishery on Puget Sound, and Food of the Chinook and silver salmon of Puget Sound." Two articles included in the 1948 Annual Report, State of Washington Department of Fisheries. 27-32.

36. Jensen, Hans M. 1956. Fisheries Research Papers. Washington Department of Fisheries. "Migratory habits of pink salmon found in the Tacoma Narrows area of Puget Sound." 1(4):22-24.

37. Senn, Harry and R. M. Buckley. 1978. "Extended freshwater rearing of pink salmon at a Washington Hatchery". The Progressive Fish-Culturist 40(1):9-10.

38. Buckley, Raymond M. 1999. "Incidence of cannibalism and intra-generic predation by Chinook salmon (*Oncorhynchus tshawytscha*) in Puget Sound, Washington.: Ecological investigations, WA Dept. of Fish and Wildlife Fish Program, Resource Assessment Division.

39. Scheffer, V. B. and J. W. Slipp. 1948. "The whales and dolphins of Washington State with a key to the cetaceans of the west coast of North America." The American Midland Naturalist. 39(2): 257-337.

40. Wydoski, R. S. and R. R. Whitney. 2003. "Inland fishes of Washington" (Second Edition). American Fisheries Society, University of Washington Press.

41. Hendry, A. P., and T. P. Quinn. 1997. "Variation in adult life history and morphology among Lake Washington sockeye salmon (*Oncorhynchus nerka*) populations in relation to habitat features and ancestral affinities." Canadian Journal of Fisheries and Aquatic Science 54: 75-84.

42. Anonymous. 2007. "Pacific salmon commission joint Chinook technical committee report. Annual report on catch, escapement, exploitation rate analysis and model calibration of Chinook salmon under Pacific Salmon Commission jurisdiction, 2006."

43. Anonymous. 2012. "Pacific Salmon Commission Joint Chinook Technical Committee. 2011 exploitation rate analysis and model calibration." Report TCHINOOK(12)-2.

44. Martin, Paul J. *Port Angeles, Washington* – A History. (No date. Washington State Library, Olympia, WA).

45. Chasan, Daniel J. 1981. *The Water Link: A History of Puget Sound as a Resource.* University of Washington Press.

46. *Time* magazine. September 16, 1940. "Paris Derby", page 63.

47. *Time* magazine. October 14, 1940. "Dead Lice", page 68.

48. The *Seattle Times.* 1940: September 30, October 2, October 3.

49. Pressey, Richard T. 1953. "The sport fishery for salmon on Puget Sound." Washington Dept. of Fisheries, Fisheries Research Papers (1)1:33-49.

50. Anonymous (Frear, Gordon S., Editor). 1960. "Pacific Northwest Fishing and Hunting Guide." Wood and Reber, Inc., 500 Wall St., Seattle 1, WA.

51. Heard, W. R., Shevlyakov, E., Zikunova. O. V., and R. E. McNicol. 2007. "Chinook salmon – trends in abundance and biological characteristics." North Pacific Anadromous Fish Commission, Bulletin 4:77-91.

52. Pressy, Richard T. 1953. "The sport fishery for salmon on Puget Sound." Washington Dept. of Fisheries, Fisheries Research Papers (1)1:33-49.

53. Haw, Frank and Raymond M. Buckley. 1968. "The ability of Washington anglers to identify come common marine fishes." Calif. Fish and Game, 54 (1): 43-48.

54. Chasan, Daniel J. 1981. *The Water Link: A History of Puget Sound as a Resource.* University of Washington Press.

55. Smith, Victor E. 1922. "The taking of immature salmon in the waters of the State of Washington during the 1922 fishing season." The thirty-first annual report of the State Fish Commission (Washington). Olympia.

56. Haw, Frank and Raymond M. Buckley. 1973. *Saltwater Fishing in Washington.* Second edition. Stan Jones Publishing, Inc. 200 pages.

57. Childerhose, R. J. and M. Trim. 1979. *Pacific Salmon and Steelhead Trout.* University of Washington Press. 158 pages.

58. Irvine, J. R. and N. T. Johnston. 1992. "Coho salmon (*Oncorhynchus kisutch*) use of lakes and streams in the Keogh River Drainage, British Columbia." Northwest Science, 66(1):15-25.

59. Bonar, Scott A., Bonding, Bruce D. Divens, Mark and William Meyer. 2005. "Effects of introduced fishes on wild juvenile coho salmon in three shallow Pacific Northwest lakes." Transactions of the American Fisheries Society 134:641-652.

60. Moring, John R. 1976. "Contributions of delayed-release, pen-cultured chinook salmon to the sport fishery in Puget Sound, Washington." The Progressive Fish-Culturist, 38(1):36-39.

61. Haw, Frank and Peter K. Bergman. 1972. "A salmon angling program for the Puget Sound Region." Information Booklet No. 2, State of Washington Department of Fisheries.

62. Phillip, D. P., Cooke, S. J. Claussen J. E., Coppenlman, J. B., Suski, C. C., and D. P. Burkett. 2009. "Selection for vulnerability to angling in largemouth bass." Transactions of the American Fisheries Society 138:189-199.

63. Robertson, O. H. 1961. "Prolongation of the life span of kokanee salmon (*Oncorhynchus nerka kennerlyi*) by castration before beginning of gonad development." Proceedings of the National Academy of Science 47(4):609-621.

64. Quinn, Thomas P. 2005. *The Behavior and Ecology of Pacific salmon and Trout.* 2005. American Fisheries Sociey in association with University of Washington Press (page 251). 378 pages.

65. O"Connor, Brad. 1974. "Masu, and interesting import from Orient." 1974. Article appearing in the *Seattle Times* (5/9/74).

66. Tuggle, Jim. Undated/unpublished manuscripts. Gillnet wars, part I (1-4), and Gillnet wars part II (1-6).

67. Whitney, R. R. 2007. Personal communications relating to activities of the Fisheries Advisory Board.

68. Vasquez, R, and D. Meneken. 2/2/05. "Makah tribe defends its larger-than-expected chinook salmon catch; state officials worried." *Peninsula Daily News* (Port Angeles, WA newspaper).

69. Conrad, Robert H., and Marianna Alexanderdottir. 1993. "Estimating the harvest of salmon by the marine sport fishery in Puget Sound: evaluation and recommendations." Northwest Fishery Resource Bulletin. Manuscript Series Report No. 1.

70. Roos, John F., *Restoring Fraser River Salmon. A history of the International Pacific Salmon Fisheries Commission 1937-1985.* 438 pages.

71. Pacific Salmon Commission. 2011. Joint Chinook Technical Committee. Report TCCHINOOK (12)-2.

72. Haw, Frank and Peter K. Bergman. 1972. A salmon angling program for the Puget Sound

73. Hume, Stephen. The *Vancouver Sun* (daily newspaper), Tuesday, August 11, 1998.

74. Fisheries and Oceans Canada. 1999. News release: Pacific Northwest Salmon Recovery Efforts and the Pacific Salmon Treaty (4/30/99).

75. Waldeck, C. A., and E. H. Buck. 1999 (updated September 14). "The Pacific Salmon Treaty: The 1999 Agreement in Historical Perspective." Congressional Research Service. The Library of Congress.

76. Pacific Salmon Commission. 2012. Joint Chinook Technical Committee. Report TCCHINOOK (12)-2 and (12)-1.

77. The Columbia Basin Fish & Wildlife News Bulletin. "Agencies outline salmon recovery costs past and future." September 7, 2007.

78. Paquet, P. J. and fifteen other co-authors. 2011. "Hatcheries, conservation, and sustainable fisheries – achieving multiple goals: results of the Hatchery Scientific Review Group's Columbia River Basin review." 2011. Fisheries, Vol. 36(11):547-561.

79. Weeder, J. A., Marshall, A, R. and J. M. Epifanio. 2005. "An assessment of population genetic variation in Chinook salmon from seven Michigan Rivers 30 years after introduction." North American Journal of Fisheries Management 25:861-875.

80. Quinn, Thomas P. and M. J. Unwin. 1993. "Variation in life history patterns among New Zealand Chinook Salmon (*Oncorhynchus tshawytscha*) populations." Can. J. Fish. Aquat. Sci., Vol. 50:1414-1421.

81. Becker, L.A., Pascual, M. A. and N. G. Basso. 2007. "Colonization of the southern Patagonia Ocean by exotic chinook salmon." Conser. Biol. Oct;21(5):1347-52.

82. Pascual, Miguel, Bentzen P, Riva C., Mackey G. Kinnison, M. T, and R. Walker. 2001. "First documented case of anadromy in a population of introduced rainbow trout in Patagonia, Argentina." Transactions of the American Fisheries Society 130:53-67.

83. Brown, Bruce. 1982. *Mountain in the Clouds*. Simon and Schuster, New York. 239 pages.

84. Wagner, Henry R. 1933. *Spanish Explorations in the Strait of Juan de Fuca*. AMS Press Inc., New York, N.Y. 10003. 323 pages.

85. Lichatowich, Jim. 1999. *Salmon Without Rivers*. Island Press. Washington D.C. Covelo, California. 317 pages.

86. Jordan, D. S. and E. C. Starks. 1895. *The Fishes of Puget Sound*. Leland Stanford Jr. University.

87. Smith, G. R., Montgomery, D. R., Peterson, N. P., Crowley, B. 2007. *Spawning sockeye salmon fossils in Pleistocene lake beds of Skokomish Valley, Washington*. Science Direct. Quaternary Research 68(2007) 229-238.

88. Quinn, Thomas P. and M. J. Unwin. 1993. "Variation in life history patterns among New Zealand Chinook Salmon (*Oncorhynchus tshawytscha*) populations." Can. J. Fish. Aquat. Sci., Vol. 50:1414-1421.

89. Wydoski, R. S. and R. R. Whitney. 2003. *Inland Fishes of Washington*. University of Washington Press. 320 pages.

90. DeHaan, P. W., B. A. Adams, R. A. Tabor, D. K. Hawkins, and B. Thompson. 2014. "Historical and contemporary forces shape genetic variation in the Olympic mudminnow (*Novumbra hubbsi*), an endemic fish from Washington State, USA." Conservation Genetics doi:10.1007/s10592-014-0627-7.

91. Washington Department of Fisheries. 1953. Sixty-third Annual Report.

92. Davis, H. S. 1970. *Culture and Diseases of Game Fishes*. University of California Press. Berkeley, Los Angeles, London. 332 pages.

93. Mobrand, L. E.; J. Barr, L. Blankenship, D. E. Campton, T. P. Evelyn, T. A. Flagg, C. W. Mahnken, L. W. Seeb, P. R. Seidel, and W. W. Smoker. 2005. "Hatchery reform in Washington State: principles and emerging issues." Fisheries 30(6):11-23.

94. Reimchen, T. E. and N. F. Temple. 2004. "Hydrodynamic and phylogenetic aspects of the adipose fin in fishes." Can. J. Zool. 82: 910-916.

95. Beacham. T.D., and Murray, C. B. 1983. "Sexual dimorphism in the adipose fin of Pacific salmon (Oncorhynchus). Can. J. Fish." Aquat. Sci. 40: 2019-2024.

96. Nandor, G. F., Longwill, J. R. and D. L Webb. 2010. Chapter 2. "Overview of the coded wire tag program in the Greater Pacific Region of North America. Tagging, Telemetry and Marking Measures for Monitoring Fish Populations." Pacific Northwest Aquatic Monitoring Partnership – Special Publications.

97. Kurlansky, Mark. *Cod: A Biography of the Fish that Changed the World*. 1997. Walker Publishing Company, Inc.

98. Natural Resources Consultants (NRC), Inc. 2007. Northwest Strait Commission/ Foundation derelict fishing gear program. NRC – 1900 W. Nickerson, Seattle, WA 98119-1650.

99. Kappenman, K. M. and B. L. Parker. 2007. "Ghost nets in the Columbia River: Methods for locating and removing derelict gill nets in a large river and an assessment of impact to white sturgeon." North American Journal of Fisheries Management 27:804-809.

100. Vander Haegen, G. E., Ashbrook, C. E., Yi, K. W., and J. F. Dixon. 2004. "Survival of spring chinook salmon captured and released in a selective commercial fishery using gill nets and tangle nets." Fisheries Research 68; 123-133.

101. Anonymous. 2007. Two gillnetters cited for keeping nets in too long. Newspaper article from the The Daily Astorian, 4/4/07.

102. Anonymous. 2007. Council FW Committee Recommends Five 'Innovative' Projects. Columbia Basin Fish & Wildlife News Bulletin, 8/30/07.

103. Thompson, David. 1994. Columbia Journals. Edited by Barbara Belyea. University of Washington Press.

104. Anonymous. 2012. Oregon voters say no to gill-net ban, states continue discussions on alternative 'off-channel' plan. Columbia Basin Fish & Wildlife News Bulletin, 9/9/12.

105. Pollock, M. M.; Pess, G. R. and T. J. Beechie. 2004. "The importance of beaver ponds to coho salmon production in the Stillaguamish River Basin, Washington, USA." North American Journal of Fisheries Management 24:749-760.

106. Felt, Margaret E. 1986. *Reach for the Sky*. Maverick Publications, Bend, Oregon. 161 pages.

107. Lichatowich, Jim. 1999. *Salmon Without Rivers*. Island Press. Washington D.C. Covelo, California. 317 pages.

108. Grette, G. B. and E. O. Salo. 1986. "The status of anadromous fishes of the Green/ Duwamish River System." Draft report submitted to: Seattle District U.S. Army

109. Review of 2011 ocean salmon fisheries. Pacific Fishery Management Council. Table B-43 (p. 255).

110. National Oceanic and Atmospheric Administration, National Marine Fisheries Service, Northwest Region. 1/19/07. 5-Year Review: Summary & evaluation of Puget Sound Chinook, Hood Canal summer chum, Puget Sound Steelhead.

111. Haw, F. and S. B. Mathews. 1969. "Recreational use of surplus hatchery coho salmon." Transactions of the American Fisheries Society, 98(3):487-496.

b. At this writing, no fewer than four other Franklin H.S. graduates are currently prominently involved in Washington salmon management: Dr. Conrad Mahnken – WA Fish and Wildlife Commissioner, Phil Anderson – Director of the Department of Fish and Wildlife, Frank ("Larry") Cassidy – influential/tireless salmon proponent and Frank Urabeck- a veteran recreational fishing advocate.

c. Chinook and coho salmon less than a foot in length were called salmon trout.

d. Notable among these were Ken McLeod, an avid steelheader and fly fisherman, and Don S. Johnson., President of the Washington State Outdoor Council.

e. In response to 1947 inquiry from the Director of Fisheries, Attorney General Smith Troy ruled that a lottery involving fish tag returns was illegal.

f. Personal communication from Dr. Whitney.

g. Personal communication from Dr. Whitney.

h. A condition coinciding with approaching maturity, characterized by maximum size, fat content and bright silvery lateral coloration.

i. The many examples include the waters below Greer's Ferry Dam, White River, Arkansas (producing a world record brown trout); Navajo Dam, San Juan River, New Mexico and Flaming Gorge Dam, Green River Utah.

j. Dr. Richard Whitney, technical fisheries advisor to Judge Boldt, indicated to me that his understanding is that the ruling of the U.S. Supreme Court in the Puyallup II (1969) established that the State of Washington has the right/responsibility to regulate tribal fishing when conservation of the fish resource is clearly the issue. Whitney is unaware of a modification of that ruling.

k. Not to be confused with trawlers that drag sack-like nets targeting other species.

l. A stock is a specific river interbreeding population (e.g., lower Columbia River fall Chinook salmon).

m. Hatchery-origin salmon taken in the commercial fisheries are marketed as "wild" fish.

Index

Page numbers in bold type refer to illustrations.

About the Author

Born during the depths of the Great Depression, Frank Haw has spent his life within the Puget Sound Area. He became addicted to fishing at an early age while living in Seattle's Rainier Valley, developing his skills on the shores of Lake Washington, nearby docks of Puget Sound, and waters of the Snoqualmie Valley. Since 1963 he has resided in Olympia, Washington.

Upon discharge from the U.S. Air Force, he enrolled at the University of Washington receiving a B.S. in Fisheries Biology in 1959 when he was immediately hired by the Washington Department of Fisheries to investigate the State's salmon sport fishery. At that time, the Department's activities primarily involved commercial fishing and salmon hatcheries but Frank played a key role in implementing aggressive programs that focused on recreational fishing. His involvement with the salmon sport fishery resulted in catch and participation levels reaching a record high.

During the waning years of Governor Evans' Administration, he was appointed Deputy Director of Fisheries and served in this capacity through Governor Ray's term of office. Due to the implementation of the so-called Boldt Decision, this was most likely the most difficult era in the history of the agency.

Following retirement from State Service, he joined Northwest Marine Technology as a senior biologist working on fish identification systems and various salmon management issues. For many years he has been a staunch supporter of fishery and hatchery reform.